SPY

MASTER

THE REAL-LIFE KARLA, HIS MOLES, AND THE EAST GERMAN SECRET POLICE

LESLIE COLITT

Addison-Wesley Publishing Company

Reading, Massachusetts   Menlo Park, California   New York
Don Mills, Ontario   Wokingham, England   Amsterdam   Bonn
Sydney   Singapore   Tokyo   Madrid   San Juan
Paris   Seoul   Milan   Mexico City   Taipei

Library of Congress Cataloging-in-Publication Data

Colitt, Leslie.
    Spymaster: the real-life Karla, his moles, and the East German secret police / Leslie Colitt.
        p.   cm.
    Includes bibliographical references and index.
    ISBN 0-201-40738-8
    1. Wolf, Markus, 1923–   . 2. Spies — Germany (East) — Biography.   3. Germany (East). Ministerium für Staatssicherheit — Biography.   4. Intelligence service — Germany (East) — Biography.   5. Germany — Politics and government — 1945–1990.   I. Title.
DD287.7.w65C65   1995
943.1087'092 — dc20
[B]   95-25065
                                                                                CIP

Jacket design by Linda Kosarin
Text design by Ruth Kolbert
Set in 11-point Electra by Pagesetters, Inc.
1   2   3   4   5   6   7   8   9-MA-98979695
First printing, September 1995

Prologue

I first heard about General Markus Wolf, head of East Germany's foreign intelligence service, shortly after I came to Berlin in late 1959. Wolf was held by friend and foe to be the cold war's most successful espionage chief. But he was doubly intriguing to me because, although we were on opposite sides of the barricades, we shared a common uprooting experience. Both of us were the sons of German-Jewish fathers and had fled the Nazis with our families, he to Stalin's Soviet Union and I to America. Little did I imagine that in only a few years' time the Stasi, the secret police of which Wolf was deputy chief, would begin pursuing me.

Not long after arriving as a postgraduate student in Berlin, I struck up a friendship with Armin, a likable young East German refugee who had lost a leg and both his parents as a boy in Danzig (known also as Gdańsk) during the Second World War. Unknown to me, my new friend's destiny was already entwined with that of Markus Wolf. But whereas Wolf would soon achieve legendary fame as a spymaster, my friend Armin would be much less fortunate.

Armin knocked on the door of my room at the Student Village of Berlin's Free University in early 1960, only a few months after I had moved in.

"Armin is my name," he said offering his hand. "I've just arrived from the DDR."

He used the initials for Deutsche Demokratische Republik — East Germany. I was struck by his carefully articulated, refined German, which seemed unusual in someone from the proletarian German Democratic Republic.

"I heard you are American," he said, fixing me with his intensely blue eyes. "Do you know, Lenin said that if you took Russian intelligence and added American inventiveness you would have the ideal Soviet man."

I must have looked impressed, because his pale, bearded face broke into a grin that contrasted oddly with his sad gaze. The smartly cut gray woolen overcoat he wore struck me as being a touch too elegant for a refugee from the East.

I glanced at the cane draped over his arm. He removed it with his free hand and gave his left leg a powerful whack.

"Wooden, it's my peg leg," he said, laughing. Although later he often joked about his artificial leg, the result of a severe injury he'd suffered as a boy during the last months of Hitler's war, it had clearly played a crucial role in his past.

Armin and I spent a great deal of time together. Fresh from a small college in provincial Maine, I was impressed by his worldliness, although he had never travelled outside the GDR. It was fascinating to hear the stories of his youth in Nazi Germany — tales that he sometimes embellished with a parody of Joseph Goebbels ranting and raving as in the old newsreels. His account of how he, the son of a prosperous Nazi manufacturer, joined the Communist Party in the GDR, was expelled by it, and then fled to the West, epitomized the political extremes within which an entire generation of Germans lived.

I enjoyed Armin's stories about Café Schmalfuss, his favorite haunt in Leipzig, which, as he told it, was filled with a never-ending supply of the most enchanting Saxonian women. I was fascinated, too, by his ability to quote Marx, Engels, Lenin, and, if need be, Stalin on virtually any subject we discussed from women to religion.

Armin had been thrown into prison in Leipzig on contrived charges of economic crimes, and, by the time of his release in 1959, shortly before we met, he had decided to flee the GDR. More than a thousand East Germans were escaping to the West every day, most of them through the largest hole in the Communist world, Berlin. The Berlin Wall was still only a dream in the minds of its Communist builders when Armin prepared to commit the official crime of "fleeing the Republic."

He told me the details of the day of his escape. He had packed his small brown vinyl suitcase, propped his spare wooden leg under his arm, and boarded the streetcar to Leipzig's imposing main railway station with its twenty-two platforms. Displaying his disability pass at the ticket counter in the vaulted West Hall, he bought a reduced-rate round-trip ticket to East Berlin's Ostbahnhof. A round-trip ticket was essential for convincing the uniformed controllers patrolling the train that he was only visiting friends in East Berlin and would be returning to Leipzig in a few days.

The controllers passed through the train before it entered East Berlin but only glanced at the small blue GDR identity passes held up by Armin and his fellow passengers. Two hours and thirty minutes after leaving Leipzig, the train pulled into the Ostbahnhof, East Berlin's peeling main station. Armin walked to the platform on the opposite side of the station where the S-Bahn urban railroad linked East and West Berlin. From here it was only five stops to Lehrter Bahnhof in West Berlin.

The train, with a hiss of compressed air, entered Bahnhof Friedrichstrasse, the last station in East Berlin. Trembling, Armin looked out to see border guards with German shepherds posted every ten yards along the platform. The two-minute but seemingly endless stop was broken only by an announcement crackling over the loudspeaker: "*Achtung, letzter Bahnhof im Demokratischen Sektor*" (Attention: last station in the democratic sector). It was a warning to East German soldiers, policemen, members of the State Security Ministry, and all other officials that they were forbidden to travel to the West and were to immediately leave the train. Ironically, nearly everyone in Armin's compartment could scarcely wait to get to West Berlin.

The doors finally slammed shut, and the train rolled out. A few passengers pointed at the hulking ruin of the Reichstag in the distance, but hardly anyone spoke during the three minutes it took to reach Lehrter Bahnhof in West Berlin. None of the Easterners who sat with small suitcases pressed under their legs dared get out this close to the border. They waited until Zoo station, where they would be quickly swallowed up in the rush of Western commuters.

Armin spent the first few nights with an acquaintance in West Berlin and then moved into the Student Village where we met. Like all those who fled from the GDR, he had to be processed at Marienfelde reception center by West German and Western Allied counterintelligence officials before being issued a West Berlin identity document. At that time Marienfelde, located in a suburb of West Berlin, was overflowing with East German refugees of all ages. The cream of the German Democratic Republic was being skimmed off, and left behind were the state's most submissive citizens.

Armin said he was interrogated by the representatives of West Germany's Federal Intelligence Agency (BND) and its counterintelligence agency (BfV), as well as the three Western Allied intelligence services. They were satisfied that he knew nothing of interest about the Soviet army in the GDR, and that as a just released former prisoner he had personally suffered at the hands of the Communist regime. He was given permission to reside in West Berlin, where he planned to begin studies at the Free University.

Several months after Armin's escape, we sat in my room on a Saturday, drinking warm vodka and debating what to do in the evening. On an impulse, I suggested that we might go over to East Berlin, completely forgetting that Armin would risk arrest if he set foot in the East again. But he was enthusiastic about the idea and suggested just the place for us, a cultural center run by the Freie Deutsche Jugend (FDJ), the Communist youth organization.

The evening we spent there was especially memorable. We debated with young East German Communists about the mass exodus from their country and the future of the Soviet Union under Nikita Khrushchev and drank sweet Bulgarian wine while trying to obtain the addresses of two pretty young students. Armin pretended to be an ethnic German from Argentina and entertained us at the piano with German student songs that had long been banned in East Germany. The alcohol took its toll, and we recalled little of what happened afterward. When I woke up later that morning in the West, I realized just how dangerous our foray to East Berlin had been for Armin and wondered why he had taken the risk. But I concluded that this was something only he could decide.

On a gloomy winter afternoon several months later — it was less than a year before the building of the Berlin Wall — I was waiting outside East Berlin's Friedrichstrasse station for my girl-friend (and future wife), who lived in the East Sector, when I caught sight of a familiar figure in a smartly tailored gray overcoat. As he limped on his cane across the dimly lit street, I wondered why he had again taken such a risk.

Tanja watched anxiously as her father read the note from her principal, a stern 150 percent female Party activist who was head of the elite secondary school Tanja attended in East Berlin's Greifswalder Strasse.

"Comrade Major General! There are some matters we must talk about pertaining to your daughter Tatjana's behavior. Please call for an appointment. With socialist greetings!"

General Markus Wolf looked sharply at Tanja, intending to question her, but was instead filled with pride in his comely and intelligent daughter.

"What is this all about?"

"Pappi, you know how petty the Germans are. I only brought the pop records that you gave me — remember the ones with Cliff Richard and Petula Clark — to a party, and we played them. One of the boys taped them, and the principal found out about it and confiscated the records. She started lecturing us about Western cultural barbarians undermining our socialist order." Her father had bought the records during a visit to a "fraternal" East European country where, unlike East Germany, Western pop music was not reviled.

"*Mein Gott,*" he muttered. "Sometimes our people are al-most as bad as the . . ."

He swallowed the word "Nazis," scribbling a date on a piece of paper for Tanja to bring back to school.

The general and his wife Emmi were often critical of the Germans, but they would speak rapidly in fluent Russian so that the children would not understand. Tanja, her elder brother Michael, and even the youngest, Franz, however, were used to hearing Russian at home and understood a great deal. The children worshiped their father, who treated them as his equals while looking every inch the major general of the GDR People's Army when he wore his elegantly tailored uniform on the national holidays of the German Democratic Republic and the Soviet Union.

A few days later the general parked his Volga car outside Tanja's school, which resembled a Wilhelminian fortress. It was not far from their home in Berlin-Pankow, a borough of East Berlin where nearly all the members of the Party's ruling Politbüro lived in large prewar homes on closed streets.

Emmi was right, he thought, locking the door of the Volga and inhaling deeply. The car's vile-smelling Soviet plastics and adhesives and its undulating ride were probably the cause of her frequent attacks of intense nausea in the backseat.

Seated in the principal's office, he listened patiently as the principal, a member of the borough Communist Party committee whose father was rumored to have been a Nazi, expressed her deep concern about Tanja's depraved pop records.

"Comrade Principal, are we building socialism or a sanatorium?" he began firmly. "Can we expect our young people to believe in the humanistic values of Communism if we isolate them from the rest of the world? An international outlook is the mark of a true Communist, not nationalism."

She looked at him, stunned. Here was Comrade General Markus Wolf, head of the Central Intelligence Administration and deputy minister of State Security of the GDR, lecturing her that exposure to Western pop groups was not harmful to socialist morality and actually helped young East Germans to become better Communists. What would the Politbüro say to such impartiality, such a lack of class viewpoint?

"Remember that we want to raise intelligent young Communists, not mindless robots," Wolf said with a curt nod as he turned to leave.

Less than two miles away, in the sprawling headquarters of the State Security Ministry — better known to ordinary citizens as the

Stasi — a lieutenant colonel in Department 20 pored over a report by one of the Stasi's informers. The colonel was a member of the nearly 100,000-strong officer corps of the Stasi. His informant, a teacher code-named Blackboard who lived in the Köpenick district of East Berlin, was one of nearly 150,000 Stasi informers who composed a network with tentacles reaching into the remotest kindergarten and provincial playhouse.

Blackboard's report was on a fourteen-year-old boy named Olaf who had been entertaining his fellow pupils with accounts of what he had seen on forbidden West German television, and his parents, who were clearly exerting a "destructive" influence on him.

Based on Blackboard's account, Olaf was called in by the school principal, a devoted Party member who blacklisted young people for wearing forbidden "Ami" (American) jeans and chewing gum. Students knew that once their social deportment records were blotted, they stood little chance of being admitted to the university.

Another man in the room, who failed to identify himself, fired questions at Olaf about his parents' contacts in the West. But the boy only stared in bewilderment at his interrogator. Glancing at a sheet of paper, the man demanded to know about the Schroeder family in Hannover. Did Olaf's parents not correspond regularly with them, and did these people not visit his family every year and send parcels for birthdays and at Christmas? Were they relatives, friends?

Olaf replied that they were friends of the family, but that he had known Herr Schroeder as "Uncle Karl" for as long as he could remember.

The man busily recorded the boy's answers in a small black notebook. He noted that Olaf's parents had failed to give the Schroeders' name to the authorities at their place of work, as was required of citizens who had family, friends, or acquaintances in the West. That lapse was suspicious in itself.

Olaf was ordered to find out everything he could about Herr Schroeder: where he worked and what he did when he visited the GDR. He was also to write down the Western TV programs his parents watched. Above all, under no circumstances was he to let anyone know about this conversation. The man asked whether Olaf understood that if he violated the trust placed in him by State Security, it would have a negative impact on his future and could cause trouble for his parents.

"*Jawohl*," the boy replied meekly. He knew that the man opposite him wielded immense power and would use it against him if he did not inform on the Schroeders and his parents.

"Of course, Olaf, if we are satisfied with your information, it will be of great benefit to you in your future life," the man said.

The boy realized he had little choice, and nodded in agreement. He had joined the ranks of those who were both victims of the system and instruments of its control.

The colonel inserted a sheet of paper in his typewriter and wrote that additional reports on both parents were to be obtained by informers at the parents' workplaces and in their neighborhood, and that further evidence of "antistate activities" was to be investigated.

Markus Wolf did not wish to know about Olaf or the other "unofficial collaborators" of the Stasi who were being used to control their fellow East Germans. As chief of the Central Intelligence Administration (HVA), dealing with foreign intelligence, Wolf operated on a more lofty level. He was the supreme tactician, as capable of hooking up his agents with lonely secretaries in the West as he was of conversing about Dostoyevsky and Tolstoy. His was the mind behind the audacious plan to introduce long-term "sleeper" agents into the stream of East German refugees entering the West. The strategy entailed years, sometimes decades, during which time the new citizens of West Germany worked their way into key positions and supplied him with the innermost secrets of the "class enemy."

But Wolf was also deputy head of the Stasi, which took over where the Nazi Gestapo had left off: informing on, compromising, and grinding into submission millions of East Germans. Many of its victims were to take revenge when the Communist dictatorship later collapsed. Xenophobia and neo-Nazism, which always lurked just below the surface in East Germany, would erupt into the open, as countless East Germans, like young Olaf, suddenly became a volatile political element in united Germany.

Yet Wolf rejected any blame for the deep moral wounds inflicted by his Stasi on East Germans. He claimed that he was responsible only for espionage, that internal suppression was the function of his titular boss, the odious Erich Mielke. Dubbed the "Man without a Face" by Western intelligence services, which for decades were unable to get a photo of him, Wolf was a study in contradictions: a calculating exploiter of human weaknesses whose personal warmth and concern for his nearly four thousand staff officers and spies gained him their unshakable loyalty; a product of Stalinism who rejected its excesses but suppressed his doubts only to become a glowing supporter of Mikhail Gorbachev; a descendant of orthodox Jews who alternately concealed and resurrected his Jewish background; a victim of Nazi persecution who served to preserve a Communist police state.

Just as the seeds of Germany's division were sown by Adolf Hitler and nurtured by Joseph Stalin, the origins of Markus Wolf's tragically divided self lay in the past.

Markus Johannes Wolf's birth was a family affair.

Dr. Friedrich Wolf, his father, supervised the event in the parental bedroom. His mother Else's great-aunt, Ella, acting as midwife, yanked the baby from the darkness of his mother's womb into the pale winter light of his new home. They lived in a modest rented house in the shadow of Hohenzollern Castle, which loomed over the medieval town of Hechingen, in southwestern Germany.

Dr. Wolf's hand still stung from the bite Else had given him at the peak of her labor pains. He glanced at his watch. It was 12:20 P.M. on January 23, 1923. Markus "screamed vigorously," Friedrich wrote afterward in the first entry of a diary begun at his son's birth.

Births were normally routine events for Dr. Wolf, a social-minded physician who was also a radical leftist playwright and an advocate of free love and abortion. At the age of thirty-four he already had a son and daughter by his first marriage, which had recently ended in a bitter divorce. But this was no ordinary birth. Markus was the outcome of Friedrich's passion for the fair-haired, vivacious Rhineland beauty, Else, ten years younger than he, who had broken with her parents and the world of bourgeois morality to join her handsome, dark-eyed suitor.

Friedrich never stopped wooing Else until he died, shortly after his seventh child was born to yet another mistress. He poured out his innermost feelings for Else in thousands of letters of the kind most women could only dream about. She returned his devotion and remained loyal to him despite his countless infidelities across the face of Europe.

Dr. Wolf spent the morning before Markus's birth on a house call to one of his impoverished patients. The poor farmers and workers of Hechingen understood little of Herr Doktor's eccentric views, but they revered him for treating them against a token payment of potatoes or, equally often, without charge. The medical authorities frowned on his basic homeopathic cures and his habit of wearing sandals and shorts while making house calls in the summer. The waiting room of his practice, furnished with crates and rough-hewn boards, was "scandalous," they complained.

Friedrich's oppositional streak arose out of an ingrained sense of justice and equality. As a child he had rebelled against his father, Max, an orthodox Jewish businessman who ran his household like a Prussian army quartermaster. Tyrannized by his father, Friedrich swore that when he had children of his own he would treat them as his equals.

His parents were orthodox, the descendants of Spanish Jews who had been given refuge in the Rhineland some four hundred years earlier. They sent him to a strict Jewish school that, predictably, heightened his awareness of being a Jew but, at the same time, caused him to abandon Judaism. On completing his medical studies, Friedrich rejected the Jewish faith, severing all ties with the "Israelite" religious community, and further alienating him from his family.

Friedrich was typical of the many German Jews in believing that he was fully assimilated into German society. German-Jewish children grew up singing "Stille Nacht, Heilige Nacht" ("Silent Night, Holy Night") on Christmas Eve just like their Christian playmates. The proud German-Jewish minority that the Wolfs belonged to was a mirror image of German society.

Friedrich's rebellion against the political establishment began in earnest when he served as a young medical officer in the German Army during the First World War. At first, he patriotically supported Germany's "just war" like most other male German Jews. Younger Jews, like Friedrich, flocked to volunteer for the

Kaiser's army while their fathers moved colored pins representing the German and Allied armies across the giant maps of Europe that covered their living-room walls. Later the Jews of Germany demonstrated their arrogance and insecurity by rejecting as uncultured rabble the hundreds of thousands of Jews from Poland and Russia who found refuge in Weimar Germany.

After he was severely wounded several times, Friedrich's enthusiasm for the war gave way to hatred of the slaughter he had witnessed on the western front. Repelled by the insolence of the upper-class officers corps, he gave up his own officer's quarters and moved in with the infantrymen who served as cannon fodder in the trenches.

Friedrich Wolf's rejection of his father's blind nationalism was rooted in the tradition of nonconformist German Jews, men such as the poet Heinrich Heine and the political philosopher Karl Marx, one of the greatest Jewish revolutionaries. Unlike Heine and Marx, though, Wolf did not convert to Protestantism. Defiantly, he registered with the authorities as a "dissident," a nonbeliever. Thus it was only fitting that Friedrich later struck out the word "religion" on Markus's birth certificate and left the space blank.

Markus became one of his father's greatest delights, even though Friedrich was rarely home. Markus was a thoroughly "charming little fellow" who laughed and was happy when spoken to, Friedrich wrote in his diary. He added, though, that his son's piercing early morning screams gave a hint of another, more stubborn side of his character. Markus at nine months was as active on his "little stompers" as a one-year-old, his father bragged. He was especially pleased that Markus played with the chestnuts his inventive father had strung on a chain across his bed.

"He tells incredible stories, and at the moment is a dadaist, expressing his whole world in *da da*," Friedrich quipped.

One of the many Wolf family photos shows a sturdy, handsome child reaching confidently for an object in his father's hand. The boy radiates the kind of self-assurance that convinces doting parents that their child is destined to play a special role in life. Another photo shows Markus as a one-year-old standing on a table, an arm resting tenderly on his mother's breast. Else,

smiling, her pretty features framed with her golden braided hair
and clad in a peasant blouse and smock, resembles a demure
young woman in a Dürer painting.

Markus's first memories were of the lonely log house in
Höllsteig, near Lake Constance, on Germany's southern border
with Switzerland, where the Wolfs moved when he was three. He
recalled the farm horse that carried him out to the fields and the
peasants who barely scratched a living from the earth. He also
remembered the fall from the window of the log house to the
pavement below that left him unconscious and close to death.
Above all he could never forget the cold-water baths, mudpacks,
and strict vegetarian diet enforced by his father, who was convinced that faulty diet was the main cause of illness. The family
milled its own whole meal grain and baked its own bread. Later
Markus helped undermine his father's crusading vegetarianism by
swapping his salad-and-tomato sandwiches in school for a classmate's liverwurst sandwiches.

In Höllsteig, far from the ills of urban life, his father wrote
the remarkable book that was to gain him far wider fame among
ordinary Germans than did any of his ideologically saturated plays
and novels. It was his popular medical book, Nature as Healer and
Helper. The best-selling book, with its photos of Markus, his
younger brother Konrad, and their mother and father — often
posing in the nude — soon graced the bookshelves of hundreds of
thousands of German households. Remarkably, it even managed
to survive the Third Reich's purge of all books written by Jews.

Friedrich dedicated the book to an uncle, Dr. Moritz Meyer,
who was more of an ersatz father. Meyer, a justice official and a
disciple of natural healing, had inspired his nephew to study
medicine. Friedrich, in gratitude, had dedicated his doctoral
thesis on childhood multiple sclerosis to his beloved uncle. In an
act of tragic naiveté, Dr. Meyer sent a brochure he had written on
vegetarianism to the most renowned vegetarian of the time, Adolf
Hitler, with a personal dedication. His reward was to be put to
death by the Nazis in Mauthausen concentration camp.

Friedrich was a socialist and early Green with a mission: to
help better the lot of the common man by teaching him how to
eat, dress, and think in a healthier way. Mind and body were

intrinsically bound together, as he never tired of demonstrating in his medical book, which was filled with pictures of Friedrich sprinting, performing a cartwheel, being hosed down with cold water by three-year-old Markus, and standing outdoors at his tall homemade writing desk, a broad-shouldered Picasso-like figure clad in sandals, shorts, and a wide straw hat. His wife's sister, Grete, and a woman dancer friend posed in the nude doing dance exercises. Three-year-old Markus could be seen riding bareback on a large horse in one photo labeled "Training for courage." In another he was shown balancing on his father's knees: "Fathers, do not neglect your children!" the caption exhorted.

Studying the photos many years later, Markus could not help smiling at this advice. The truth was that he seldom saw his famous father in those years. When he was not caring for his patients, Friedrich was writing feverishly or was away attending performances of his plays. But Else made sure that even in her husband's absence, Markus and Konrad were made aware of Friedrich's views on all important questions of life. His letters to them throughout their boyhood years and into their early manhood were filled with paternal advice on how to conduct themselves as upright socialists.

Hechingen, surrounded by lush fields and meadows in the romantic, southwestern corner of Germany, was an unusual place for an intellectual like Friedrich Wolf. He once referred to it disparagingly as the German version of "Central Africa," but it was here, far from the chattering, left-wing intellectuals in the cafés of Berlin, that he was able to put into practice at least a small part of his remarkable social vision.

As a result of the relentless operation of capitalism, the proceeds from Friedrich's medical book made him financially independent for the first time. Pooling the money with a loan from a building society, he realized a middle-class dream, his own home. The Wolfs moved from the isolation of the country into a large white cube-shaped house in Stuttgart built by a Bauhaus architect hired by Friedrich. They were to spend five years in their new home, which was expropriated after the Nazis took power. The new buyer had to pledge that he would replace the "flat Jewish roof" with an "Aryan pointed roof."

Growing up with a father who campaigned tirelessly against the political and social injustices of Weimar Germany left a deep mark on the Wolf boys. Even more than Bertolt Brecht, Friedrich used the theater for agitprop — agitation and propaganda — which he was convinced would lead to radical social change. He became a cause célèbre when his highly charged, proabortion play, Cyanide, swept the theaters of Germany in 1929 and landed him in jail briefly. Cyanide propelled Friedrich to nationwide prominence. He lectured and campaigned nonstop against paragraph 218 of the penal code, which stipulated a prison sentence of up to five years for women who aborted their pregnancies and anyone aiding them. He became Germany's most prominent proabortion crusader, a hero to the entire left-wing movement. Cyanide was followed by *Sailors of Cattaro*, a powerful antiwar drama.

In tune with the growing polarization of political life in Weimar Germany, Friedrich, like other intellectuals of his time, renounced the relatively moderate Social Democrats in 1928 and joined the Communist Party of Germany, the KPD. But he was not content to theorize. As the Party's candidate for a seat on the Stuttgart municipal council, he gained a sensational forty-two thousand votes, nearly 20 percent of the ballots cast.

Along with a fellow physician, Dr. Else Kienle, Friedrich was arrested in January 1931 and accused of performing abortions for personal gain. After spending several weeks in a detention cell, Friedrich was released on bail. He then spearheaded a campaign to gain Dr. Kienle's freedom, which culminated in a rally in February 1931 for their legal defense, at which Brecht and Albert Einstein lent their support. After being ultimately cleared of the charges, Friedrich and Dr. Kienle embarked on a triumphal tour of the Soviet Union.

Sportsman that Friedrich was, he visited Moscow's Dynamo sports stadium, which was run by the secret police. He even performed a cartwheel in front of a shapely, admiring female swimmer, who reciprocated with a cartwheel of her own. In his letters to Else back home in Stuttgart, he enthused about the "wild but marvelous life" he found in the world's first socialist state.

Living with a father like Friedrich, everything seemed clear-cut to Markus and Koni, as his brother was nicknamed. The Communists were people like their father and his friends who were struggling for the rights of the oppressed working people. Capitalism was in its last gasp, and the future lay in the East, where socialism was being built in the young Soviet Union. Markus accepted without question his father's idealized vision of the proletariat: heroic and noble, like the monuments being raised in the Soviet Union to the handsome workers striding confidently into the future.

In Stuttgart the Wolfs were able to afford a nursemaid for Markus, and later they sent him to a progressive school that stressed the arts and crafts. Unlike at other German schools, there was no homework, and boys and girls sat together in class. He was also allowed to retain his unusual habit, for a German, of writing with his left hand. He had had to give up on his right hand after a wintertime accident. While out sledding with Koni, the brothers had smashed into a wall near their home. Koni ran screaming into his father's practice, although he had barely been scratched. Markus was pale but said nothing despite the intense pain in his broken right arm.

At supper that evening, Markus ate with his left hand. His father admonished him to use his right hand, but then, seeing Markus freeze momentarily, he took him to be X-rayed. Typically, Friedrich saw to it that the injury was treated with strenuous exercise. He made Markus use his right arm daily for three months to lift a heavy sandbag that hung from a rope and pulley he had rigged over a window.

At school, Markus's teachers showed remarkable tolerance for the boy's frequent ill-tempered outbursts, which were the reaction to his father's often violent fits of anger. The child was, after all, the son of a celebrated playwright. As a result Markus developed into a headstrong child who refused to excuse himself for anything.

Yet in spite of his father's theatrical outbursts, usually directed at Else for being too lax with the children, Markus recalled that life at home was harmonious. Visitors to the Wolfs never failed to be impressed by the spirit of tolerance and equality between parents and children. "The turbulence in the house was genuine democracy. Wolf never took on paternal airs or gave orders to his sons," one old Communist friend of the family observed admiringly. She added that Markus and Koni also owed a great deal to their remarkable mother, who was the classic "comrade at the side of a Communist intellectual, artist, and campaigner."

Else was always ready to meet her genial but moody husband halfway. When Friedrich decided to abolish Christmas one year, she argued that the children had a right to a Christmas tree. They compromised. On Christmas Eve, Markus and Koni were led into the living room, where a large fir tree stood crowned not by the star of Bethlehem but by a glowing red star like the revolving ones Stalin had mounted atop the Kremlin towers. Instead of the traditional German Christmas carols, Friedrich cranked up the gramophone and played "Higher, Higher, Higher," the Soviet aviator's song.

In the summer, the Wolf boys attended the German Communist Party's Young Pioneer camp. There they sang strident hymns to the Party and its leader Ernst Thälmann, who seemed confident of assuming power in the midst of a deepening depression. But although the Communists were the third most powerful party in the Reichstag of 1930, German workers would soon abandon them for the Nazis.

A group photo taken at the camp in 1930 showed Markus and Koni giving the Young Pioneer salute with their companions. The two boys were togged out in smart matching checked jackets that contrasted starkly with the rough woolen sweaters of their companions from working-class households. But their father, too, had long since taken to wearing well-cut suits, ties, and even smoking cigarettes when the children were not around.

The boys adored their troop leader at the Young Pioneers, Lotte Rayss, a young Party activist who had, inevitably, fallen in love with their father. Friedrich needed little encouragement, having already set down in his book Comradely Marriage his lifelong principle that neither marital partner should constrict the other. Friedrich was compulsively open in all his extramarital relationships, which to him were an irrepressible natural phenomena. He hid nothing from his beloved Else, who suffered silently. She remained faithful to him until the end. Suffering deeply from his many affairs, she had chosen to undergo treatment in a mental clinic rather than desert her godlike husband.

Impulsive, extraordinarily charming, erudite, and physically attractive, Friedrich fascinated women. He was pliable in their presence, unable to resist their advances. Women were attracted by his darkly handsome appearance and his typical Rhineland bonhomie. His missionary zeal inspired loyalty to him and his causes long after he had become entangled in another affair.

After Cyanide, Friedrich basked in his newly found fame. Besieged by actresses who hoped to gain a role in one of his propagandistic plays, he did nothing to discourage their advances. His apparent humility and shyness, which contrasted so sharply with his otherwise soaring egotism, seemed only to heighten his mysterious appeal.

"I was fascinated by his superb body. He was the most handsome man I ever met," an actress friend of Friedrich's recalled. Markus, with his father's dark brown eyes, would soon have a similar magnetic appeal for the opposite sex.

Friedrich's body was his "favorite creation," a Russian friend remarked after observing the delight with which Friedrich displayed his muscular frame. Markus would also share this trait, which often bordered on narcissism. From his mother he inherited an extraordinary devotion to family. Surrounded by family members who had no secrets from each other, it was not surprising that Markus was raised to abhor secrecy and all forms of intrigue and deceit.

The comfortable if turbulent life of the Wolf family was demolished on February 27, 1933, the day the Nazis set fire to the Reichstag, the German Parliament and accused the Communists of arson. Only a few weeks earlier, Adolf Hitler, attired in a respectable morning coat, had assumed the office of chancellor of the Reich after a democratically won election. Within months,

Dachau and Sachsenhausen concentration camps, designed to hold the political enemies of the new National Socialist regime, were being built in full view of the inhabitants of Munich and Berlin.

Friedrich soon learned that he was on the list of opponents of Nazism who were to be arrested. Doubly endangered as a Communist and a Jew — his earlier rejection of Judaism was irrelevant to the racially obsessed Nazis — he fled to a cabin in the Austrian mountains and was not to set foot on German soil again for twelve years.

Markus and Koni were taken from Stuttgart to their mother's relatives in the Rhineland. Friedrich entrusted Else, who as a non-Jew was in less danger of arrest, with winding up his affairs in Germany. He instructed her that his books were to be left with trustworthy custodians until his return. In 1933 Else and the boys were smuggled across the border to neutral Switzerland with the help of comrades from the illegal German Communist Party.

Thus began the exile of the Wolf family, four centuries after their ancestors came to Germany. Unlike most other refugees from Nazi Germany, they did not seek asylum in America, Britain, or another Western haven. Wolf's first family, however — his ex-wife Kaethe and Markus's half-brother, Lukas, and half-sister, Johanna — escaped to England.

Always the optimist, Friedrich convinced himself that the masses in Germany would soon rise up against their fascist oppressors. In a letter to the Theatre Union in New York, he expressed the hope that he would be "back in Germany again in 1934."

Rejected by his beloved fatherland, Wolf was welcomed with open arms by his new spiritual motherland, the young Soviet Union. Like so many other Western intellectuals, he had sung its praises after an earlier visit. In Moscow, this time at the invitation of the influential Soviet Writer's Union, he was rewarded for his pro-Soviet views with a flat for his family in the Arbat section, the old merchant's district of Moscow, which was inhabited by the new intelligentsia of Soviet writers and scientists.

Before settling down in Moscow, though, after almost a year

of separation, the Wolfs spent an unforgettable summer together on the isle of Bréhat off the coast of Brittany. It was one of the rare periods when Friedrich was together with his family for more than a few consecutive days.

Here Friedrich wrote his powerful anti-Nazi drama, *Professor Mamlock*, which played to packed houses from Moscow to New York. Many years later it was made into a striking film by his son Koni. The story was Friedrich's simplistic solution for the crisis of Germany's Jews. Professor Mamlock, a renowned Jewish surgeon in Berlin when the Nazis took power, believed, as did many patriotic German Jews who had come of age before the Weimar Republic, that his medals for bravery as a soldier during the First World War would save him from Nazi persecution. But Mamlock's son, a firebrand Communist who ridiculed his father's liberalism, proved to be right in his predictions about the future of Jews under Nazism. Mamlock was stripped of his hospital post and, rejected by his former colleagues who now supported the Nazis, he killed himself. Wolf's message was clear: the Jews of Germany were to throw off their chains and unite with their natural allies, the Communists.

That summer of 1933 in Brittany was not all hard work. Friedrich paddled with Else and his sons off Bréhat Island in the kayaks they had had sent from Germany. Else would later wistfully recall those marvelous months together in a letter to her husband. But Friedrich was not tamed quite that easily. Lotte Rayss, his earlier fellow-Communist flame from Stuttgart, and a close friend of the family, was invited to visit them. The old romance was rekindled as the two paddled together in the secluded coves of Bréhat. Their child, Lena, was born in 1934 in Switzerland, where Lotte had escaped from the Nazis. The ordeal that lay in store for Lena and her mother would leave an indelible impact on Markus when he was a teenager.

After the summer vacation Else returned with the boys to Switzerland, where they learned Russian while waiting for the Soviet entry visa that would allow them to join Friedrich in Moscow. Shortly before his eleventh birthday, Markus wrote his father a touching letter from Basel. "Pappele," he began in Swabian dialect, "do you remember how you told me that all sailors can knit? Now I can too." He wrote that he had sprained his ankle in gymnastics at school and was home knitting Christmas presents for his aunts and a cap for "Lotte's little baby."

"I want to go to the CCCP as quickly as possible," he told his father, using the Russian initials for "USSR." "If you don't want me to, then I will simply come on my own."

A few months later the Wolfs were reunited at 8 Nizhni Kislovski Pereyulok, in a small two-room apartment that was luxurious by Moscow standards in 1934. Lotte and her baby arrived soon afterward and moved in with them. A family photo showed Markus seated below a large wall map of the Soviet Union, gazing down tenderly at his infant half-sister while giving her a bottle. Lotte and her child, however, were soon ordered by the exiled German Communist Party to move to Engels, the capital of the ill-fated Soviet republic of ethnic Germans at the Volga River in southern Russia. Later she was arrested by the secret police in Engels on trumped-up anti-Soviet charges, separated from her child, and incarcerated in one of Stalin's forced labor camps, or gulags, in Kazakhstan.

Else Wolf was horrified to learn of Lotte's arrest and Lena's placement in a secret police orphanage. No one could deter Else from seeking to rescue the child. She set out on the long, arduous rail trip to the orphanage and demanded to talk with the director. Summoning up all her courage and newly gained proficiency in Russian, she convinced him to release Lenutchka into her custody. Her return to Moscow with the child was seen as nothing short of miraculous.

"Only later did Koni and I realize how much courage was needed to act in such a way," Markus recalled. In this respect, too, Else was different from their father. She did what her conscience demanded of her while he temporized. Friedrich had constantly urged his sons to "act on the courage of your convictions," but, although refusing to howl with Stalin's wolves who denounced accused fellow writers, he had never dared criticize Stalin's crimes beyond the safe confines of his family and close friends.

Else took Lenutchka back with her to Moscow and the

warmth of the Wolf apartment. Markus and Koni were overjoyed to see their sister again. In an almost unearthly demonstration of devotion to her husband, Else cared for Lena as if the child were her own flesh and blood. Markus would never forget this example of humanity. He told himself that one day he, too, would care for and be loyal to others who depended on him.

Friedrich insisted that the boys become Soviet children as quickly as possible. "Eat the kasha and the black bread, it is good for you," he advised them. The quicker the boys assimilated, the better, he argued. It had been the motto of his own young years in Germany. The children on the street in Moscow poked fun at the Wolf boys, who still wore shorts as in Germany. "*Nemets, perets, kolbassa, kislaya kapusta* (Germans, pepper, sausage, sauerkraut)," they chanted derisively. Markus and Koni soon took to wearing trousers and were quickly given the Russian names Mischa and Kolya. From then on Markus was known to his family, friends, and later, even his foes, by this nickname.

Mischa entered the Karl Liebknecht School for the children of German, Austrian, and other German-speaking Communist emigrants. He soon learned to cope with the turbulent life of everyday Moscow, such a change from the orderly life his family had known in Stuttgart, and grew accustomed to the gruff but warm-hearted Muscovites — who habitually spat out the shells of sunflower seeds wherever they happened to be — so different from the stiff Germans he had known. Simply getting to school in Moscow was an endurance test. The Wolf boys clung to the outside of the overflowing streetcars and balanced on the coupling mechanism between the cars. School itself was loud and undisciplined. Once Mischa's math teacher, Mrs. Fainberg, fled from the classroom in tears and never returned.

Mischa marched in the November revolution ceremonies on Red Square with his friends, shouting the praises of Stalin with the crowd as they filed past the leader. Stalin, a tiny figure muffled in a greatcoat, waved to them from the top of Lenin's tomb. They lined Gorky Street to cheer the first Soviet airman to fly across the North Pole to America. Mischa dreamed of becoming an aeronautical engineer for one of the famous aircraft design bureaus of Ilyushin or Tupolev.

Just as he was beginning to feel more Russian than German, Mischa was reminded that his Jewish-sounding surname automatically stamped him among Russians as an *Evrey*, a Jew. His father's contacts with the West made the family appear even more cosmopolitan and therefore increasingly suspect to their Russian neighbors. The Wolfs' attempts to overcome this knee-jerk Russian anti-Semitism with ever greater displays of loyalty to the Soviet cause were met only with suspicion.

Stalin was in full control of the Party and state apparatus by 1934 and gazed down benevolently on his subjects from portraits and posters. Life was still harsh, but there were signs of a better future. Rationing was abolished, and the newspapers were filled with Stalin's plan to raze old Moscow and build a ring of skyscrapers that would eclipse those of New York City.

Mischa spent the summer of 1934 with other fellow schoolchildren in the Ernst Thälmann Young Pioneer camp at Kaluga on the wooded banks of the Oka River. Tall and gregarious, mature beyond his years at age eleven, he was anonymously picked to be a group leader. It was much the same ritual that he was to experience later as a member of the Party nomenklatura. Members of this elite cadre were recommended for positions of responsibility by someone from above and then confirmed by acclamation.

The camp's adult supervisors were more interested in leading numbing drills than in expanding the minds of their charges. In a letter to his parents, Mischa complained bitterly about the senseless discipline, primitive sanitary conditions, and miserable diet of kasha gruel. His father replied with a flood of well-meant advice that, typically, was of little practical use.

> In order to combat abuses you need to form a commission and meet with your Pioneer supervisors. Make clear to them that if you aren't rested up then you won't be able to keep up with studies in the winter. . . . Also tell them that Comrade Stalin and the Party theses do not condone such haste. Quality is the byword! You can tell your Pioneer administration that I said this as a Communist doctor. But under no circumstances are you, as a good

Pioneer and especially a Pioneer leader, to bicker! You and the other group leaders should speak collectively with the administration. Do you understand, Mischa! And don't be despondent my boy! A big kiss from your Pappele.

Mischa had long been aware of his father's utopian view of human perfectibility, which entailed repressing whatever did not conform to this vision. As for life as a Young Pioneer, he later recalled mainly the positive aspects: "Everyone had a certain duty as well as responsibilities to society. . . . It was the feeling of belonging to a larger community, knowing that one was not alone and being there for others. . . . The word 'solidarity' never lost its meaning and content."

The alarming reports from Nazi Germany, where friends of the Wolfs were being arrested and imprisoned for opposing Hitler, heightened the family's gratefulness for having gained asylum in the Soviet Union.

Mischa never once doubted that wise Comrade Stalin had only the best interests of the Soviet people at heart. "Stalin's words were beyond any questioning for us Young Pioneers and future Komsomol [Communist Union of Youth] members," Mischa said, summing up those years.

He and Koni by now were almost indistinguishable from the other Russian boys who lived in the Arbat. In the summer the boys wore gym shirts, sneakers or sandals. In the winter they had heavy overcoats, a fur hat, and felt boots for the coldest days. They were now acting and thinking like Russians and had almost shed their German past.

Mischa came to admire Russians' openness and hospitality, their readiness to share everything with a guest or neighbor. Russians trusted their friends and did everything possible to help them. He was equally impressed by the nonchalance of the Russians he knew, their disdain for order and discipline and, not least of all, their love of company and alcoholic celebrations. Else, on the other hand, despaired that her sons had become *peyanitsi* (drunkards), especially since she had been strongly opposed to alcohol in her youth. "I guess that is dialectics," she remarked half-jokingly.

The Wolf family's vegetarianism became increasingly unworkable in Moscow, where vegetables and fruits were rare. They ate meat whenever they were fortunate enough to get it. Violating one of the cardinal pieces of advice in his medical book, Friedrich smoked heavily, a habit Mischa soon picked up as well.

Friedrich's unflagging support for the Soviet cause was rewarded when he received official permission to lease a plot of land and build a summer house in Peredelkino, the elite literary colony just outside Moscow. Mischa spent glorious summers with his family in their sprawling wooden dacha surrounded by birch trees. The house was filled at all times with visitors, and many a member of the German exile community in Moscow found refuge there during what they euphemistically called politically "complicated" times.

The great Russian writer Boris Pasternak lived nearby, and he would occasionally emerge from his dacha to watch his wife, Sinaida, play volleyball with Mischa and his friends. Mischa was already a favorite among the girls. He learned to dance with Nina Fedin and Zilya Selvinski, the daughters of noted Soviet writers, to the melodies from their old windup gramophone player.

As for Friedrich, he had no intention of being confined to the Soviet Union. He wangled permission to visit New York in 1935 for a performance of his *Sailors of Cattaro* at the Theatre Union. Brooks Atkinson of the *New York Times* hailed the production as the "most trenchant melodrama in town," and Friedrich reveled in the publicity the *Times* gave him as "Hitler's Public Enemy No. 1."

Fresh from Moscow, he was plainly awed by what he saw in New York but could not openly write about. In a letter to Else and the boys he praised Rockefeller Center as the "progressive side of capitalism of which Marx speaks. And the giant city library next to my hotel on Fifth Avenue where everyone can enter free of charge without a *propusk* [Russian for "an official permit"] . . . Granted this system is foul within, . . . but there is much to learn here, also for us," he remarked in one of his frequent flashes of insight.

Mischa's thoughts were being distracted elsewhere. His first serious adolescent love interest was Margit Knipschild, an intelligent and pretty young blonde girl from Berlin. A classmate at his school, she lived in a nearby home for the children of Austrian and German Communists whose parents had suffered under the Nazis. In spite of Margit's passionate letters to him, sex played no role in their relationship, he clearly recalled. But abstinence was not unusual in those prudish times, and in the overcrowded living conditions of Moscow.

Mischa and Margit looked on as many of their teachers vanished without a trace during the terrible purges of 1936 and 1937. After the Soviet secret police (the NKVD) arrested Herr Krammer, the school director, the Karl Liebknecht School was shut down, and the adolescent lovers parted. Margit was sent to the 592nd Moscow School and began studies in 1940 at the Pedagogic Academy. When Germany invaded the Soviet Union in June of that year, she and her fellow students were assigned to the civilian air defense. They were given pails filled with sand and a pair of tongs to dispose of incendiary bombs the Luftwaffe might drop on Moscow.

Shortly after Margit's return to her student room on September 19, 1941, after a long night's vigil on the rooftop of a Moscow building, she was taken into custody by NKVD officers and brought to secret police headquarters in the hulking Lubianka building. Without being informed of her alleged crime, she and a number of prisoners were led aboard a rail transport headed for Novosibirsk. After barely surviving the twenty-two-day trip, she boarded another transport to Frunze in Kirgizia, where she was informed of her sentence and crime — eight years for anti-Soviet agitation — and thrown in prison.

She refused at first to sign her sentence papers but gave in when the authorities made it clear that the alternative was to be tortured. From Kirgizia she was taken to a camp that belonged to the giant Karaganda gulag complex in Kazakhstan. One of Margit's girlfriends learned that Margit was in the same camp as Lotte Rayss, little Lena's mother, and informed Else Wolf. Both of them wrote to Margit, but she was forbidden to answer. She languished in the broiling summers and suffered during the bitterly cold winters of Kazakhstan for what seemed like an eternity.

Mischa, years later, spoke about his sense of guilt over what happened to Margit, of how he wrote to friends who knew her trying to get news of her. But it was only in January 1945 that Margit received a letter from him, the first that the prison authorities allowed her in four years. This time she was permitted to respond, and she wrote him of her "delirious joy" at receiving this sign of life from her friend. She told him that she had a two-month-old boy, Mischka, fathered by another prisoner, and that she was desperately trying to keep the baby alive. Could Mischa possibly send her a package with dried milk for the child and perhaps another letter? Half her sentence was over, and only four years remained, she wrote.

But on her release from prison in 1949, Margit was sentenced to seven more years of banishment and hard labor in Karaganda. She spent that time under the harshest conditions deep underground in a mine; at the end she was a locomotive engineer. After fifteen years of prison and internal exile she was permitted to return to the GDR in 1956. She met her Mischa again in East Berlin, but by that time they had both changed. Margit had lost her faith in Communism; Mischa seemed more convinced than ever.

Mischa had heard his parents speak in hushed tones about the arrests and secret trials of their friends, neighbors, and acquaintances during Stalin's reign of terror. Friedrich Wolf, while deeply worried that the purges were narrowing in on him, found an explanation for them. He told Else and the boys that socialism had been forced to take on such a brutal face because the Soviet Union, the world's only socialist state, faced a mortal danger in Nazi Germany. The state had to defend itself against this external enemy as well as against Stalin's opponents within the Party who sought to weaken socialism. Sometimes, regrettably, errors were made and the wrong people were arrested. Loud public protests, however, would achieve nothing and would only play into the hands of the enemy. Instead one had to try to convince influential comrades that a mistake had been made, he told them.

It was a lesson that Mischa never forgot. From the start, he had noticed that people did not mention the arrests when they spoke with members of the affected families. Nearly everyone believed it was all a mistake, that the arrests were the result of malicious denunciations. Yet life went on, and it was far from an unmitigated terror for a young person such as Mischa who was active in sports, popular among his friends, and anything but a brooder. Mischa never once doubted that the Soviet Union was a haven for the oppressed and downtrodden.

Mischa and Koni were fortunate in being transferred to the 110th Moscow School, not far from their apartment. Their parents saw this Russian school as a means to turn the boys into Russians as quickly as possible. Ivan Kusmitch Novikov, the school director, was a Russian humanist who encouraged political discussion even during those dark years. Mischa devoured Pushkin, Yesenin, and Mayakovski along with Heine, Galsworthy, and Hemingway. He and his classmates attended magnificent concerts in Tchaikovsky Hall and studied the works of the masters in Tretyakov Gallery.

In mid-1937, without warning, one of Friedrich's closest friends in Moscow, Wilhelm Wloch, was arrested. Wloch had fled to Moscow with his wife and two children after engaging in dangerous underground work for the Comintern (Communist International) against Hitler. In the early morning of July 27, he was taken away from the family's tiny apartment in the Hotel Lux by the NKVD. His wife Erna never forgot his last words to her: "Comrade Stalin knows nothing of this."

Afraid that he would be next on the list, Friedrich stepped up his efforts to leave the Soviet Union, using the pretext of wanting to join the pro-Soviet Republican forces that were fighting Franco in the Spanish Civil War. But his request was turned down with no explanation. His application to become a citizen of his adopted country was also denied, although Else and the boys were granted Soviet citizenship. Friedrich grew ever more nervous. He started whenever the doorbell rang at night. Then, mysteriously, as the purges reached a crescendo, he was given permission to leave the Soviet Union temporarily. Although his German passport was valid for only a few more days, he left on the first possible train for Paris, where he arrived stateless but immensely relieved. He had managed to escape the seething cauldron of Moscow, and by this time the Spanish Civil War was over.

Not long afterward Mischa got a postcard for his fifteenth birthday from his father in Paris: "Do you remember when we were in Paris five years ago on our way to Bréhat? Pappele is sitting on exactly the same square, Place Danton, and is thinking of his boys," Friedrich wrote. As far as it went, this was true. But Mischa sensed that there was more.

While Friedrich worked feverishly on new plays and books in France, he managed to fit in what was colloquially known in his circles as a *"techtelmechtel,"* an affair. His flame was Ruth Hermann, a German Communist who had worked illegally in Germany. He met her at the party he threw in Paris on his fiftieth birthday, and he was unable to resist her. Their child, Catherine, Mischa's third half-sister, was born in 1940. Mother and daughter escaped to Cuba from German-occupied France.

Alone with the boys in Moscow, Else Wolf took in Erna Wloch, the wife of the arrested Wilhelm Wloch, and their two children, a gesture that won her enormous sympathy. The cramped Wolf flat resembled a refugee camp. The two mothers slept on couches, Margot Wloch on a folding cot, and her brother Lothar bedded down in the kitchen. Mischa and Koni slept in their tiny connecting room.

Erna Wloch was never allowed to see her imprisoned husband and was permitted only to bring fresh underclothes to a side entrance of the Lubianka building. On one occasion she was handed an ominous bundle containing his blood-soaked laundry. It was only by chance that she and her children found out in 1939 that Wilhelm Wloch had died that year on his way to a forced labor camp. As with so many other disgraced soldiers of the Party, he was rehabilitated twenty years later.

Looking back, Mischa said that he was convinced that had Wloch survived, he would have worked to build socialism just like the others who survived Stalin's camps. "He would have been on their side and on ours," he argued. He was probably right. Many of those who survived the gulags continued to faithfully support every twist and turn in the Party line until the bitter end.

Despite her experiences with Stalin's reign of terror, Else Wolf, too, retained her faith in the Communist vision. For her, though, that vision was inexorably bound up with her unwavering belief in her husband's missionary role as a writer.

Erna Wloch, however, was so embittered by the loss of her husband that she was determined to return to Germany even under Nazi rule. Hitler and Stalin's nonaggression pact of 1939 allowed her request to return to Germany with her two children to be granted. In a supremely ironic twist of fate, her son, Lothar, who had spent his formative years in Moscow under Stalin, joined the Luftwaffe and fought for Nazi Germany against his former Soviet homeland.

Shortly after his sixteenth birthday, Mischa received a long letter from his father in Paris. As so often before, Friedrich excused himself for forgetting his son's birthday. "I hear you are getting your own Soviet passport. Congratulations on becoming a real citizen of the great Soviet people," he wrote. He proceeded to tell Mischa exactly how fortunate he was. He described the hopeless lives of the emigrants of his son's age in France who were condemned to aimless wandering and were unable to learn anything. "You can see how much more meaningful your life is," he remarked pointedly.

He also told Mischa of the Jewish woman he had met, a wonderful *"yidische Mamma"* who had given shelter to and clothed ten German Jews. Equally important, though, she was taking them the next day to see the film version of his play *Professor Mamlock*, which had been made in Moscow. She spoke with such pride about the Soviet Union, although she had never even been there, he wrote admiringly.

"You are fortunate to be where you are," he wrote. "You boys are lucky enough not to know anything else: no economic crises, no unemployment, no lock-outs. . . .

"Did you read the novel I wrote, Misch? What's your analysis? You are a very *kulturni chelovyek* [cultured man], so please write in detail about what you didn't or did like about it."

Typically, Friedrich also reminded Mischa of his responsibility to Lenutchka as her big brother. If his sister did not obey him, Mischa had the right to spank her "little ass," Friedrich said.

Always the dramatist, he closed with words calculated to bring tears to his son's eyes.

> Now Mischa, good night. It is late. I often think back on that winter day in Hechingen when you, tiny midget, came into the world. . . . Meni [as Mischa called his mother] bit me in the hand, you were causing her so much pain. It makes me feel good to remember all that. I wish I could experience it all over again. Give Meni a big fat kiss and be my big, brave boy. Your Papp.

Friedrich spread the word to his friends that he planned to return to his family in Moscow by the autumn of 1939, provided that he could work undisturbed on his new play during the summer. He also spoke wistfully of returning one day to "our beloved, liberated Germany," where he and his friends would help create a "wonderful German theater" in Berlin, Hamburg, and Stuttgart.

It would be two years before Friedrich was reunited with his family. Following the Nazi invasion of Poland and France's declaration of war on Germany, Friedrich was arrested in France as a stateless alien and taken to the infamous concentration camp of Le Vernet. Among his fellow prisoners was Arthur Koestler, who by then was deeply disillusioned with Communism. *Darkness at Noon*, Koestler's seminal novel about Stalinism, marked him in Friedrich's eyes as a traitor to the Soviet Union. Nothing could destroy Friedrich's faith in the Soviet Union, not even the Hitler-Stalin pact. While languishing in Le Vernet camp, Friedrich was given an opportunity to emigrate to America. But he refused, since it would have meant writing in the U.S. application form that he had never been a Communist. Faced with extremely harsh living conditions in the camp and the prospect of being turned over to the Nazis, he displayed an unflagging optimism that was a source of inspiration to the other prisoners.

Else, with the aid of the family's influential friends in Moscow, lobbied the Soviet authorities ceaselessly, asking that they help gain Friedrich's release by granting him Soviet citizenship.

In August 1940, two months after France's capitulation to Germany and only a month before he was scheduled to be turned over to the Nazis and certain death, Wolf was told that he had been made a Soviet citizen. The following spring he was deported to the Soviet Union along with Soviet veterans of the Spanish Civil War.

Markus, Koni, and their mother welcomed him at Kiev station, which, in a macabre reflection of the times, was sealed off for the event by troops supplied by the secret police. Nazi Germany and the Soviet Union were now allies, and not too much was to be made of the veterans' return from Spain.

Mischa by now was nearly six feet tall and peered down on his father with less awe but with greater respect because of the ordeal his father had been through in France. His own boyhood dream of designing and building planes was coming closer to reality. He was accepted at age seventeen as a student of the aeronautical academy in Moscow and now spent long hours bent over his drawing board in a corner of the Wolfs' apartment. Much of his free time was occupied by military training. One day Mischa was mysteriously summoned to a meeting of Party officials, where he was asked questions by the father of a schoolmate. Unknown to him at the time, he was then placed on a confidential nomenklatura list that would accompany him wherever he went in coming years.

With Hitler's invasion of the Soviet Union in June 1941, the Wolf family dismissed whatever qualms they had had about Stalin's terror. Friedrich knew that the Nazi secret police would include him among the dangerous persons to be taken into custody if German troops succeeded in taking Moscow. Shortly before Lenutchka was evacuated to a home for the children of writers in Tchistopol, Else gave her a word of caution: she was never again to speak German, the language of the enemy. Lena obeyed.

As the Wehrmacht rolled to within twenty miles of the Soviet capital in October 1941, Friedrich and other members of the Writer's Union and their families were ordered to board a military train and permitted to bring one rucksack per person. Their destination was Alma-Ata, the capital of Kazakhstan. The three-week journey was one of indescribable hardships.

The train proceeded at an agonizing crawl across the Ural Mountains, constantly shunted aside on the single track by other trains packed with Soviet troops heading for the front. Flatcars piled high with machinery from factories being evacuated to Siberia, along with workers, also had priority over the train carrying the writers and their families. With some luck, the group obtained bread and other basic foods at the stations along the route using vouchers issued them by the authorities.

Once again, Else Wolf rose to the challenge during their evacuation. Each day she distributed 400 grams of bread per person and helped soothe the tempers that flared in the cramped railroad cars. Washing was out of the question, and the toilets were clogged. The other, less hardy members of the group stared in amazement as Friedrich and Markus ran into the snow piled at the side of the tracks in −20-degree temperatures and rubbed themselves clean.

Although he did not have his instruments, Friedrich tended to the sick who lay apathetically in their bunks stacked three high in the hot, stinking cars. Mischa helped care for the frail Anna Akhmatova, the greatest living Russian poetess. Two of her husbands had vanished during Stalin's purges, and her son was interned in a labor camp. For more than a year, she had stood in line each day, together with other mothers and wives, to learn of his fate. Mischa was unaware at the time that she was officially disgraced.

Hildegard Plevier and her husband, Theodor, who later wrote the best-selling novel Stalingrad about the destruction of the German Sixth Army in 1943, were also among those evacuated from Moscow. She had nothing but praise for Else and Friedrich Wolf's selfless devotion to those in need.

Mischa successfully completed the fifth semester of his studies in 1942 at the relocated aeronautical academy in Alma-Ata. Koni, now seventeen, joined the Red Army and was assigned to work at the front in a propaganda unit whose mission was to persuade German soldiers to desert. He was part of the Forty-seventh Soviet Army that fought its way into the heart of Germany in 1945. Friedrich was assigned to the front lines to help in the denazification of those captured German officers who agreed to reject the Nazis. A number of them joined the pro-Soviet National Committee for a Free Germany, which Friedrich had helped found. Again, as during the First World War, Friedrich seethed with anger over the arrogance and privilege of the senior German officers. Even as prisoners of war, they retained their manservants.

Only Else returned to Moscow, where she coped with the hardships of the home front. She attempted to keep the family together with an unbroken flow of letters to her husband and sons, written in Russian so that they would pass military censorship. She suffered stoically in the knowledge that Friedrich was in the midst of an affair with the wife of a close Russian friend.

On his nineteenth birthday, Mischa was accepted as a full member of the exiled Communist Party of Germany. The Party had other things in mind than aeronautics for the lanky bilingual youth who was displaying keen intelligence and resourcefulness in every task he was given. He was ordered to leave the academy and report to the Comintern school at Kushnarenkovo, near Ufa, an important industrial city on the banks of the Belaya River. Mischa obeyed like a loyal soldier of the Party.

The elite school, located on a prerevolutionary farming estate, was run by the Comintern (Communist International). The students, who came from countries occupied by Nazi Germany or allied with it, were to be molded into Communist functionaries. As members of the Party's elite nomenklatura, they were to be placed in key positions after their countries were liberated from Nazi rule.

Mischa was quickly initiated into the school's clandestine rules of behavior: students were given a cover name; their real names and past lives were to remain a carefully guarded secret. He was given the pseudonym Förster and was chosen, on the basis of the Party's list of names, to be leader of the student group.

Shortly after his arrival, Mischa ran into an old friend from Moscow, Wolfgang Leonhard, in the school dormitory. They had known each other since 1935, when they both entered the Karl

Liebknecht School. Leonhard recalled their terse greeting in the dormitory more than a decade later in his book, *Child of Revolution*, which described his break with Communism: Mischa casually extended his hand to his friend and introduced himself as Förster; Leonhard replied with his new code name, Linden.

A day at the Comintern school began with roll call in the courtyard and sports before breakfast: gymnastics, cross-country running, and broad-jumping. Each student's performance was carefully recorded, and Mischa did well in sports.

Since all the men had gone to war, he and his fellow students were assigned to the machinery maintenance crew on the nearby state farm. They also unloaded the stream of barges that docked on the Belaya River.

The teachers were highly trained Communist functionaries from each country represented in the school. Their real identities were known neither to the pupils nor to each other. Mischa was impressed by the enormous theoretical knowledge of his teachers. Their explanations were always concise, conforming precisely to the official line in *Pravda*, the Soviet Party newspaper.

Comrade Klassner, one of his teachers, whose real name was Paul Wandel, was typical of the new breed of functionaries, who were replacing the older, less educated, working-class revolutionaries who had led the armed uprisings and mass strikes after the First World War. Klassner had the uncanny ability to anticipate ideological shifts in the Party line and then to effortlessly argue the exact opposite of what he had previously taught. Although he was German, his main allegiance was to the Soviet Union and, above all, to Joseph Stalin. After the war he became an important East German functionary.

Comrade Mikhailov, the Bulgarian school director, personally lectured on the history of the Comintern. He was an inspired teacher who described the Party's revolutionary struggles in each country so graphically that Mischa and the other students almost felt as if they had taken part in the action themselves. Years later they would learn that Mikhailov's views were the unadulterated Stalinist version of history. They were told virtually nothing about the mortal enemies of the Bolsheviks, except their names: Trotsky and Bukharin.

By now it was clear to Mischa that he and his fellow students were being prepared to be dropped behind German lines before the end of the war. He was instructed in the use of rifles, machine guns, and pistols and trained in guerrilla warfare. He was taught, and told to commit to memory, the procedures for producing illegal leaflets using the most primitive means. Taking notes was prohibited. Together with the others he also learned how to react "correctly" and without directives from above to all political questions relating to the Soviet Union. But, he asked himself, what if he were caught and tortured so that he would be forced to reveal his real identity? He was certain that as the son of the Jewish writer Friedrich Wolf the Nazis would swiftly eliminate him.

The students were given access to sources of information that ordinary Soviet citizens had no idea existed. The school library contained information bulletins put out by the Comintern containing articles and broadcasts from the Western media. They were numbered and could be read only in the library, and the students had to sign their names when given a copy.

Mischa was grateful and proud that the Party regarded him as politically mature enough to be exposed to the views of what was, after all, still the "class enemy," despite Moscow's wartime alliance with the Western powers.

Long afterward, the Comintern students learned that the few graduates of their school who had been actually sent behind the German lines were quickly caught by the Gestapo and executed. This outcome was not surprising since the young Communists had been poorly prepared for guerrilla fighting. But conditioned by the morbid Stalinist suspicion that traitors lurked everywhere, many suspected that the executed guerrillas had been betrayed by someone in their own ranks; whoever it may have been was never revealed.

Mischa and the others were repeatedly warned by their instructors that those comrades who did not correctly toe the Party line would face expulsion and worse. Klassner demonstrated this in the most drastic manner by testing whether his students were totally subservient to the Party. During a class discussion, he turned to Willy, an older student and former worker, who had fought bravely in the International Brigade in Spain against the Fascists and was well liked among the students, and asked him to answer a hypothetical question: What would he do if he, as head of an illegal Communist group operating within the German invasion forces inside the Soviet Union, was ordered to burn down the houses of Soviet civilians and shoot the women and children?

Willy swallowed hard and stammered what he had been taught. "It is essential to preserve the secrecy of the illegal group," he responded.

"Even if this meant committing atrocities against the Soviet population?" Klassner probed.

Willy admitted that he was not entirely sure, but repeated, as he had learned, that the illegal group was not to be betrayed under any circumstances.

Klassner lashed out at the hapless Willy, accusing him of treason against the Party and the Soviet Union. All the students, except Wolfgang Leonhard, according to his own account, joined in the teacher's assault. Willy was thrown out of Comintern school and expelled from the Party. Under the circumstances, there was little doubt that he would end up in prison or in one of Stalin's gulags.

Nearly fifty years later, Mischa provided his own version of the event, recalling that Willy had been accused of violating Party discipline and had foolishly blurted out: "I shit on Party discipline." Mischa said that he and the others had tried to save Willy by getting him to engage in "self-criticism." Pausing for a moment, Mischa recalled that Willy had indeed ended up in Siberia — not for political reasons but because he was German — and was returned to East Germany after the war. The incident, Mischa admitted, had long remained with him as a "very unpleasant memory."

Although the students were warned against the ravages of alcohol and intimate contacts with the opposite sex, Mischa flaunted both bans. He was attracted by a shy nineteen-year-old dark-eyed and fair-haired girl, code-named Stern, who had a reputation as the most copious notetaker in the entire class. Her real name was Emmi Stenzer. Her father, Franz, a Communist deputy in the Reichstag from Bavaria, had been murdered by the Nazis in Dachau concentration camp.

In a macabre twist of fate, Emmi's mother was among the first German emigrés to be arrested in Moscow in 1937 and subjected to ceaseless interrogation. Miraculously, she managed to convince the NKVD of her innocence and was released. But she did not tell her daughter (who at the time was in the international children's home in Ivanovo) about her ordeal until after the war. Frau Stenzer, too, was certain that the Soviet authorities had made a tragic mistake.

Wolfgang Leonhard would never forget his own interrogation—more like an inquisition—at the Comintern school. It was conducted by Director Mikhailov, Klassner, an unnamed woman, and, to his total surprise, Emmi Stenzer, alias Stern. Leonhard was accused of "unbolshevik behavior" and "arrogance," but he was never told what he was actually supposed to have done.

"Nonetheless, I already felt guilty of having committed an offense," he recalled.

He described how Emmi Stenzer rose at this point and glanced at her notes on a sheet of paper. In a calm, steady voice she quoted all the "suspicious" remarks her fellow student had made since entering the school. Leonhard was bombarded with criticism and then told to state his position. Bewildered, he could reply only that the criticism was justified and that he would try to improve himself.

The next day in class, Emmi Stenzer sat as always in the row in front of him. Leonhard reflected that her informing on him had been detestable, but he resolved to be very careful about his remarks in the future. Mischa and the others were meant to learn the same lesson.

Although the female and male students lived in separate dormitories, Mischa recalled that "intimate contacts" were nonetheless possible. He and Emmi were able to steal moments for themselves in the midst of their packed schedules. Summer harvests on the state farm, where the students worked, offered many opportunities to be together.

In the autumn of 1942, the students were told that a

common front had to be forged with the Western Allies and all political forces opposed to Hitler. Mischa quickly grasped the implications. After the war was won against Nazi Germany, the Soviet Communist Party would work together with bourgeois and left-wing political movements previously denounced by the Party in order to build an antifascist Germany. Both he and Emmi learned a cardinal lesson from their nearly ten months at the Comintern school: individuals erred, but the Party never did.

The Comintern school was closed down in May 1943, having outlived its purpose. Emmi was sent to the front to work with the National Committee for a Free Germany, where she helped produce leaflets urging the German troops to surrender. She later admitted that they were worthless.

A fearless young woman, she was seriously wounded at Gomel when shrapnel from a German grenade almost tore off her leg. The lingering pain from the wound would remind her of the war for years to come. Mischa was ordered by the Party to return to Moscow and work as an editor and commentator for the radio station of the exiled German Communist Party, which targeted German troops and the civilian population. There was no mention of his resuming studies as an aeronautical engineer when the war was over, and he no longer asked.

One day in 1944, when his father was home on leave, Mischa told his parents that he and Emmi were going to marry the next day. Friedrich, forgetting his own hasty marriage to Else, replied tongue in cheek how nice it was that Mischa was letting him know. The following day, September 24, the strikingly handsome Mischa married the petite, watchful Emmi in the marriage bureau opposite the Moscow Zoo. There were no witnesses, but the couple later made up for the lack of ceremony by taking part in an all-night celebration at home with family and friends. Even Wilhelm Pieck, the head of the exiled German Communists and later president of the German Democratic Republic, sent his warmest congratulations.

Long after his divorce from Emmi, Mischa remarked that he and Emmi had married so that the authorities would not separate them. "It was almost a marriage of convenience, but there was also love," he reminisced. The Party separated husband and wife anyway. They could come together only on special occasions in Moscow.

Hitler's invaders would soon be hurled back by the Red Army, and the following year Mischa and Emmi would return, not home, as Soviet Russia had become their home, but to their native Germany, which lay vanquished and in ruins.

C H A P T E R
2

Markus Wolf gazed down fascinated at defeated Germany several thousand feet below the droning Soviet military plane that flew him toward Berlin. On this brilliantly clear day in May 1945, he was amazed to see that the red-roofed villages and towns appeared to be intact despite the fierce fighting that had just ended.

As the plane flew low across the serene Oder River, Wolf saw other towns flattened by Soviet artillery in the most massive bombardment the world had ever seen. Tens of thousands of dead Soviet soldiers still lay unburied in the ground below him.

During the remaining half hour of the flight to Berlin he saw undamaged settlements in the midst of the forests and lakes of Brandenburg. A shimmering white ribbon, the Autobahn, sliced through the green countryside, a sharp contrast to the rutted roads in the Soviet Union.

Wolf, seated with Emmi and their comrades from Moscow, was mentally bracing himself for his arrival in Berlin. Only two weeks had passed since Nazi Germany's unconditional surrender on May 8. Wolf was the second member of his family after Koni to return. In the eleven years since the Wolf family had fled the Nazis, the Soviet Union had become their motherland. So Wolf was intensely curious about what he would see and experience in Germany and, most of all, what the Germans would be like in defeat.

From the air, even the suburbs of Berlin looked remarkably

untouched by the recent battle. But then as the plane winged low over the center of the vast city, he received a shock. As far as he could see, there was nothing but the jagged, empty shells of buildings. Only an occasional moving truck or car reminded him that this vast field of ruins was actually Berlin.

Wolf and the other German Communists in the aircraft had been assigned by the Soviet leadership to join the Ulbricht Group, which was already installed in the Soviet Zone of Germany. Walter Ulbricht, a wily, goateed functionary of the exiled German Communist Party who had survived the Moscow purges, had been chosen to rebuild the Party in the Soviet Zone and then, Stalin hoped, in all of defeated Germany.

Wolf and his fellow male passengers bound for Berlin all looked strangely alike. They wore the same serge suits, identical coats, and hats, issued them at a special store near Red Square. He was one of the tallest men in the plane, slender and athletically built like his father had been as a young man. With his horn-rimmed glasses, searching gaze, and fine features he looked more like an intellectual than a Party functionary. His sensual mouth, though, betrayed another side of his nature.

The plane jolted onto the hastily patched runway of Tempelhof airport. As Wolf walked through the badly damaged terminal, he heard several workers speaking German. It was strange: the language was so familiar, but the people were remote. The group was driven in a military bus through the streets of the nearly eradicated city. Wolf was convinced that the center of Berlin could never be rebuilt. A new city would have to be erected in the suburbs, where the cherry trees were in bloom that warm spring.

Things looked much better in Berlin-Friedrichsfelde, where the Soviet officers' hotel was located. The houses were intact, and the shops were filled with bread and other basic foods. Compared with people in Moscow, the Germans in the streets were remarkably well dressed. Berlin's sprawling subway and elevated urban rail systems had resumed punctual service. Beer had begun to flow again in the taverns.

A few days after his arrival, Wolf was standing at a bridge in Berlin-Lichtenberg when he spotted a familiar figure wearing a Soviet officer's uniform. The officer, who had a shock of black hair, was trying to repair a motor bike. It was Koni. He had survived after fighting with the Red Army across Russia, Ukraine, and Poland, earning six medals for bravery on the long road to Berlin. The brothers' reunion was entirely unsentimental — no hugging or kissing despite their closeness. They laughed as Koni told of his brief interlude as the Soviet commandant of Bernau on the outskirts of Berlin. But soon Koni grew tired of playing occupier, and returned to the Soviet Union to attend the Moscow film academy.

Markus had been handpicked by the Party to serve as the chief foreign policy commentator of Berlin Radio, which only a few weeks earlier had been trumpeting the Nazi leadership's last fanatical appeals to hold out against the "Bolshevik barbarians." Even though his broadcasts calling on the Germans to surrender had fallen on deaf ears, Wolf had been highly recommended for this new post by Robert Korb, his superior at Radio Moscow.

Shortly after arriving in Berlin, Markus was taken to the Soviet-controlled radio station in what was soon to become the British Sector of Berlin. His pseudonym would be Michael Storm. He would also control the political content of broadcasts to make absolutely certain that they were in Moscow's interest.

Markus and Emmi were assigned a spacious five-room apartment nearby, which had been requisitioned by the Soviet Army. The young Wolfs also had a country house at their disposal at Glienicke Lake just outside the city. Life for them in postwar Berlin had its drawbacks — they encountered many diehard Nazi sympathizers — but they were still a good deal more comfortable there than they had been in Moscow, where they had been only junior members of the Party's privileged nomenklatura. In Berlin they were entitled to the perks enjoyed by the most senior Soviet officers in occupied East Germany.

Nothing, though, prepared the Wolfs for their encounters with the Germans. "Strange as it sounds, the Berliners I have gotten to know in this part of the city near the radio station completely fail to realize that Germany is a defeated country and that they bear all the blame for the war and the terrible crimes," he wrote in his first letter from Berlin to his parents in Moscow.

Emmi was shocked by the reply she was given by her German landlady when she asked about the Nazi concentration camps: "German men would never do such things," the woman said irritably.

"When I heard them talk, I often thought it would have been better not to return to Germany," Emmi said of those years. Markus complained that the Germans were so ungrateful for the selfless help the Soviet army gave them that they even grumbled about getting green coffee beans instead of roasted coffee. The Social Democrats had the audacity to protest against their members being "taken away" by the Soviet authorities.

He neglected to mention that the Soviet occupation authorities were carrying out mass arrests of both ex-Nazis and opponents of Stalinism, and that they were sentencing the prisoners to forced labor camps, strangely enough, at the former Nazi concentration camps of Buchenwald and Sachsenhausen. Not until forty-five years later did the Soviet Union admit that nearly forty-three thousand Germans had died in these camps between 1945 and 1950, many of them former Social Democrats who had resisted Communist totalitarianism. Their families were forbidden ever to reveal what had happened.

Wolf spent ten months covering the Nürnberg War Crimes Trials that began in November 1945. His first child, Michael, was born during the trials. Nicknamed Mischenka, Michael closely resembled his father but had the blonde hair and gray eyes of his grandmother, Else.

Over those months Wolf mingled with the Western correspondents who lived with him in Nürnberg in a castle requisitioned by the U.S. Army. There he met a young German-born journalist, Willy Brandt, who wore the uniform of a Norwegian press officer. Their paths would cross again in the future.

Wolf's impatience with the Germans reached its height in Nürnberg. As an accredited correspondent for Berlin Radio, Wolf sat with the other correspondents in the press section of the tribunal, gazing at the nineteen Nazi leaders who were accused of ordering the deaths of nearly forty million people. These cowardly, pitiful creatures refused to accept any responsibility for their crimes, Wolf brooded. After the trial ended on October 1, 1946, in a commentary by "Herr Markus Wolf of Berlin Radio," broadcast in the Eastern and Western occupation zones and heard by millions of Germans, Wolf said Nürnberg had shown that the Germans could not escape responsibility for the mass crimes, committed in their name, simply by claiming that they had only followed "orders from above."

"If our people draw the consequences from this trial, then the sentences today could go down in history as the beginning of a newly created, free and peace-loving Germany," Wolf said. Strictly speaking, Wolf should not have spoken of "our people," since he was still a Soviet citizen.

Official Soviet policy in postwar occupied Germany was still based on Stalin's directive that the Communists were to cooperate with all antifascist political groups. Social Democrats, Liberals, and even Christian Democrats were elected as city mayors and regional leaders in the Soviet Zone. Walter Ulbricht's Communist functionaries were to remain discreetly in the background to make sure that the democratic process did not veer out of the Party's control.

Many of the older Party officials who joined Ulbricht had fought against Hitler as exiles in the Soviet Union and the West and remained idealists in spite of Stalin's purges. Encouraged by the Party's slogan after 1945 — "A Special German Road to Socialism" — they were confident that they would be able to avoid the tragic "errors" of Stalin's Byzantine Soviet state.

Wolf had first learned of the "Special German Road to Socialism" at Comintern school, so he was not in the least surprised when the Party line was reversed, leaving the "bourgeois" political parties in the GDR to mutate into lapdogs of the Communists. Nor was he surprised by the humiliating fate of the East German Social Democrats. Logic had told him that their influence would fade from the day in 1946 when they were merged into the Communist Party to produce the Socialist Unity Party of (East) Germany (SED).

Both Wolf and his father still spoke with fervor of the ideals of the Party and identified with its goals of social justice. But Friedrich Wolf had seen too much and remained silent too long under Stalin to remain true to his earlier ideals. As for Markus, a hard shell had grown around his emotions ever since the wanton arrests of his teachers, friends, and acquaintances in Moscow and the relentless dialectic of the Comintern school. He had once dreamed of building aircraft for the Soviet Union, but instead he had become an adept and agile member of the Party nomen-klatura.

Friedrich Wolf waited impatiently to be allowed to return to Germany and was convinced the delay was owing to Stalin's mistrust of the Jews. Only after appealing to Stalin himself was he given permission to return. Friedrich joined his son in Berlin in 1946, leaving Else to pack their belongings and dispose of the dacha in Peredelkino. But his elation at first setting foot on German soil was soon dampened when the conquered Germans refused to swallow the bitter medicine he had in store for them. His anti-Nazi play You Shall Reap as You Sow was rejected by East German theaters as being too harsh on the Germans. Just as he had repressed his knowledge of Stalin's crimes, the Germans wanted only to forget the Nazi era.

Friedrich's praise of Stalin in the early 1950s, even as the dictator unleashed a wave of anti-Semitism in Moscow, brought him political rewards. He was appointed East Germany's first ambassador to Poland. Schools and units of the National People's Army bore his name, and his chest was covered with medals. Yet all the official adulation could not make up for the loss of the Germany that he had once so loved. He died in 1953, disillusioned, shortly after the young woman he fell in love with while taking a spa cure gave birth to Thomas, his seventh child.

Else telephoned Markus early on October 5, 1953, to tell him that his father had died. Markus drove his Soviet-built Pobyeda car from his home in Berlin-Pankow to Lehnitz, north of Berlin, where his parents lived. The sunlight played on the yellow autumn foliage of the birches lining the road. He wanted to remember his father as the unblemished hero he had been to him in his youth, but he knew that Friedrich had been all too human. At the house he found his father still lying on the floor next to his bed, where he had collapsed of a heart attack. Else was despondent but remained calm, just as she had always been in difficult situations.

Like Friedrich Wolf, most of the several thousand German-Jewish communists and socialists who settled in postwar East Germany came to realize that there could be no return to the Germany of the past. Those who had survived the death camps or, like Friedrich Wolf, had been in exile were mistrustful and suspicious. Impoverished East Germany, not West Germany with its economic miracle, became a magnet for these Jewish survivors. They were attracted by the German Democratic Republic's claim to be the antifascist, socialist German state. And in many respects this promise rang true in those early postwar years. Unlike in West Germany, former Nazis were barred from assuming administrative posts, teaching, and working in the justice system, although some turncoats evaded the ban. In the 1950s the Central Committee of the East German Socialist Unity Party was filled with Jews who, despite their ordeal under the Nazis, tried to suppress their Jewish origins.

Young East Germans flocked to join the Party that gave land to the poor and opened the universities to the working class. But after Ulbricht tightened his grip on the Party, antifascism was replaced in practice by a new motto: Learning from the Soviet Union means learning to win. The seeds of a future right-wing backlash were being planted in East Germany; alienated for years by having to praise the Soviet Union, younger East Germans were attracted to the neo-Nazis after the demise of Communist rule.

To the traumatized Jews who returned to East Germany, even totalitarianism in the East seemed preferable to democracy in West Germany, where former Nazi "writing desk murderers" were restored to high positions in the government. One of the most prominent of these was Dr. Hans Globke, Chancellor Konrad Adenauer's state secretary from 1953 to 1963. Globke had served until 1945 as a senior official of the Nazi Interior Ministry, where he had helped prepare the intellectual climate for the Holocaust. He was the author of the legal commentaries to the notorious Nürnberg racial laws of 1935 that, among other things, excluded Jews from public life and banned their marriage to non-Jews. The Jews who returned to Communist East Germany told themselves that because West Germany installed ex-Nazis in senior government and judicial posts, it presented the greatest of all dangers.

Among the prominent Jews who came to the GDR were Anna Seghers, the writer whose best-selling anti-Nazi novel, *The Seventh Cross*, was made into a Hollywood film; Stephan Hermlin, postwar Germany's most gifted poet. Ernst Bloch, a leading Marxist philosopher, and Hans Mayer, the literary historian, were appointed professors at Leipzig University. Even the novelist Arnold Zweig, a Zionist, succumbed to emotions about Germany and returned to East Berlin. A few, a very few, such as the writer Stefan Heym who returned from America to praise Stalin in his East Berlin newspaper column, recognized the folly of their choice. Heym later condemned the hypocrisy of the Communists who banned his novels but never dared to expel him.

Some of the German Jews who rose to the top of the political heap remained unbending dogmatists: Gerhart Eisler, the propaganda chief whose brother Hanns composed East Germany's national anthem (the text with the words "Germany, united Fatherland" was later banned, and only the melody could be played); Albert Norden, a rabbi's son and Politbüro member, whose propaganda department was, ironically enough, located in Joseph Goebbel's old Nazi Propaganda Ministry, and who said that the GDR would never pay restitution to Zionist Israel; Hermann Axen, a survivor of Auschwitz and an influential Politbüro member until the GDR's collapse; Kurt Hager, a member of the ruling Politbüro in charge of ideological purity; and Hanna Wolf (no relation to Markus), the dogmatic head of the Communist Party academy. Hager provided one of the more memorable footnotes to history in 1988 by remarking that merely because Gorbachev was hanging up new "wallpaper" — a disparaging reference to perestroika in the Soviet Union — East Germany did not have to do the same.

Even the first head of the Handelsorganisation (HO), the huge state retail trade organization, was Jewish, although this did not save him from being arrested for alleged economic crimes.

Nor did being Jewish help Paul Merker, a member of the Politbüro who was arrested in 1952 as an agent of Zionism and the
"U.S. financial oligarchy." Released from prison in 1956, Merker
managed to survive in a publishing house in East Berlin and was
even awarded the Fatherland Order of Merit in Gold for toeing
the line.

The Party had bigger things in store for the talented and disciplined Markus Wolf. After the German Democratic Republic
(GDR) was proclaimed with Soviet backing on October 7, 1949,
in East Berlin — in retaliation for the founding of the Western-
backed Federal Republic of Germany on May 24 of that year —
Wolf was appointed first councillor at the new GDR Embassy in
Moscow. A diplomatic career was scarcely his goal in life, but
obeying the Party's orders was by this time second nature to him.

Markus and Emmi were still Soviet citizens, but they also
possessed West Berlin identity papers, since they still lived in the
British Sector of Berlin. But retaining his Soviet citizenship was
out of the question given Wolf's new assignment as a representative of East Germany in Moscow. It was with a heavy heart that the
couple applied to the Supreme Soviet to be relieved of their
Soviet citizenship. In spite of the new East German diplomatic
passports they were issued for the trip to Moscow, the Wolfs still
felt more like Russians than Germans, and they were happy to be
going back home to Moscow. They had always spoken Russian
with each other, sometimes switching to German for the benefit
of their young son, Michael. Tatjana, who was born in 1949 and
spent the first two years of her life in Moscow, was a favorite with
her father. Emmi disliked accompanying Wolf to diplomatic re-
ceptions, where he cut such a fine figure, so instead, she attended
evening classes in Slavic languages and literature at Lomonosov
University. Like most other East European diplomatic families,
they were assigned a comfortable apartment and had a maid, a
Volga German, who minded the children and did the housework.

Wolf was astonished the first time he saw Stalin, his childhood idol, close up and realized how small he was. Gazing down
on Stalin from the diplomatic gallery of the Supreme Soviet, Wolf

also detected a bald spot on the leader's pate, which was always retouched on Stalin's photos. The revelation, however, did nothing to dispel the awe Wolf felt in the leader's presence.

He never forgot the reception Stalin gave for Mao Tse-tung at the Hotel Metropol after a Soviet-Chinese summit meeting in Moscow. Stalin entered the hall wearing his simple military tunic without medals. Not a sound could be heard among the hundreds of guests. Stalin raised his glass in a toast to the Chinese leader and praised him as a leader whose roots were in the people. Wolf and the others who were present immediately understood the inference: Stalin, too, was a man of the people. Such modesty on the part of the genial leader of the world Communist movement was proof to Wolf that all the talk about a personality cult developing around Stalin was the work of the leader's opponents. Stalin had no part in it.

As first councillor of the new GDR Embassy in Moscow, Wolf was in charge of processing the applications of thousands of German Communists who were still trapped in the Soviet Union. Simply by withholding his signature of approval for emigrants whose politics he disagreed with, Wolf could prevent their return to the GDR. He sometimes did so, telling himself he was acting in the interests of the GDR.

In 1951 the Party approached Wolf once again with a new assignment. This one took him completely by surprise. He was to return to Berlin and help build a new foreign espionage service using Soviet intelligence as a model. Moscow recognized that as the cold war intensified it needed trustworthy East German agents because they could penetrate West Germany far more effectively than its own spies could.

A senior position in foreign intelligence required someone with an acute mind whose allegiance to the Soviet Union was beyond question. Few other younger East German Communist Party members had such qualifications. Wolf, on the other hand, had already proven himself to be a loyal protégé of the Soviet Union. His command of Russian and his understanding of Russian ways was so complete that Soviet officials regarded him as virtually one of their own.

Only one doubt lingered in their minds: the Jewish past of

the Wolf family. Being Jewish was a potential liability in 1951, when Stalin's anti-Semitic campaign was attaining new heights. But the Soviet decision makers also knew that Markus's father had chosen that German nationality and not Jewish nationality be entered into the family members' internal Soviet passports. Markus Wolf's links with his father's Jewish past were, in any event, tenuous at best. The only Jews he knew were atheists, and like most of them he was critical of Zionism and Israel. A Soviet officer, a good friend of Wolf's, had once remarked to him that Jews in the Red Army's quartermaster corps were responsible for shortages in army supplies. Wolf recalled years later that he had felt "personally affected" by the remark and had objected, but he could not remember whether he told the officer about his own Jewish roots.

Wolf concealed his first negative reaction to the intelligence assignment. Espionage work, like the Comintern school, meant secrecy, which ran against the grain of his outgoing nature. But he quickly overcame his initial doubts and became determined to live up to the trust the Party had placed in him. Espionage was vital, he told himself, especially as the cold war intensified. The work involved was not always pretty, but it was necessary in order to counter the aggressive aims of the enemy in Washington and Bonn. The cause of peace and socialism justified the use of all means.

Above all, it was important that East Germany be able to counter the Western Allied threat. The Americans had already installed Hitler's former general Reinhard Gehlen to head West Germany's new foreign intelligence agency, Organisation Gehlen. For Wolf this appointment only confirmed that former Nazis and aggressive American leaders had linked up in an attempt to roll back the new Communist governments in Eastern Europe.

General Reinhard Gehlen had commanded the Wehrmacht's military espionage unit against the Soviet army. In the closing days of the war the wiry little general had beat a hasty retreat from Berlin to the Bavarian Alps, where he hid rolls of microfilm containing thousands of files on all his spies and informers in the East, as well as analyses of Soviet military capabilities. After Germany's surrender, Gehlen presented a selection of this priceless treasure to American officers and was whisked off to Washington, where he was welcomed like a godsend by the CIA. The Americans cared little that he spoke neither English nor Russian. His aura of expertise managed to convince the CIA officers that he was an intelligence fox. In return for Care packages and CIA promises of financial and moral support, Gehlen relinquished his store of information to the Americans and was made head of his old organization.

Gehlen also swapped his Wehrmacht uniform for his new sartorial civilian trademarks: black hat, white scarf, and sunglasses. He was able to peddle the myth of his genius far and wide. Gehlen realized that the best way to justify an expensive intelligence service was to wildly exaggerate the capabilities and aims of the enemy. He excelled in constructing dire scenarios and managed to convince the CIA that a Soviet military strike against Western Europe was imminent. By the late 1940s he had four thousand officials under his command at the Organisation Gehlen in Pullach, a suburb of Munich. It was a motley crew, including ex-officers from the Wehrmacht general staff, SS hatchetmen, and anticommunist specialists from the Third Reich's Central Security Agency. They were an embarrassment for Washington, but American intelligence was drooling for the information that only Gehlen could provide.

In 1956 the Organisation Gehlen was taken over by West Germany and renamed Bundesnachrichtendienst (BND), the Federal Intelligence Agency. Although the agency initially netted a series of espionage coups against East Germany, the truth was that Gehlen's network of agents in the Soviet Union had all but melted away by this time. One by one his amateur spies had been caught, sentenced to death, or "turned around" by the Soviets. Information on the Soviet Union from tens of thousands of returned German POWs was much overrated. Furthermore, KGB moles inside the BND revealed nearly everything to Moscow. Years passed before the BND recovered from the ravages of the Gehlen era. The agency consistently lacked the ideological impetus, sheer imaginativeness, and perseverance that made East German intelligence so successful. Equally serious, it grossly underestimated the number of East German spies operating in the West.

The beginnings of East German espionage were modest in the early postwar years. Two old-guard Communists, Bruno Heidt and Franz Dahlem, directed intelligence operations against the West. Soon they had agents gleaning information from the Western Allied military establishments in West Berlin and from West Germany's new ministries, Parliament, armed forces, and the Bundesamt für Verfassungsschutz (BfV), the obtusely named Federal Office for the Protection of the Constitution, whose real function was counterespionage.

When Wolf joined the GDR's fledgling intelligence service in late 1951, the agency was still camouflaging itself under the name the Institute of Economic Research. Housed in a former school in Berlin-Pankow, and then in a prewar building on Rolandufer in central East Berlin, it was nominally under the control of a state secretary in the Foreign Ministry, Eugen Hanisch, alias Anton Ackermann. Nearly everyone in a senior position in East German espionage in those early days had been a prewar Communist and had engaged in undercover work for the illegal Communist Party during Hitler's Third Reich. Each had an alias, adopted during the Nazi era, which stuck with him for a lifetime.

Wolf immersed himself in a world where everything was the opposite of what it seemed to be, a world of distorting mirrors, where treason was good as long as it was the enemy that was betrayed. He spent the first six months as deputy head of the analysis section under Robert Korb, his former wartime boss at Radio Moscow who had gained firsthand experience as an "illegal," a Communist agent in Nazi Germany.

After proving his mettle in analysis, Wolf was moved into the more challenging sphere of counterintelligence. In addition to detecting enemy agents, counterespionage attempted to plant its own agents in the center of the enemy's intelligence operations in order to detect the information the Westerners were seeking, how they were trying to get it, and from whom. Here Wolf acquired the mental agility that was needed to control double agents and triple agents and to keep track of who had been given what information and for which purpose. He was quickly confronted with the realities of espionage in a divided Germany when two East German agents were uncovered as double agents of the West. This

episode was a reminder to him of the need to strictly compartmen-
talize intelligence in order to limit the information a double agent
or possible defector could get his or her hands on.

After a time Wolf realized that Anton Ackermann was in
political hot water. In addition to attracting fire for expressing his
political differences with Ulbricht, Ackermann had violated the
prudish East German leader's moral code by having an affair with
his maid that ended in his wife divorcing him. After the East
German uprising of 1953 was suppressed, Ackermann was
stripped of his position. Head sunken, Ackermann admitted that
he had held "hostile" views. The Party rewarded him for his self-
criticism with a writing desk, an office with a title on the door, and
a lifetime salary. Years later Ackermann was rehabilitated and
awarded the Fatherland Order of Merit for keeping his views to
himself.

Two other former Communist "illegals" who ran the Institute of Economic Research — the legendary prewar spy Richard
Stahlmann and Gerhard Heidenreich — played an important role
in Wolf's swift rise to the top.

Heidenreich was the sole founding father of East German
espionage to survive the end of the GDR. When I met with him in
the summer of 1993 he was nearly blind and lame and lived in a
spacious apartment in east Berlin's Roedernstrasse that was
crammed with personal mementos of his espionage past. But his
memory was his most important asset. Heidenreich recalled that
Wolf, while privately expressing support for Ackermann, had not
openly opposed Ulbricht. It was a duality that Wolf was to display
throughout his career.

"He was a friend of the Soviet Union and absolutely trustworthy," Heidenreich explained admiringly.

Wolf not only survived Ackermann's demise, but at the age
of thirty he replaced him as head of East German espionage. The
tall, well-mannered, and very intellectual-looking young man
who now wore nickel-framed spectacles came with an enthusiastic recommendation from the Soviet State Security police. Born
into middle-class German surroundings but hardened in the cru-
cible of Stalin's Russia, Wolf appeared to Ulbricht to be the ideal
person to understand the mentality and habits of the bourgeois

Western establishment that he would work to penetrate. Ulbricht personally informed Wolf of the appointment in December of 1952.

The Soviet advisors of East German intelligence had praised Wolf as a worthy German heir to the traditions of the Cheka, the first blood-soaked Soviet secret police, which later evolved into the KGB. But if there was one thing Wolf was determined to do, it was to keep his hands free of any trace of blood. "Rather a thousand beads of sweat than a single drop of blood," he boasted.

With the help of his Soviet friends, Wolf was determined to transform the still rudimentary East German espionage apparatus, then known as Central Department 4 of the State Security Ministry, into the proverbial "sword" of the Party. His aim was to develop unassuming agents who would be able to latch onto top secret information from the new American-backed West German government as well as the armies of the three Western Allies — the United States, Britain, and France — in West Germany and West Berlin. Moscow and East Berlin were obsessed by the belief that the Western Allies were secretly planning to mobilize "their" Germans to attack the massive Soviet forces in Germany and Eastern Europe. To get his hands on the intelligence needed to thwart such a threat, Wolf needed to train a new type of intelligence officer.

East Germany's first espionage school for officer training was located in a villa in the leafy Tschaikowskistrasse in Berlin-Pankow. The first batch of thirty recruits was not even told the purpose of their training. Secrecy was an inviolable principle, and each of the young men attending the course chose a code name for himself.

The participants were instructed in Marxism-Leninism and the basics of intelligence work. But they were also taught correct table manners and social behavior at parties, which were arranged by a teacher of English. The future intelligence officers had to be convinced Communists in order to instill the necessary revolutionary zeal in their agents, but they also had to teach their prospective agents in the field how to blend in perfectly with their surroundings in the West so that they could operate undetected in "enemy" territory.

Graduates of the espionage school were sent for on-the-job training to West Germany, where they emptied dead-letter drops and arranged clandestine meetings between their agents and couriers who smuggled the information back to East Berlin. But the new intelligence officers made mistakes too, costly ones, that landed them in West German prisons. For one thing, Wolf had underestimated the lure that Western consumer goods would represent for his elite espionage corps. A number of his officers attracted unusual attention in the West by acting like pfennig-pinching Eastern bureaucrats. They ate sandwiches in their cheap West German hotel rooms in order to save up their hard currency allowance, which they spent on purchases for themselves and their families back home in East Germany. All too often, the price of such parsimony was detection and arrest by West German counterespionage officials.

Wolf worked closely with the six "liaison officers" from the huge Soviet intelligence community in Berlin-Karlshorst who were assigned to him as advisors. They shared many secrets of the long Soviet espionage tradition and at the same time made sure that Moscow was kept abreast of every move made by East German intelligence. The Soviet advisors automatically received a copy of all the important information that the East Germans were able to gather. Moscow also maintained its own network of agents in East Germany, which it jealously kept for itself. Sometimes the Russians called on Wolf to reveal details of his operations so that the "German comrades" would not make any mistakes. Wolf would object, arguing that in doing so he would be exposing his agents to the danger of being revealed to the West by potential Western moles inside Soviet intelligence. But such differences of opinion with his Soviet advisors were usually dissolved in glasses brimming with vodka.

Those formative years of GDR espionage were not unlike those of the ambitious East German sports program. Espionage and sports were among the few fields of endeavor in which the GDR was able to prove itself superior to the West.

The first East German agents were anything but socialist paragons. One was an East Berlin physician with a weakness for drink, and another was a struggling businessman who badly needed the money. Both were instructed by their controlling officers to attend the regular drinking revels of Ernst Lemmer, a jovial conservative politician in West Berlin. Lemmer originally headed the Christian Democratic Union (CDU) in East Germany, but by the early 1950s he played an important role in Chancellor Adenauer's CDU in the West. He bubbled over with inside information on the Bonn government and his own contacts with the three Allied commandants in West Berlin.

Lemmer was unaware that East German intelligence had been given a copy of a pledge he had signed earlier agreeing to work for Soviet intelligence. But Wolf, after weighing the pros and cons, decided against using the pledge to compromise Lemmer. He firmly believed that compromised informers and agents were inherently unreliable, even though a remarkable number of Stasi agents were trapped into working in GDR counterespionage by one unsavory means or another.

Unknown to each other, the doctor and the businessman reported back the results of their evenings with Lemmer to their controllers in East Berlin. As is so often true in espionage, the value of the clandestine information was debatable. Invariably, many of the same top secrets cropped up soon afterward in the West German press.

Staff officers of East German intelligence, like their Soviet models, were given military rank and were issued army uniforms, which were kept in their office closets to be worn on special occasions. After an initial shudder, Wolf got used to wearing a general's uniform that was almost identical to those that had been worn in Hitler's Wehrmacht. In May 1954 he was promoted to major general, a meteoric rise for a young man who had never seen combat.

Among Wolf's earliest agents were former Wehrmacht officers who had been captured on the Eastern Front and had joined the Soviet-sponsored National Committee for a Free Germany that his father had helped found. These agents would visit their former Wehrmacht buddies in the West and dutifully submit intelligence reports back to the GDR.

Espionage headquarters in East Berlin also obtained a steady flow of information from East German engineers and technicians who were instructed to discover the secrets behind West Germany's economic miracle from their old friends and acquaintances in the West. A surprising number of Westerners required little coaxing to supply secrets. Many strongly opposed the rearming of West Germany and Chancellor Adenauer's policy of giving former Nazis influential positions in the Bonn government.

East German intelligence had one enormous built-in advantage in its undercover operations in the West: West Germany was an open society, and its fifty-seven million people shared the same language, history, and customs with the eighteen million East Germans. Dressed in Western clothes and shoes, an East Berliner could not be distinguished from a West Berliner.

Only a few months after taking over as espionage chief, Wolf suffered his first setback. In April 1953 Johann Krauss, one of his officers responsible for economic espionage, defected to the West, bringing with him the files on more than thirty East German agents in the West — who were promptly arrested. But the coup was not quite as spectacular as it first seemed to West German counterespionage. Many of the alleged agents named in Krauss's files turned out to be prospective recruits who had not yet been approached by East German intelligence.

Alarmed by the disclosure of their espionage activities on Rolandufer, the East German authorities ordered the emergency evacuation of headquarters and its dispersal throughout East Berlin. In scenes worthy of a low-budget spy film, dozens of trucks carrying files guarded by controllers, analysts, and communications officers lurched through the nearly deserted nighttime streets of East Berlin. Seeking to shake off any Western observers, the drivers took circuitous routes to the new buildings they were to occupy. As it turned out, the political espionage department landed in Klosterstrasse, only a few hundred yards from the former headquarters.

Wolf survived the defection remarkably well. Blame was placed on Ackermann. In 1956 East German intelligence was renamed Hauptverwaltung Aufklärung (HVA), or Central Intelligence Administration, under the direction of Major General Markus Wolf. Still virtually unknown, his name would soon instill fear and respect among his rivals in the West.

When the next East German intelligence defector, Capt. Max Hein, absconded to the West in 1959, he informed West German counterespionage that the HVA was a booming enterprise. He claimed it had thousands of agents in the West — a gross exaggeration — and that the agency had been merged with the State Security Ministry, which was true. State Security, the secret police, was known to some East Germans by its German initials MfS — standing for Ministerium für Staatssicherheit. But most citizens simply called it, with varying degrees of contempt, the Stasi. If someone half-jokingly mentioned the "Look, Listen, and Snatch Company," everyone knew the person was referring to the Stasi.

Captain Hein confirmed for Western intelligence that the HVA was headed by a certain Markus Wolf, known as Mischa to his Russian advisors. West German intelligence feverishly searched for a photo of the mysterious Wolf but came up with nothing better than childhood pictures and a fuzzy photo taken shortly after the war. Hein disclosed that Wolf recruited many of his agents from among East Germans who had family in West Germany, giving them a legitimate excuse to visit the West, but he was unaware of Wolf's latest strategy, which was designed to allow the HVA to penetrate to the core of the enemy's bastion of power.

Wolf had begun to riddle the three most important West German political parties, as well as the leading industrial companies and scientific institutions, with his agents. He also took care to plant low-level agents in the registry offices that recorded every change of address by West Germans, including moves abroad. Later, his spies were even located inside lonely hearts clubs, providing the names of promising female prey for East Berlin's Romeo agents.

Moles strategically placed inside the West German Defense Ministry passed on everything from troop deployment plans to technical details on the latest NATO weapons. This intelligence was augmented by information from agents located within the leading West German defense contractors. The spies were mainly native West Germans or East Germans who had "fled" to the West. Normally, they sent their espionage material to East Berlin headquarters via couriers or instructors — both East and West

Germans — who worked part-time for the HVA while maintaining their cover with ordinary jobs. Some moles had their secrets transmitted to East Berlin in the daily interzonal trains running between the two Germanys. Film capsules containing their photographed information would be deposited behind a removable wall panel in one of the train's toilets.

Every mole had a controlling officer in East Berlin who supervised and conferred with him or her in East Germany or neutral countries at regular intervals. The controller received all the mole's reports, which were then evaluated in the analysis section. The analyses were graded according to the quality of the information and then sent to senior HVA officers. Information deemed of special importance was passed on to Erich Mielke, head of State Security, and circulated to members of the ruling Politbüro.

Wolf routinely read the analyses of reports from his most important moles. Out of the more than one thousand HVA spies who operated in the West in the 1970s and 1980s, no more than fifty were high-level moles. He could recall their code names and locations years after East Germany had ceased to exist. For Wolf it was immensely exhilarating to command a clandestine network of dedicated moles who were divulging the West's innermost secrets to him. He had learned in Comintern school that knowledge and information were power, and now he had access to the secret information about his foes that the Politbüro and the KGB were eager to get. He came to the conclusion that espionage was, after all, a fascinating and suitably elite occupation, even if it did involve preying on the weaknesses of human beings.

Only a few years after taking command of the HVA, Wolf scored his first major coup by netting Hans-Heinz Porst, the millionaire head of a prospering West German camera-store chain who became an important mole in the liberal Free Democratic Party (FDP). Porst, who secretly joined the Socialist Unity Party (SED) of East Germany in 1958 during one of his visits with Wolf, was captivated by Wolf's unobtrusive friendliness, his readiness to discuss topics that were normally taboo in the Party, and his flashes of humor. Porst considered it an honor to work for a man of culture and refinement whose well-cut suits attested to his good taste. Porst's vision of German unity and his fascination with Wolf motivated him to deliver detailed information on the FDP and its key role in the conservative-led coalition that governed West Germany.

In time, and drawing on the patience he had learned from the Russians, Wolf would use his ubiquitous sources to glean top secret political, military, and industrial information from West Germany as well as from its American superpower protector and NATO.

Ironically, in those early years the West turned out to be a less formidable opponent for Wolf than was Erich Mielke, his superior and the minister of State Security. Mielke was the father of East German counterespionage, which he saw as the key function of State Security. To him, foreign intelligence was a dangerous waste of time. Born in 1907, the son of a wheel maker, in a tough working-class neighborhood of Berlin-Wedding, Mielke became a forwarding clerk and glowing Communist who slugged it out with the Nazis in the streets of Berlin in the early 1930s. A squat, boorish man, Mielke personified what many East Germans disparagingly meant by the word "*Prolet*," a proletarian lout.

Mielke had eyed Wolf with suspicion from the day Ulbricht appointed the thirty-year-old to head East German intelligence. The two men were exact opposites in almost every way. Wolf was extroverted, urbane, and towered over the dumpy and paranoically suspicious Mielke. Wolf's vastly superior learning automatically tagged him as a member of the intelligentsia, which Mielke instinctively mistrusted. Wolf was a cosmopolitan, part of an extended family that had been dispersed around the globe from Moscow to New York, whereas Mielke's horizon ended at the sector border of East Berlin. They had only two things in common: their zealous allegiance to the Soviet Union, and their conviction that if State Security lowered its shield against the enemies of socialism, the GDR would be lost.

In the course of time, Wolf learned a great deal about Mielke's checkered past. He discovered that Mielke kept evidence locked in his safe about the day in 1931 when he shot dead two policemen in Berlin before fleeing to the Soviet Union. He also knew about Mielke's habit of collecting information on the pasts of other East German functionaries who might one day prove dangerous to him. Mielke had once told a close associate the "naked truth" about Erich Honecker, the Communist youth leader who later drove Walter Ulbricht from power. After the Gestapo arrested him in 1935 on charges of treason, Honecker was rumored to have betrayed several of his Communist colleagues. In return, Mielke claimed, Honecker had been given "certain benefits" by the Nazi secret police while serving his ten-year prison sentence.

Mielke reluctantly left foreign intelligence to Wolf while controlling the Stasi's main activities, counterespionage, and, most important, the political police, who were responsible for internal control and surveillance of the population. Although the Stasi had taken over from the Gestapo, its job was more difficult, perversely enough, since the Communist system was far more unpopular among East Germans than the Nazis had been.

Back in 1952, when Mielke was still a state secretary in the MfS, the Stasi had numbered little more than 4,000 employees. The uprising of 1953 jolted the leaders into realizing just how unpopular they were, and the Stasi began to increase its ranks. The secret police had mushroomed to 52,700 in 1973 and grew by some three thousand each year until the agency was dissolved. After thirty-four years as head of State Security, Mielke would rule over an empire of nearly 100,000 staff members and some 150,000 informers. The annual cost of this secret police and foreign intelligence apparatus in the 1980s mounted to 3.5 billion GDR Marks (East German marks; $2.5 billion at the official exchange rate), a heavy burden for a country as small as the GDR.

In the mid-1960s, by contrast, the BfV had still been a medium sized-agency with 900 staff members and a modest budget of DM 20 million. By the mid-1980s, the agency had accumulated 2,150 employees and a budget of DM 175 million, not including the corresponding agencies that operated in each West German state. Yet all this was paltry in comparison with Wolf's HVA in East Berlin, which had 4,128 officers in 1989 and an annual budget of 1.4 billion GDR Marks (nearly $800 million). That was a great deal of money for a population of just over 16 million. The CIA's estimated budget, for a nation of 265 million people, was $3 billion.

Mielke could nearly always be found in his first-floor office, with the lights, like those in the Kremlin office of his idol, Stalin, burning late into the night. In times of crisis he often slept on a cot in a room adjoining his office. Conferences attended by Wolf and other senior officers turned into monologues; at one Mielke spoke for seven and a half hours. Mielke gorged himself on his power and the flattery he received from his subordinates. His vanity was such that he would boast about every award he received from home and abroad, and he wore his medals Soviet style, like a shield of armor across the jacket of his white dress uniform.

Just as he demanded total surveillance of the population, Mielke exercised minute control over his own apparatus, ordering his fifteen regional Stasi chiefs to report to him personally by telephone whenever they entered or left their district headquarters. The large telephone console on his desk was crammed with buttons enabling him to immediately summon his senior officers to his side.

Personally he led a spartan life, steadfastly refusing to have his 1950s-style office refurbished. Unlike his hard-drinking KGB counterparts, nearly all of whom he would outlive, Mielke neither drank nor smoked. He was a health fanatic, rising at 5:00 A.M., doing exercises, and swimming. His annual medical checkup in the Stasi hospital routinely ended with Mielke asking the chief physician, a general, whether he was fit for service and then receiving the standard reply, "*Jawohl*, Comrade Minister." Mielke's only real passions were his Stasi football team, Dynamo, and hunting. Wolf was incensed when Mielke, who lived in perpetual fear of anti-Stasi outbursts during Dynamo games, assigned HVA officers to stadium duty — a blow to the prestige of the elite intelligence officers. Wolf eventually succeeded in extracting his men from this duty by persuading Mielke that such exposure was dangerous for the clandestine service.

Like many members of the leadership in Moscow and East Berlin, Mielke was addicted to hunting, a pastime that had once been reserved for the aristocracy. A pure kitsch painting of a hunter and his dog, with deer bounding from a meadow into the woods, hung in the room next to his office. Wolf also took up hunting, but he preferred not to shoot game together with his loud-mouthed superior.

Wolf came to know Mielke as an incorrigible braggart who would wildly exaggerate the effectiveness of GDR foreign intelligence in the presence of his Soviet colleagues. Wolf cringed inwardly when Mielke told his guests that if the Party leadership were to order him to capture West Berlin during the night, he would have "GDR identity papers" issued to West Berliners by the time they woke up the next morning. He even went so far as to claim that State Security could take control of West Berlin without any outside help.

Although Wolf masked his distaste for Mielke's crudeness, he stood up for his opinions when attacked by his superior. Once, in the early 1960s, Mielke openly berated Wolf at a council meeting of senior State Security Ministry officials, accusing "Comrade Wolf" of practicing appeasement.

Wolf had argued against the campaign to remove rooftop and balcony TV antennas that faced west in order to pick up West German television. The distortions of the Western media could be more effectively combated by greater openness in the GDR media, he suggested.

"You mean we should let the class enemy broadcast his lies into every living room in the GDR?" Mielke asked.

"Comrade Minister, we should counter them with our own truths," Wolf replied.

"Comrade Wolf, I am afraid you have forgotten that we are not engaged in a philosophical debate, but that we are dealing with a vicious class enemy," Mielke said, glaring at his deputy from the head of the conference table.

The two men also disagreed on the question of how much security was needed to protect the Wolf family from the enemy. Wolf stubbornly refused to obey Mielke's orders that he and his family be given round-the-clock security protection by the Stasi. Mielke finally agreed to allow Wolf's driver, First Lieutenant Fiete Henning, to double as a bodyguard. Wolf, however, habitually sat next to Fiete in the front seat of the Volga car and not in the rear of the car as did Mielke and most other senior East German officials. A strong bond developed between Wolf and his officers because he treated them as equals.

Col. Klaus Eichner was one of Wolf's officers, and, like most staffers, he revered Wolf for the concern he showed for his subordinates, his keen intelligence, and his quiet self-control. Eichner had never once seen Wolf act arbitrarily, in contrast to Mielke's hysterical outbursts. Eichner never forgot Wolf's words at an HVA celebration marking the anniversary of the end of the Second World War. He began a speech to the assembled officers by reading from the letters he had written from Berlin as a young man in 1945 to his parents in Moscow. Eichner and the others were deeply moved. Even the occasional office rumors about Wolf's extramarital affairs only made him seem more human to Eichner and his fellow officers.

At the end of what was usually a long day, Fiete would drive Wolf home to Majakowskiweg, where a guard would salute and raise a red barrier pole to let the car pass. The street was sealed off from East Berlin proper, as was the rest of the Niederschönhausen section, an area dotted with large prewar homes. Several of the dwellings were occupied by members of the ruling Politbüro, but later, in the early 1960s, the families were moved to the Wandlitz compound outside Berlin.

The Wolf family — Markus (when he was home), Emmi, the three children, and a housekeeper — lived in a comfortable two-story house. Fiete, the driver-bodyguard, was like a father to the Wolf children, who were accustomed to their father's late hours and frequent absences from Berlin. The Wolfs' housekeeper, Friedel, doted on the children.

Franz, the youngest, had been born in 1953, the year of the fateful workers' uprising when the last vision of a just socialist society in East Germany was crushed by Soviet tanks. At that time Wolf reflected that a socialist Germany had once been his dream, as it had been his father's. But he remained silent about his doubts. To have voiced opposition to this distortion of socialism would have played into the hands of the West and cost him his job, he told himself. This was the lesson he had learned from his father.

Wolf often recalled the extraordinary way the house on Majakowskiweg had come to him. The prewar dwelling had been previously occupied by Anton Ackermann, Wolf's ill-starred boss when he joined East German intelligence in 1951. After losing his position as state secretary, Ackermann subsequently offered to swap houses with Wolf, who found the offer too good to refuse. Ackermann moved into Wolf's former small dwelling, and the Wolf family moved into the spacious house in Majakowskiweg.

Once he got home from work at night, Wolf made a conscious effort to leave behind all thoughts of Mielke and the other cares of the day. Lighting up a cigarette (he remained a chain-smoker despite several attempts to break the habit), he delved into the daily newspapers. Most of them were from West Germany, the area he needed to know the most about. Fittingly, the Western newspapers were regularly picked up by a government disposal service so that they did not fall into the hands of naive East Germans, who tended to believe everything they read in the Western media.

Wolf, like his father, rarely helped around the house, but he was a talented cook, a hobby he had picked up by watching his mother in the kitchen. All his specialties were Russian dishes: ucha, a Siberian fish soup; borscht, beet soup with sour cream; and *pelmeni*, meat-filled dough. These he would prepare with great gusto and serve to guests, including the top moles who visited him from the West.

Just as the Wolfs never felt themselves to be part of the East German leadership, they also looked disparagingly on the petit bourgeois lifestyle of the Politbüro members. Granted, an unmarked truck did deliver groceries to the Wolfs' home, and they had access to a well-stocked shop in the State Security Ministry, which always had scarce bananas and oranges, as well as low-priced Western clothing and appliances. But this was the extent of their privilege, Emmi later recalled. In any event, she said, the State Security shop was nothing compared with the special stores for the Politbüro leadership in their compound at Wand-litz.

At home, Wolf almost never talked shop, since he was sworn to secrecy along with every other officer of the HVA. On the rare days when he was home for supper, the family discussed the children's school activities and Emmi's work at the Culture Ministry, where she was responsible for contacts with the Soviet Union. She had completed studies in Slavic languages and successfully defended her doctoral thesis on Dostoyevsky. But the strains in the marriage were growing, not least because Wolf was frequently away on inspection trips to the regional HVA bureaus, and Emmi strongly suspected that, like his father, Markus was being distracted by comrades of the opposite sex.

CHAPTER

3

There could have been no starker contrast than that between Markus Wolf's triumphant return to Germany in May 1945 and the arrival of my friend Armin as a refugee in what was left of the war-torn Reich in late 1945.

Expelled from his native Danzig (Gdańsk) by the Polish victors in late 1945, Armin was an orphan when he set foot in the Soviet Zone of Germany. It was the first stage in a postwar German odyssey that would lead him to a pinnacle of recognition by the all-caring Communist Party and to the hopelessness of a prison cell.

Armin was born in Danzig in 1932, the youngest son of a prosperous burgher. The ancient and Free City of Danzig, a glittering jewel of the Baltic seacoast, was under the jurisdiction of the League of Nations after having been separated from the Reich after the First World War. More than 90 percent of the inhabitants were German. Less than a year after Armin's birth, a sea of Nazi flags blanketed the city to mark the election victory of Hitler's party.

Armin's father owned a thriving metal products factory together with a Jewish partner. The two got along well, Armin told me as we sat talking about our boyhoods in my room in the Student Village a few months after Armin's escape to West Berlin from the East. His father had never believed the anti-Jewish

71

propaganda of the Nazis but had discreetly helped his partner to escape from Nazi Germany in the late 1930s. By that time his father had joined the Nazi Party and his mother, the Nazi women's organization.

As a boy in the German city of Danzig, Armin had proudly worn his Hitler Youth uniform: brown shorts, brown shirt, and belt buckle emblazoned with the swastika. When he was ten years old, Armin stood only a few feet away from the Führer on one of his visits to the Gauleiter (the Nazi provincial ruler) of Danzig. Armin never forgot Hitler's piercing eyes.

Armin and his elder brother, Harald, led sheltered lives behind the magnificent facade of a patrician apartment building. But this privileged existence was abruptly ended with the Allied bombing of Danzig. During the brothers' evacuation to the countryside, their train had an accident that left Armin's left leg severely crushed. A veterinarian who tried to save the leg bungled the operation, and Armin had to be fitted with a wooden peg leg.

Just before the Red Army entered Danzig in early 1945, both of Armin's parents took their lives by drinking methylated alcohol. Such suicides were widespread among influential Nazi officials just before the enemy arrived. But Armin insisted that his father had been only a "nominal" member of the Nazi Party, that throughout the war his father had secretly listened to the BBC's broadcasts from London.

When the first drunken Russian soldier staggered into the family's shell-pocked apartment building in Danzig, Armin was huddled in the cellar, clinging to the sole survivors of his family, Harald and their grandmother, who was in her seventies. Armin still wore his Hitler Youth uniform. His thin, solitary, right leg dangled from his shorts. Only minutes before, Armin's brother had been out on the street launching a mortar at a Soviet tank, which he did not hit. A Russian officer leapt out of the tank and shouted at him in broken German: "Du Kind, nicht Woyna" (You child, no war). The drunken soldier who entered the cellar yelled the only Russian word the Germans understood, "Uri" (watch). Armin and Harald handed him their wristwatches. Suddenly, another Soviet soldier grabbed their grandmother and raped her in front of their eyes. Armin bolted up the stairs and out into the street where he found a Soviet officer who understood German. Sobbing and gesticulating, Armin told him about the rape of his grandmother. The soldier was found, summarily tried, and executed by a firing squad for having acted on what Ilya Ehrenburg, the Soviet writer, had told his countrymen: "The hour of revenge has come!"

In the wake of the Red Army, Polish forces occupied the rubble-strewn remains of Danzig. The panic-striken master race unfurled white flags from bedroom windows where the swastika banners had hung before. From that time on it was every German for himself. Armin and Harald were arrested by the Poles for possessing pistols that had belonged to their father. Armin suspected that a German had informed on them, perhaps even a Nazi trying to save his own neck. They were thrown into prison. Armin was maltreated, and his older brother was severely beaten. It was the first of five denunciations that he was to experience. Over the course of time he came to realize how readily his fellow Germans would betray their convictions, each other, and even their country to save their own skin.

The brothers were ordered expelled from Danzig in the autumn of 1945, along with the remaining Germans. Their grandmother was allowed to remain because of her age. She accompanied the boys to the train. Armin's last glimpse of Danzig was of the red brick railroad station with its fantasy castle turrets, which had somehow survived the flattening of the city.

"I was born into the bourgeoisie, and in 1945 I was reduced to being a proletarian," Armin told me, recalling his devastating youth.

Armin would never forget the plump, smiling face of Frau Kelling, the kindly matron who took pity on him when he arrived in the northern village of Krakow, in what was Soviet-occupied East Germany. The East Germans had been called on to take in the hundreds of thousands of refugees from the lost German lands in the east who were streaming across the Oder and Neisse Rivers. Armin had just arrived from Danzig with his brother when Frau Kelling caught sight of the pale blonde boy of thirteen with a wooden leg standing in the market square. He was clutching a small brown vinyl suitcase.

Frau Kelling had a spare room in her house because her husband, a former soldier in the elite Waffen SS, had been reported missing somewhere in the Soviet Union. Childless, she took in Armin and his brother and gave them the affection she would have shown her own children. The brothers attended school in Krakow and were taught history by a former Nazi who suffered lapses of memory when he reached the period 1933 to 1945.

Frau Kelling managed to get the boys hard-to-find apprenticeships in the nearby town of Güstrow. Armin was taken in by a watchmaker who had a thriving business with Russian soldiers, repairing the watches they had taken from the conquered Germans. Armin's brother, Harald, did not remain for long in Güstrow because the rape of his grandmother had inspired in him a blind hatred for the Russians. He left for West Germany to search for relatives in the Ruhr, where their father had come from.

Armin moved into the Haus des Kindes, a home for orphans set up by the German Communist Party in a makeshift barracks.

"We were seventy homeless boys, many of us thieves without a goal in life. The Party took us in like a mother and tried to mold us into a new young generation," he recalled to me.

The other children taunted Armin mercilessly about his peg leg, wounding his self-respect. Depressed, he sought the company of ordinary Russian soldiers, who were allowed to fraternize with German children but were forbidden contact with German adults. Far from home and harassed by their officers, the soldiers were even worse off than he was, he decided. He liked their spontaneity and complete lack of guile. They swore in the name of the Virgin Mary but spoke Lenin's name with awe. He would never forget the afternoon in Güstrow when a Russian officer quoted Heinrich Heine to him, verse after verse from memory.

One warm summer day in 1946, Armin hobbled to a lakeside café that had been requisitioned by the local Soviet commandant. A Russian soldier was playing his harmonica, and, as the pace of the music rose and the rhythm entered his bloodstream, Armin for the first time began to dance, his peg leg whirling in the air.

Armin also spent much of his time with Gerhard Haberecht, the caretaker at the orphanage who later joined the Communist Party. Together with Haberecht, whose leg had been shot away when he served in the war, and another older man with an artificial leg, Armin took part in a peace march on crutches. The three cripples were hailed by the Party as examples to be emulated.

As an orphan Armin was forced to be resourceful, once stealing a bicycle from a Russian who had stolen it from a German. He took off the left pedal to make room for his wooden leg, and strapped his good leg onto the right pedal.

He proudly passed his journeyman's examination as a watchmaker in 1949, the year the German Democratic Republic was born. Armin felt himself to be a child of this new socialist Germany, which pledged to root out every last trace of fascism. He was deeply ashamed of having once worn the brown uniform of the Hitler youth.

Armin hurled himself into the activities of the Party's youth organization. The Free German Youth (FDJ) gave him the recognition he hungered for and kept him and other teenagers occupied and out of trouble. In return they sang the FDJ's optimistic songs about the "Land of Happy Children" and "Building the World Anew." Armin enjoyed a warm, pleasant feeling of security as part of the group. It was a feeling of warmth and belonging that he had not known since he left Danzig.

In addition to his skill as a watchmaker, Armin realized that he was gifted rhetorically and academically. He won an FDJ gold medal after completing a course in classical German literature. At the age of eighteen the FDJ delegated him to attend a course for educators in a former hotel at the once elegant Baltic Sea resort of Kühlungsborn. His teacher, Jan Vogeler, an ardent Bolshevik, was the son of the renowned painter Heinrich Vogeler.

At this point, the lives of Markus Wolf and Armin intersected for the first time. Heinrich Vogeler and Friedrich Wolf had been close friends, and in the early 1920s they had invested much of their idealism in creating an ill-fated socialist artist colony at Worpswede, where Markus was conceived. Heinrich Vogeler emigrated to the Soviet Union in 1925, but, unlike Friedrich, he never got out again. He was arrested by the NKVD and died in 1942 in a gulag in Kazakhstan. His son Jan, who had been a classmate of Wolf at the Comintern school, never told his pupils a word of this.

Armin joined the new Socialist Unity Party of Germany (SED) at the age of eighteen in a brief, unceremonious act. He had studied Marxism-Leninism as a candidate of the Party and knew the catechism of Communism to the letter. Like many intelligent young East Germans he was impressed by the number of prominent German emigrés who had returned to settle in the GDR, the "better Germany." Armin plunged into Party studies on the history of the Soviet Union as rewritten by Stalin. More than ever he realized that a command of dialectical materialism and Soviet history opened up untold opportunities in East Germany. This was a society where money bought virtually nothing. Knowledge of the laws of history and economics, on the other hand, could bring one great influence.

Discouraged by his teaching experiences, Armin spent a year working in the income tax department of the Finance Office in Güstrow. The work was incredibly boring, but he hoped the job would help qualify him for higher studies. Armin's mind raced with ideas of ways of getting ahead in this egalitarian society. He knew that Hilde Benjamin, the Stalinist Justice Minister, urgently needed prosecutors and judges who were untainted by fascism. Armin suggested to his friend Haberecht that they apply to take a one-year correspondence course followed by a six-month practical course at the newly established State Law Academy in Potsdam-Babelsberg; after eighteen months they would be qualified as full-fledged judges. But Armin, who was only nineteen, was rejected for being too young. Haberecht took the course, passed it with flying colors, and went on to become the chief public prosecutor in the town of Teterow. In private a kindly man, he did not have the slightest qualms about passing harsh sentences on opponents of the new socialist order.

Armin caught wind of another promising career opportunity. The Culture Ministry had set up a school for cultural enlightenment where adult education teachers were trained in a former castle in the medieval town of Meissen. After studying at the school for nine months, Armin was qualified to teach Marxist philosophy. Brimming with ambition, he went on to study at the Workers' and Peasants' College in Leipzig, where he could earn the secondary school diploma required for teaching regular university studies. Normally, children from middle-class families were excluded from the university, but Armin's watchmaker trade had made him a worker. It was all quite simple if one followed the rules of the game, he told himself.

But he quickly ran afoul of the Party's inviolable principle that its members were never to oppose the leadership's directives. Armin criticized the government's decision in 1953 to raise the price of staple foods. Angered by higher prices for basic foods and more stringent wage regulations, tens of thousands of protesting workers poured into the streets of East Berlin and East Germany on June 16 and 17, 1953. For a moment, millions of East Germans believed the time had finally come when the unloved system would collapse. But the uprising was crushed by Soviet tanks and dismissed by the East German leadership as an attempted imperialist coup against the Workers' and Peasants' State.

The Party lodged charges against Armin, and he was censured. He was finding out the hard way what Mischa Wolf had learned about Party discipline as a young man at the Comintern school in the Soviet Union. Normally, this transgression would have been enough to bar Armin from further university studies, but thanks to an old-time Communist in Leipzig who successfully intervened with the authorities, Armin was able to begin formal studies at Karl Marx University in 1954.

Alone among East German universities, Leipzig's Karl Marx University enjoyed an international reputation. Among the professors were Ernst Bloch, Hans Mayer, and Emil Fuchs, the theologian and father of the A-bomb spy, Klaus Fuchs — names that meant something in Western academic circles. It was a time of relative cultural tolerance in East Germany, and Armin soaked it all in. He began his doctoral thesis on Leonardo da Vinci. But the liberal spell did not last long. Ulbricht ordered Bloch thrown out in 1957 for "mystification" of Marxist philosophy. Mayer never returned to East Germany after the Berlin Wall was built. One of Armin's logic professors hanged himself in a forest near

Leipzig after a young informer for the new State Security Ministry learned that in the 1920s he had been a Communist dissident.

Armin, too, was beginning to get on the nerves of the Party organization at the university. The Party arranged for one of his friends to denounce him for being politically untrustworthy, spreading "Titoist" views, and general troublemaking. Party proceedings against him in 1958 determined his expulsion from the university.

"They said I could never become a socialist as I represented a bourgeois morality. I was without work and desocialized for the second time in my life," he said, looking back on that decisive year.

Armin's faith in socialism was badly dented but still not lost. The ideal itself continued to shine. He was positive that the bureaucrats, that army of yes-men who were in charge of implementing socialism, were to blame. Carefully considering his options, he decided to write to the Yugoslav Embassy in East Berlin and ask for political asylum. Since contact with revisionist Yugoslavia was as dangerous as ties with the West, he hid the red postal registration receipt for the letter in the drawer of his portable chess set.

As he mulled over the possibilities for making money until he could get to Yugoslavia, Armin hit on the idea of setting up a private, and thus illegal, technical translation service together with a Belgian Communist who lived in Leipzig. Yearning more than ever for recognition and affection, Armin spent evenings in Café Schmalfuss, a rollicking den of iniquity peopled by jazz musicians, homosexuals, and informers for the State Security Ministry. It was here that he fell into conversation with a young man, a frequent visitor to the café, who kept one ear attuned to Armin and the other to the remaining patrons. He was an "informal collaborator," an IM, as the Stasi called its informers. After drinking too much one evening, Armin told the young man about his plan to escape to Yugoslavia. A few days later, Armin was denounced to the authorities—for the third time since Danzig. But this time the consequences would radically alter the course of his life.

Armin was awakened early in the morning by the shrill,

incessant ringing of the doorbell. The two men at the door identified themselves as policemen, but it was obvious to Armin that
they were from the Stasi. An interrogator later that day accused
him of setting up an illegal private translation service. The GDR's
penal system moved swiftly, and Armin was sentenced to one year
in prison for fraud and tax evasion.

Through the barred window of the cell he shared with six
other inmates in the Stasi prison, Armin could see a corner of the
Karl Marx University institute where he had studied.

Armin's account of his escape from East Germany after being
released from prison greatly impressed me. He was the first refugee from Communism I had ever met, and I was as fascinated by
his tales about life in the GDR as I had been earlier by my father's
stories about his own boyhood in Germany. Unlike most American boys who grew up in the 1950s, I was excited by the cold war
and especially by Berlin, which was at the heart of the East-West
conflict. I had longed to see Berlin ever since I was a teenager.

In the summer of 1952, I visited the city for the first time
with my parents. We walked past the bombed-out ruins in West
Berlin's inner-city borough of Schöneberg to the apartment house
in the street where my father had once lived. He told me that as a
boy he had spit cherry pits onto the balcony of Albert Einstein's
apartment below. Miraculously, the building was one of the few
that still stood in the nearly leveled neighborhood. But to my
father's dismay, the street was still called Nördlinger Strasse, the
name given it in the 1930s by the Nazis. They had changed
the street name from Haberlandstrasse, because Haberland, the
founder of the section, had been Jewish.

Wherever we went in Berlin in that summer of 1952, I
wondered about nearly every adult German we encountered. Had
they witnessed the degradation and expulsion of the Jews and
looked the other way? But I was also intrigued by the clashing
images I saw: the vast Soviet war memorial in East Berlin, built by
German workers from the ruins of Hitler's Reichs Chancellery;
the ornate buildings rising in Stalinallee, impoverished East Berlin's monumental new boulevard; West Berlin's outdoor cafés

filled with well-fed patrons who seemed oblivious to the four occupying powers.

I was determined to come back. By the time I returned to Berlin as a graduate student of political science in 1959, my obsession with the city's Nazi past was replaced by an awareness of the true nature of the cold war. I was drawn into the distorted, truncated world of East and West where people and things often turned out to be far different from what they seemed to be.

I came across a slew of organizations in West Berlin that were fighting tooth and nail against the Communist threat. One of them was the militantly anticommunist Investigating Committee of Free Lawyers, known by its German initials UFJ. Armin mentioned that he had visited UFJ headquarters several times to get legal advice. Later he even worked for Informationsbüro West, an organization that analyzed East German publications and was linked with the UFJ.

The UFJ was a child of the cold war, and it operated under the auspices of the American occupation authorities, ostensibly to provide legal advice to East Germans. But its real purpose was to gather information for the West from inside East Germany, where even the most basic statistics were classified as secret. The information was supplied to UFJ by its network of East German informers who occupied sensitive positions in East German industry, foreign trade, science, and other areas. They were repelled by the havoc the Soviet system was wreaking on East Germany and yearned for a united Germany. Some of them were even prepared to risk long years of imprisonment by committing acts of sabotage in East German factories and offices.

The informers supplied their information to UFJ headquarters in the leafy West Berlin suburb of Zehlendorf, where I lived. But not all the East Germans who visited UFJ headquarters were what they appeared to be. Neither were all the UFJ staff members. East Germany hated and feared the UFJ and did everything in its power to infiltrate and undermine its activities, as I later discovered. Informers on both sides were motivated by idealism, and over time I would learn how easily idealists were manipulated in the fierceness of the cold war struggle.

It was in the spring of 1960 that I had my first encounter with the alleged Communist enemy, in the guise of Yuri, the exuberant head of the Komsomol (Communist Union of Youth) at Moscow University. Yuri and I met on a bus tour through East Germany arranged by the East German Free German Youth. Through him I discovered the extent of the Russian yearning for an end to the dangerous and debilitating conflict with America. We privately ended the cold war on the bus after Yuri produced a liter of warm East German vodka and drank half the bottle in huge gulps. I downed the rest of the fiery liquid while the East German organizers in the bus eyed us warily. We arranged to meet the next day at his student hostel in East Berlin to continue our talk. But when I arrived there, the hard-line East Germans refused to allow me past the front gate.

I spent far more time exploring East Berlin and surrounding East Germany than I did attending classes on the theory of Communist economies at West Berlin's Free University. But it was in the crumbling streets and towns of the GDR that I discovered the true nature of the Communist system.

In April 1961, Sachsenhausen, the former Nazi concentration camp for political prisoners, which was located in Oranienburg, north of East Berlin, was dedicated as a memorial against Fascism. Built in 1936, Sachsenhausen served as a model for the death camps erected later in the east. The organizers in East Berlin were only too pleased to accredit me as a newspaperman covering the dedication ceremonies, although, in fact, it was something of a ploy, as I was not yet a full-time journalist. The press bus that took us to Oranienburg joined a long column of buses filled with blue-shirted FDJ members and soldiers of the National People's Army. East German flags and red Communist banners hung from apartment buildings and houses along the road from East Berlin. Shortly before arriving at the former concentration camp, we passed a long row of steep-roofed houses occupied by officers of the East German Army. The houses had been built in the 1930s for the SS guards and commandant of the camp.

The GDR had erected a museum at the concentration camp with exhibits from all the countries whose citizens had been imprisoned there. The first display was an eye-opener. DEUTSCHE DEMOKRATISCHE REPUBLIK stood out in large red letters over the exhibit, replete with East German flags and slogans proclaiming the GDR to be the antifascist German state. The organizers seemed genuinely hurt when I suggested that to include the GDR among the victims of Nazism was not only ludicrous but an insult to the real victims.

We walked onto the roll-call grounds of the former camp where the prisoners had been forced to stand for hours, where they had been beaten and executed. The grounds were lined by young blue-shirted FDJ members waving small GDR paper flags as we passed. Rows of East German soldiers flanked the path to the monument erected to the nearly 100,000 prisoners who had perished there while the inhabitants of nearby Oranienburg looked away. A booming loudspeaker voice hailed the role of the Communist Party and the Red Army in liberating the camp in 1945. With the playing of East Germany's anthem and the Communist Internationale, the ceremony was virtually indistinguishable from the May Day celebration in East Berlin. Only the tanks and missiles were missing.

I was witnessing the perversion of East Germany's original antifascism into the glorification of the GDR. Any thought of mourning the victims of the Nazis was stifled by the massive display of uniforms and the martial language of the speakers. Seemingly the Communists who came to power in East Germany, including Jews, had been morally crippled beyond recognition, first by Nazism and then by Stalinism. Older East Germans, plagued by guilt for the Nazi crimes, had submitted willingly as the Communist leadership rammed the antifascist propaganda down their throats. They were convinced that Stalinism and the Soviet occupation of their country was the price they had to pay for Germany having lost the Second World War. But what about the young East Germans, who had no personal memory of the war and few feelings of guilt? How much longer could they be expected to bottle up their emotions and remain silent?

Not long after I met Armin in 1960, two middle-aged Americans appeared, uninvited, in my room at the Student Village.

"You could do something for your country and yourself by helping us," one of the men said. Thin and pale, he peered at me, expressionless, through rimless glasses. "By doing some interviewing for us," he explained.

I assumed that "us" was the CIA, which had a massive presence in West Berlin, and said I was busy with my studies. But he insisted that it would not take much of my time.

The other man tossed me a German newspaper and asked me to read a paragraph. When I finished he nodded his apparent satisfaction without asking for a translation. I wondered if this was the test for recruiting agents.

"Think it over and I'll call back in a few days," the thin man said.

In the following days I mulled over the proposal. In my final year as an undergraduate at Colby College in Maine, I had intentionally avoided making an appointment with the visiting CIA recruitment officer because I wanted to become a journalist and not an intelligence official. But now I decided that doing something for one's country, as the thin man had put it, was not such a bad idea. After all, Nikita Khrushchev's Berlin ultimatum to the West was still hanging over the divided city. I was convinced that the Soviet leader's threat to turn West Berlin into a "free city" and evict the Western Allies was a bluff, since such action would only provoke a war that Moscow did not want. But could anyone be certain what the Soviets would do?

I agreed to meet the thin man in his German Ford just off the Clay Allee (the wide thoroughfare named after the hero of the Berlin Airlift, General Lucius D. Clay), where U.S. Berlin Command headquarters were located. Looming over the sprawling gray complex that had once housed the Nazi Air Defense Ministry was a tower bristling with satellite communications dishes. I assumed that at least one of them linked the CIA with its most important Western outpost.

The thin man's car had green U.S. forces license plates, which struck me as not being the most convincing cover for an intelligence operative. We drove to a coffeehouse where he explained that I was to report one evening later that week to a house in Podbielskiallee, a residential street in the nearby suburb of Dahlem. A housekeeper would open the door, and I would find a questionnaire on a table in the living room. A number of

Germans had been invited to come to the house under the pretext of a public opinion poll, and I would ask them questions. All of my guests, who would appear individually, had some connection to East Germany or one of the other Communist countries. I would be paid DM 200 (deutsche marks) — $50.00 at the time — a month for asking the questions one evening a week. But I suspected there was more to it than that.

A few minutes after I arrived at the large house, the first candidate rang the doorbell. He was a Berliner with relatives in the GDR, and he answered the questions on my list in a straightforward manner. By now I surmised that the aim was to find out more about the pollees' Eastern relatives. Shortly after he left, a woman who had relatives in Poland was shown into the living room, and I asked her the same questions. After a few such sessions I gathered that my employers must have found the names of the people I was "interviewing" by surveillance of the mail entering West Berlin from East Germany and Eastern Europe. I learned later that the three Western Allies who enjoyed occupation rights in West Berlin had an office in the main West Berlin post office and telephone exchange, and that their people opened letters and tapped telephones at will. Obnoxious though it was, this snooping post was dwarfed by the Stasi's sprawling mail surveillance and phone-tapping facilities in East Berlin and the rest of the GDR.

Snooping and informing for one or the other intelligence service was so widespread in Berlin that even the British Broadcasting Corporation, highly respected for its objectivity, was entangled. The BBC office at 6 Savignyplatz, in the heart of West Berlin, was one floor below the Reuters news agency, *Time* magazine, and several other British and American correspondents (I worked there from 1968 to 1987 as a correspondent for *The Observer* (London) and then the *Financial Times* of London.) The Berlin correspondent of the BBC reported for the radio station's German Service, which beamed programs into the GDR, as well as for the BBC's World Service, financed directly by the British Parliament. The resident BBC correspondent was sponsored by the British Military Government (BMG), which did everything to make him feel like one of its dependents. The BMG provided him and his family with a house, British Forces car registration, and license plates. The BBC's mail to and from London was picked up and delivered each morning by a BMG courier. After the Berlin Wall was built in 1961, the BBC correspondent was issued a BMG pass like any other member of the British forces in Berlin. The pass entitled him under Four Power rights to drive through Checkpoint Charlie into East Berlin without submitting to the minute searches and interrogations of the border controllers. But the price of this quasi-official status was considerable in terms of the BBC's dependence on its military host in Berlin.

Several times a month the BBC correspondent was "debriefed" in London Block, the British Military Government's headquarters adjoining Berlin's Olympic Stadium. (The building was only relinquished to the Germans in 1994 when the Allies withdrew from Berlin.) British Secret Intelligence Service (SIS) officials learned about the BBC correspondent's contacts in East Berlin and, if they were of interest, followed them up on their own. This intimate relationship was common knowledge to the other journalists at 6 Savignyplatz, who accepted it as an odd but seemingly unavoidable by-product of the cold war.

My own "interviews" for the CIA went on for several months, during which time I was amazed at the willingness of the Germans to cooperate with my bogus public opinion polls. I was surprised one day while reading the (East) *Berliner Zeitung* to come across an exposé listing CIA "safe houses" in West Berlin. Among them was my house in Dahlem. I mentioned the article the next time I met the thin man. He only smiled condescendingly, as if to say, "You're not worried about the East Germans, are you?" It never occurred to him to caution me against visiting East Berlin and the GDR, which I foolhardily continued to do.

One day the thin man asked me whether I could establish contact with a certain West German student organization in order to learn more about its members. Cold war or not, this amounted to informing, pure and simple. But I was unable to muster the courage to say no, mumbling instead that I was busy with exams but would see what I could do. The organization in question was the Liberal German Student Federation, and of particular interest was its leader, a young man named Wolfgang Lüder. The thin man wanted me to find out what contacts Lüder had with citizens of the Soviet Union and East Germany. It was common knowledge that this student organization of the Free Democratic Party (FDP), along with several senior FDP politicians in West Berlin, was advocating a dialogue with the Communists. In the eyes of the CIA, this objective automatically made the group suspect.

I made no attempt to approach either the liberal students or Wolfgang Lüder. As a result, my contacts with the thin man grew more infrequent and then lapsed altogether.

The thin man also asked me something else, which I must have repressed so thoroughly that it was nearly expunged from my memory. He wanted to know whether I could recommend another student to him who might be interested in earning some money without any risk. I thought for a moment and then mentioned Ali, my next-door neighbor in the Student Village. Ali was a good-natured, extremely likable Syrian, a member of the Druze minority, who worked at odd jobs to finance his engineering studies. We got along well, and he would invite me in for coffee and to share the cakes his parents sent him. Ali had a girlfriend in East Berlin, a busty platinum blonde who worked in the HO department store. On Friday evenings he would cook magnificent meals for her, and then they would make love for the rest of the weekend. I figured that he probably could use some extra money.

Soon afterward, I left Berlin and lost track of Ali. About ten years later, when I returned as a journalist, I ran into him on the street in West Berlin. He said that he had given up his studies but had a good-paying job. Something had happened to him, though, soon after I had left the Student Village, he confided. Two Americans had approached him and asked if he wanted to earn good money by delivering a parcel for them in East Berlin. He agreed, as they assured him that it was absolutely without risk. A few days later he was taken into custody by the Stasi in East Berlin.

I mumbled words of surprise but was barely able to look him in the eye. For the rest of that day I felt as if I was being suffocated by a leaden weight on my chest. I fell asleep that night only after telling myself that I had not meant to endanger Ali and that it was the thin man who had deceived us both. After a few days, I had repressed Ali's ordeal so thoroughly that it was almost lost. The memory lay buried, deep in my subconscious, waiting for something to release it one day.

Not long after my last encounter with the thin man, I learned that the CIA was actively recruiting American students in West Berlin for espionage forays into the Soviet Union. They were given only a minimum of training for these high-risk ventures. Inevitably, one of the students, Marvin W. Makinen, was arrested by the Soviets in July 1961 for photographing military installations in the Ukraine, and sentenced to eight years in prison in Kiev. Only a few months earlier the twenty-two-year-old chemistry student from the University of Pennsylvania had bragged to his friends in West Berlin that he was working for the CIA. The news of his sentencing, less than a month after the building of the Berlin Wall, shocked the other young Americans studying in West Berlin.

Another American student, Frederic L. Pryor, a Ph.D. candidate from Yale who was studying at the Free University in West Berlin, was arrested in East Berlin in late August 1961 by the Stasi on trumped-up espionage charges. Pryor was released in an exchange of spies in February 1962 on the Glienicke Bridge between East Germany and West Berlin. The swap involved Colonel Rudolf Ivanovich Abel, the Soviet spy in New York, and Gary Frances Powers, the American U-2 pilot shot down over the Soviet Union in 1960 while on a secret reconnaissance mission. Makinen was set free shortly afterward as part of the deal.

I was shaken by the disclosures of student involvement in CIA missions and by my own experiences, as I had naively assumed that only the Communists exposed their spies to such dangers. But nothing prepared me for what I was still to encounter.

I saw less of Armin when he moved out of the Student Village into a furnished room nearby. He told me that he needed a place quieter than a dormitory so he could study. One day he returned to the Student Village and proudly showed me his first major acquisition in the West. It was parked nearby, a used Opel Rekord, light blue, with automatic shift so that he could drive it with one leg. He was taking driving lessons and hoped to get his license by the end of the year. Most West Germans in those days still did not own a car, and I was surprised at how quickly he was making his way in the West.

On a winter afternoon in late 1960, I saw him limping on his cane across Friedrichstrasse, and wondered what he was doing in the East. For the first time, I suspected that Armin might not have told me everything. But I smothered the nagging suspicion, telling myself that I was not going to be caught up in anticommunist hysteria. Not long afterward one of my housemates asked if I had seen Armin since he had moved out of the Student Village. Without hesitating, I replied that I had, only a few days earlier in Friedrichstrasse. Even as I spoke I realized my blunder. But it was too late. Everyone knew that after having escaped from East Germany, Armin had no business being in East Berlin.

I never told Armin that I had seen him in the East, and we lost contact in 1961, after the building of the Berlin Wall. I did not see him again until 1992, under very different circumstances.

C H A P T E R

4

Wolf got a sensual enjoyment from reading John Le Carré's spy novels and felt genuinely flattered at being widely regarded in the West as the model for Karla, Le Carré's Soviet spymaster.

Unlike Karla, though, Wolf inserted his moles — high-level penetration agents — not only into his foe's intelligence service, but into every important West German government department and agency, and inside NATO headquarters itself. Although some moles spied out of conviction and not for money, a blanket espionage operation was very costly, requiring large amounts of hard currency, which Wolf obtained from East Germany's foremost financial juggler and his ring of shady dealers. Such corrupt practices, as well as the Stasi's support for international terrorists, were justified, even if distasteful, Wolf was convinced.

His crowning achievement was to slide a mole into the Chancellor's office in Bonn, where the spy gained the confidence of the West German leader. Wolf's imagination and the skill of his mole not withstanding, this audacious feat would have been unthinkable were it not for the crass ineptitude and bungling of the West German security services. Paradoxically, many of Wolf's successes were also made possible by the mass exodus of East Germans to the West.

Month after month, ever larger numbers of East Germans decided that there was no future for them in a Communist-ruled land. Leaving behind their houses, farms, and businesses, they fled in waves during the late 1940s and throughout the 1950s across the green border to West Germany, or they simply took the urban railroad and subway from East to West Berlin.

Wolf recognized that the growing internal opposition to the Communists was making it increasingly difficult to recruit agents for work in the West. Agents in the future would have to be all the more highly motivated. They could convincingly conceal their mission in the West by claiming to have fled East Germany out of hatred of the Communist regime.

In 1956 the stream of East Germans escaping to the West widened to a torrent. More East Germans turned their backs on the German Democratic Republic than at any time since the workers' uprising three years earlier. Even worse for the regime, half of those who left were young people under twenty-five years of age. The GDR never recovered from this massive hemorrhage of skills and talent.

The upsurge in emigration in 1956 was triggered by a wave of show trials and new government measures against privately owned companies. The blood-soaked quelling in June of the Polish workers' revolt in Poznań and the brutal suppression of the Hungarian Revolution five months later were an added impetus. But while East Germans were driven to escape from the East, they were also drawn by the West's many enticements. The most powerful lure was West Berlin. An increasingly prosperous, glittering Western outpost located in the center of the GDR, West Berlin was more threatening to Communist rule than NATO's deadliest weapons. Each day a flood of East Germans, carefully hiding their hard-earned East German marks from the Eastern border controllers, entered this gigantic neon-lighted consumers' temple as if drawn by an irresistible force.

Clutching their tightly folded East mark banknotes, they waited patiently inside West Berlin exchange bureaus to convert the money at the market rate — 5, 7, sometimes 10 East marks for 1 West mark. With the meager proceeds they bought coffee at DM 10 ($2.50 in 1956) a pound, compared to 60 GDR Marks in the East, and rummaged in Bilka's department store and Woolworth's for cheap shoes and nylon shirts. Anyone fortunate enough to have relatives or friends in West Berlin visited them first, hoping to be slipped a few hard deutsche marks. Other Easterners came to West Berlin with the sole aim of escaping from the Workers' and Peasants' State.

Among those who fled to West Berlin in 1956 was a chubby, pleasant-looking twenty-nine-year-old photographer from East Berlin and his thin, hawk-eyed wife. Early one morning in May, Günter and Christel Guillaume sat in an urban commuter train of the East German S-Bahn that rumbled into West Berlin, its lights flickering briefly as the train passed a concrete border marker with the hammer and compass seal of the GDR. Everything the Guillaumes dared take along was in two small suitcases pressed under their legs. Still, their escape was different from that of the hundreds of others who fled that day. Günter and Christel had been loyal and ardent supporters of the East German regime, so their Communist friends were deeply shocked by their departure. Only Wolf and a few of his senior officers were aware that the Guillaumes were on the crucial first leg of their mission as long-term penetration agents in the West. In East German espionage parlance, though, agents were always Western spies. The Guillaumes were quaintly referred to as "full-time informal collaborators." Their simulated escape had been meticulously prepared by their controller, Paul Laufer, one of Wolf's most trusted officers during the espionage chief's early years in intelligence. In the prewar years Laufer had worked underground in Nazi Germany as a Communist agent, so he knew all the tricks of survival.

Germany's recent past came full circle in Paul Laufer and the Guillaumes. Günter Guillaume had become a glowing convert to the Communist Party in an act of penance for himself and his father. Guillaume senior, an unemployed musician, had joined the Nazis after Hitler's election in 1933. He committed suicide when he returned to postwar Berlin from a British POW camp and found that his wife had taken up with another man. Although his son Günter had joined the Nazi Party at the age of seventeen, and volunteered as a Wehrmacht officer's candidate, his military career consisted mainly in fleeing from the Red Army.

Günter Guillaume was a hale-and-hearty, sharp-tongued Berliner who could melt into any crowd. Given the code name

Georg by Wolf's HVA (Central Intelligence Administration), he had performed well on previous trial missions to the West before his "defection." In the future he was to serve in Frankfurt as a "resident," a controller of several of Wolf's subordinate moles in the Social Democratic Party (SPD).

What Wolf and Guillaume did not know was that buried deep in the files of West German counterespionage lay a ticking time bomb. The Investigating Committee of Free Lawyers (UFJ), the anti-Communist organization that had close ties to the West German security services, had identified Günter Guillaume as having entered West Germany on an earlier mission with the goal of "infiltrating" publishing houses and "subverting" West German citizens. If the report ever surfaced, it would destroy the Guillaumes' "legend," the bogus biography the HVA had prepared for the couple as refugees from Communism.

The day after their "escape," Günter and Christel Guillaume left West Berlin for Frankfurt on a PanAm flight packed with East German refugees. Christel's mother, Erna, met them in Frankfurt where a friend of hers had agreed to sponsor them. This meant that they could avoid being processed by a refugee camp where West German counterintelligence officials might ask probing questions.

The Guillaumes began a life of hard work, so to all appearances they were like most other refugees from the East. Their instructions were to immerse themselves completely in West German life before beginning their espionage activities. They set up a copy shop in their tiny apartment in Frankfurt, and Erna opened a small tobacco store. Thanks to their perseverance, the businesses served as a welcome source of income and a cover. The Guillaumes were as determined to succeed in West Germany as were the millions of other East Germans who had fled the GDR.

Günter worked as a freelance photographer for Social Democratic publications, and Christel got a job as a secretary to Wilhelm Birkelbach, chairman of the SPD party district for Frankfurt. Her outspoken opinions as an SPD right-winger were music to the ears of Birkelbach, who was on several influential committees in the West German Parliament. Many secret documents on NATO maneuvers crossed his desk and that of his trusted secretary Christel. Günter passed the information to HVA couriers, sometimes handing over miniature films, concealed inside a cigar tube, in his mother-in-law's tobacco shop. The Guillaumes maintained regular contact with East Berlin head-quarters using a two-way radio, which Günter called their "bridge to home." He marveled at the way Christel was able to "play" the radio waves with the dexterity of a Paganini.

Between 1956 and January 1959 the Guillaumes were flooded with coded radio messages from East Berlin, which they decrypted using endless rows of numbers. The messages were transmitted on certain days, at fixed times, and using the same frequencies, an invitation to discovery by West German counter-espionage. But it took years before the West Germans were able to crack the code. What they did discover was a cascade of messages to an agent code-named Georg whose source in West Germany was code-named Fritz. This led nowhere.

One terse message read: "Trip of club chairman is most important. We expect report on situation in first team." Birthday greetings were sent to Georg — on Guillaume's birthday in Febru-ary. For the birth of the couple's son, Pierre, in April 1957, the HVA even radioed: "Congratulations on second man." Wolf and his controllers made a habit to make such gestures in the interest of the psychological welfare of their agents.

Wolf and his controllers allowed their best agents complete freedom of action, enabling them to develop a self-confidence that was alien to ordinary East Germans. After joining the SPD, Günter Guillaume began a remarkable political career as a staunch anti-Communist. Guillaume was immensely proud of his contributions to the Social Democrats as a local politician in Frankfurt while inwardly condemning the party's dependence on the "banks and monopolies."

Their son Pierre was raised like other West German chil-dren. He never suspected that his parents were not what they seemed to be. On his tenth birthday Pierre was taken by his father on a very special trip to Berlin. They passed through a crossing point in the Wall to visit Günter's mother and afterward met two of his "school friends" from his boyhood in Berlin. In reality, it was a *"treff"* (from the German *"treffen,"* meaning "to meet"), as espionage meetings were known worldwide, with Guillaume's HVA controller. While one of the men took Pierre to the zoo, Günter gave the other officer his assessment of the SPD's new *Ostpolitik* (Eastern policy of détente) toward the Soviet Union and the GDR. On the flight back to Bonn from West Berlin, Pierre suddenly asked his father why one of his school friends from Berlin spoke with such a peculiar accent. His father was startled; Pierre had detected a glaring inconsistency. The officer's accent had betrayed him as a native of Leipzig and not Berlin. They had overlooked a small but vital detail of the kind that could one day lead to their arrest.

But it was still another incident, during one of Guillaume's covert consultations with the HVA in East Germany, that brought home the "insanity" of his dual existence, he admitted years later. He was being driven in a car outside East Berlin together with his controller and instructor, when they stopped at a railroad crossing. Guillaume spotted a familiar face among the pedestrians who stood nearby waiting for the train to pass. It was a former colleague of his at the Volk und Wissen publishing house. Guillaume was unnerved. What would the man think if he suddenly saw him, an alleged "refugee" from East Germany, being driven in an East German car? His colleague would spread the story to his friends, thus demolishing Guillaume's carefully nurtured "legend" as a refugee. If word got out to the West, he and Christel would face certain arrest. At that moment, though, the barrier went up, and the East Germans' car roared off, apparently without the pedestrian having noticed Guillaume. But he could not be certain.

"I was not home in my own country. There was no place, anywhere, where I could move freely," he later recalled. It was a fate he shared with every spy working in hostile territory, the price every spy had to pay.

Before Guillaume returned to West Germany, his controller told him that Markus Wolf himself wanted to meet him on his next clandestine visit to the GDR.

Wolf awoke as usual at 6:30 A.M., feeling rested after a short, but good night's sleep. He debated whether to do his exercises but rejected the idea after gazing into the bedroom mirror. He decided that he had a remarkably trim figure for someone who rarely exercised. His physician at State Security had recommended regular exercise as an antidote to long hours in the office and late evenings spent socializing with his senior officers and top agents. Wolf had bought a rowing machine on the doctor's advice, but after a few sessions he gave it up out of boredom.

Wolf was driven to work at the usual time, 8:00 A.M., on this day in 1964, in his black Volga car. His office was on the first floor of the drab, cramped six-story structure that served as the nerve center of the HVA until 1978, when a new, twelve-story building was erected. Mielke's office in Building 1 was only a few hundred yards away. When Mielke discovered that West German intelligence had taken photos of the courtyard of his State Security Ministry from the new high-rise apartment houses across the street, he had the entrance to Building 1 enclosed to prevent Western agents from photographing him when he entered or left his car.

On this morning Wolf was looking forward to a very special meeting later in the day with his most promising penetration agent, Günter Guillaume. After years of grass-roots toil for the SPD, Guillaume had recently been chosen to be chairman of the Social Democratic Party in the important Frankfurt region. Wolf was anxious to have a long talk with Guillaume because, in the future, it might be too risky for Guillaume to visit "home," as HVA headquarters was known to the agents.

Guillaume walked through the Berlin Wall at the Bornholmer Strasse checkpoint, submitting his West German identity card for inspection by the border guards along with the other West German visitors. He spotted the car from the HVA that was discreetly waiting to pick him up at a nearby corner. He was driven to a Stasi guesthouse located amidst the greenery of Karolinenhof on the outskirts of East Berlin. The prewar house, confiscated after 1945, was stuffed with heavy furniture.

Guillaume was deeply impressed when the casually dressed head of the HVA told him to call him Mischa. Wolf also inquired solicitously about his well-being and that of Christel and their son. The "chief" was not only compassionate but was intuitively aware of the enormous psychological problems an agent faced in the field, isolated in a hostile land.

"I sensed his heartfelt affection for his agents. He made us feel that we were his equals," Guillaume later recalled.

Guillaume was relieved that far from criticizing him, as he had half expected, for failing to consult the HVA on his career moves, Wolf praised him for his initiative and encouraged him. Wolf was impressed by Guillaume's enthusiasm, his dry Berlin humor, and his intimate knowledge of the SPD's power structure. Here was a man who was methodically climbing the rungs of the SPD ladder, who seemed fascinated by the prospect of succeeding in West German politics. The fact that Guillaume, as a young man, had been a member of the Nazi Party only seemed to heighten his allegiance to socialism.

They drank East German Radeberger beer and Nordhauser schnapps, and Wolf reminisced about his youth in Moscow and his father. He gave his agents the feeling that they were working for the Wolf family as much as for the GDR.

Wolf and his mole discussed how the HVA could reap the maximum benefit from Guillaume's important new position in the SPD in Frankfurt. Wolf said it was clear that the Adenauer era was drawing to an end in Bonn, and that the SPD would sooner or later assume power. He and Guillaume agreed that it would be advantageous for Günter to establish a strong working relationship with a successful politician in his SPD district, a man who had a good chance of gaining a cabinet post in a future SPD government. If all went well, Guillaume might even ride to Bonn on the coattails of a new cabinet minister. At this point even Wolf's fertile imagination did not conceive of the heights to which his mole would ride.

Guillaume's mental and physical batteries were recharged by his meeting with Wolf, and he returned to Frankfurt to plot his next moves. Paul Laufer, Guillaume's controller, decided that his charge from now on would be an intelligence "source" on his own and would no longer be responsible for other agents in the Frankfurt area. Guillaume was assigned a new courier who lived in West Germany under an assumed name.

Wolf's confidence in his agent was soon repaid. Guillaume

successfully managed the Frankfurt election campaign of Georg Leber, a genial labor union leader who was chosen in 1966 to be transport minister in the new Bonn coalition government of Christian Democrats and Social Democrats. In 1968 Guillaume, in addition to his post as chairman of the SPD in Frankfurt, was elected to the Frankfurt city legislature. He was the only East German intelligence officer ever to hold public office in West Germany. Wolf crossed his fingers that Willy Brandt would win the national elections in the autumn of 1969, and that Leber would offer Guillaume a position in the Transport Ministry.

In line with their much enhanced importance to the HVA, in 1968 the Guillaumes were placed under the overall operational supervision of Col. Günther Neefe, newly appointed as head of Department 2, the HVA section responsible for espionage against West Germany's political parties. Günter Guillaume was by far his most important mole in the West German political establishment. The Guillaumes' new controller was Col. Kurt Gailat, who, like Günter Guillaume, concealed his shrewdness behind a clerklike appearance. Agents and their controllers were carefully matched so that they would work smoothly together. Colonel Gailat was one of the HVA's most skilled controllers and was responsible for several top HVA moles in Bonn.

Guillaume's successful management of Leber's election campaign in 1969 led to an offer from Bonn that surpassed Wolf's wildest dreams. Guillaume was asked to join the office of the new West German chancellor, Willy Brandt, as a junior aide responsible for relations with labor unions and other political organizations. Brandt had been in Wolf's espionage sights ever since the young Norwegian press officer he met at the Nürnberg trial in 1946 became the popular anti-Communist mayor of West Berlin. Wolf had hatched out a devious plan in 1959 to compromise Brandt for allegedly having been a Gestapo agent during his Norwegian exile, but because of a lack of credible evidence, the Party leadership ordered the plot aborted. Ten years later Wolf was given the unique opportunity to plant a mole inside Brandt's office.

Before Guillaume could be hired by the federal chancellory, he faced a security check by West German counterintelligence, the BfV. Throughout the 1950s and 1960s the BfV was preoccupied with ferreting out members of the illegal West German Communist Party and exposing their contacts to East Berlin. It underestimated the real threat from Wolf's HVA and his new generation of agents. On top of this, most of the senior SPD officials who came to power with Brandt rejected the visceral anti-Communism of their Christian Democratic predecessors. They suspected that the greatest danger to democracy was not the Communists but, instead, West Germany's ultraconservative intelligence and counterintelligence community. Wolf's spies made use of the tensions between Brandt's aides in Bonn and BfV counterespionage in nearby Cologne to devastating effect.

Guillaume was interviewed for his job in Bonn by Horst Ehmke, head of Brandt's chancellory, who was responsible for the Federal Intelligence Agency (BND) and BfV. Ehmke, a lisping former law professor, turned out to be an unusual choice for the job of coordinating the security services.

(On a memorable visit to West Berlin in the early 1970s, Ehmke attended a rollicking party at the Reuters news agency bureau at 6 Savignyplatz. Among the guests were several Soviet correspondents who were widely reputed to be KGB agents. Ehmke played darts in the news ticker room with the others and drank a good deal, so much that by the time the party was over in the wee morning hours he had some difficulty locating the dart board. One of the Soviet correspondents offered to drive Ehmke back to his hotel, and, in high spirits, he agreed. It was a remarkable situation. The top official responsible for protecting the Federal Republic of Germany against Communist agents, in an alcoholic haze, was driven to his hotel by a Soviet correspondent who was widely regarded to be a KGB officer. What, if anything, transpired remains unknown, but the risk was considerable.)

Guillaume displayed no emotion as Ehmke informed him that some security problems had arisen in connection with his application to work in the federal chancellory. Egon Bahr, who was Willy Brandt's right-hand man in the chancellory, had urged Ehmke to exercise caution in hiring Guillaume. In particular, he had called Ehmke's attention to the earlier report about

Guillaume's intelligence forays into West Germany in the mid-1950s. But the source of the report was long since dead, and Ehmke was inherently skeptical about such intelligence information. Confronted with the charges, Guillaume calmly replied that it had to be a case of mistaken identity, as he had never cooperated with the Stasi. Ehmke was impressed by the applicant's apparent sincerity. After being informed of Guillaume's security clearance by counterintelligence, Ehmke gave the green light for Guillaume's employment in the chancellory. Christel, meanwhile, landed a promising job with the Hessian state government office in Bonn.

As a former East German Guillaume was deemed "especially endangered" by possible approaches by the Communist intelligence services. So he was asked to sign a statement saying that he would not travel to Communist countries. Marveling at the bungling amateurism of West German security, Guillaume willingly signed. Fifteen years after his contrived "escape" to the West, he had penetrated to within striking distance of the inner circle of Chancellor Willy Brandt.

"If you want to live among the wolves you must howl with them," was Guillaume's maxim. He lived up to it by setting up a branch of the Social Democratic Party in the federal chancellory. One of his first assignments was to take charge of communications between the SPD and Chancellor Brandt's office for the party's first convention after the election. Acting as a quartermaster for the communications specialists of the BND intelligence agency, Guillaume quickly discovered that the best way to win their confidence was to ensure that they were given a comfortable hotel room and good food and drink. In return, they made life easy for him by handing him messages of the highest security level without the slightest reservation.

Hardworking and efficient, Guillaume was promoted in October 1972 to become Willy Brandt's aide responsible for the chancellor's contacts as SPD leader with the party. He was also put in charge of organizing Brandt's trips. Both Brandt and his Norwegian-born wife, Rut, found Guillaume a touch too servile and eager to please, but they had more pressing problems. Their marriage was on the rocks, the victim of Willy Brandt's restlessness and weakness for attractive young women. It was a trait that his aide had long since registered.

Guillaume, with the help of his new courier, Arno, was able to transmit top secret documents to East Berlin, as well as a wealth of personal observations about leading members of the German government and high-level conversations he overheard about *Ostpolitik*. Wolf passed Guillaume's information on to Mielke, who made certain that it was fed, morsel by delectable morsel, to the appreciative members of the ruling Politbüro. East Berlin and Moscow were informed, well in advance, of virtually every move that Bonn planned in its dealings with the Communist countries. But this was merely an appetizer for the feast to come.

Sometimes, while shaving in the morning, Guillaume gazed into the bathroom mirror and thought he could make out the blurred outlines of his other self. But then he would grin back, confident that his mission for the GDR "in the interest of the best cause in the world" had saved him from suffering any ill effects from living a double life. When Brandt was awarded the Nobel Peace Prize in 1971, Guillaume felt a surge of pride. Brandt and he made an excellent match, he told himself: the chancellor of peace and the spy for peace.

The more inside information on the Brandt government Guillaume passed to the HVA, the more Wolf was convinced that it was in the best interests of the GDR to support Brandt's *Ostpolitik*. When the Christian Democratic opposition tried to oust Brandt in a vote of no confidence in April 1972, Wolf convinced Mielke of the need to get Politbüro approval for an audacious operation to save Brandt. A key role was played by one of Wolf's West German agents, Julius Steiner, a Christian Democratic member of the Bundestag (West Germany's lower house of Parliament) in Bonn. Steiner suggested that, when the time came for the secret ballot, he would, for a price, be prepared to switch sides and vote for Brandt and against his own party's candidate, Rainer Barzel. Wolf saw to it that Steiner, in return for casting one of the two decisive votes for Brandt, was paid DM 50,000 by Ingo Freyer, a senior HVA officer.

None of Wolf's moles, not even Guillaume, knew of the existence of the other strategically placed moles within the SPD political parties who were reporting uninterruptedly to East Berlin. The HVA adhered strictly to the principle of compartmentalization: agents were never informed about fellow agents in order to protect each other if one was caught. Controlling officers knew only about their own agents. This system was designed so that in the unthinkable event that a controller defected to the West, he could not betray spies outside his immediate area of control. Yet even the strictest rules were violated, as Wolf would later learn.

While Guillaume was buoyed by his successes in uncovering the innermost secrets of the West German government, some near disastrous mishaps took place in transmitting the information to East Berlin. One time Arno, his courier, and he had arranged an ingenious but overly complicated method by which Guillaume would pass him a microfilm containing top secret material that Guillaume did not want to hand over directly for security reasons. Guillaume hid a container with the film in the upholstery of his reserved seat on the crack IC (InterCity) express train between Düsseldorf and Frankfurt. On leaving the train in Bonn, he saw Arno boarding it as planned. Arno sat down in what was supposed to be Guillaume's seat, which he had previously reserved for the remainder of the trip from Bonn to Frankfurt. But as he frantically searched the crevices of the seat, he could find nothing.

Maybe the computer had made a mistake on his reserved seat ticket between Bonn and Frankfurt, Arno thought anxiously. Or, worst of all, perhaps West German counterespionage had laid a clever trap. The material on the film offered sufficient clues to the source of the documents and could blow the Guillaumes' cover wide open. Arno moved rapidly from one empty seat to the next, probing in the cushions while trying not to appear too conspicuous. Finally, he landed on Guillaume's actual previous seat, and to his relief he found the container buried in the corner of the seat.

The first suspicions about the Guillaumes arose by sheer coincidence in February 1972 when a BfV counterespionage official stumbled across Günter Guillaume's name on the periphery of three espionage cases. This was too much of a coincidence for even the lethargic BfV to overlook. A colleague recalled the mysterious radio messages from East Berlin that he himself had puzzled over in the 1950s. The two compared the messages with the data on Guillaume and discovered that his birthday was, in fact, on the very same day that the HVA broadcast its birthday greetings to Georg. And the congratulations on the "second man" in April 1957 perfectly matched the birth of Pierre Guillaume on April 8, 1957.

But instead of closing in on Günter Guillaume and carefully taking aim, BfV officials repeatedly shot themselves in the foot. Not until May 1973 did BfV decide it was time to begin discreet surveillance of Christel Guillaume, who they suspected was acting as her husband's courier. But to their chagrin, counterintelligence officials discovered that the Guillaumes no longer lived in Frankfurt, but had moved to Bonn two years earlier.

Hans-Dietrich Genscher, the crafty West German interior minister who was responsible for security, informed Brandt of the suspicions about the Guillaumes in early May. Genscher said that the BfV believed that Günter Guillaume was an agent, but that the head of BfV, Günter Nollau, had advised against removing Guillaume from his job so that he could first be observed. He was not. Furthermore, Brandt was given the impression that the evidence against Guillaume was thin, dating back as it did to the 1950s.

A little more than a month later, Brandt asked whether he should take Guillaume along on the vacation he planned to take in Hamar, Norway. Genscher reported back that Nollau had no objections. But Nollau, who was subsequently made a scapegoat and forced to resign, later denied that he had given his consent. Inexplicably, the BfV decided to interrupt its observation of Christel during the time the Guillaumes were in Norway, on the grounds that it would have aroused immediate attention in Brandt's remote summer retreat. A suggestion that the Guillaumes' telephone be tapped was rejected as being too risky because it would involve too many people. Wolf's opinion about West German counterespionage plummeted to a new low when he learned of its bungling. Lulled into complacency by the ineptitude of the West Germans, he fell prey to the arrogance of infallibility and failed to detect the serious flaws within his own intelligence service that one day would be dramatically exposed.

Instead of flying to Norway with the other staff members, on June 30, 1973, Guillaume, Christel, and Pierre set off in the family car for Brandt's vacation lodge. Guillaume explained that he wanted to relax for a few days with the family in Sweden after Brandt's vacation was over.

Once in Hamar, Guillaume again made use of his excellent working relationship with two accompanying communications specialists from the BND. He retained copies of all the communications from the federal chancellory in Bonn to Brandt, including top secret communications between Bonn and Washington. Guillaume hid the papers in his vacation lodge. Among the documents was a letter to Brandt from President Richard Nixon stamped SECRET AND PERSONAL in which Nixon informed Brandt that Paris had indicated its willingness to cooperate in an Atlantic partnership. Nixon proposed that an Atlantic declaration be drawn up by the United States and its closest allies, excluding the other NATO members. The message said that if Moscow learned of this tactic, it could try to drive a wedge between Washington and its European allies. Another confidential message quoted Henry Kissinger as saying that the Warsaw Pact armies had achieved a "substantial degree of parity" with NATO forces, a view that could lead Moscow to doubt the U.S. nuclear deterrent.

Guillaume was sorely tempted to personally deliver the documents to East Berlin by hopping a ferry from Sweden to Warnemünde in the GDR. But he decided against this, having no desire to end his spying career. Instead he sent a postcard to a cover address of the HVA in East Berlin calling for a courier to meet him in the bar of the hotel where the Guillaumes would be staying in Halmstad, Sweden.

Guillaume had already hatched an ingenious plan to get the stolen documents out of Hamar undetected. The idea had come to him a few days earlier when he wanted to give the Norwegian mailman a souvenir of Willy Brandt's office. Accidentally, he opened up an attaché case containing official documents instead of an identical one with souvenirs. At the end of Brandt's vacation,

Guillaume approached an official of the Federal Criminal Agency, which was responsible for the chancellor's personal security, and asked the official to carry back an attaché case to his secretary in Bonn on the chancellor's plane, because the case contained important papers that he did not want to have in his car when he drove back.

What the official did not realize was that instead of the attaché case with the documents, Guillaume handed him the one with the souvenirs. Guillaume would discover the "mistake" when he returned to Bonn and, switching the attaché cases, would return the copies of the communications to the secrets registry. Driving back to Germany, the Guillaumes stopped at the hotel in Halmstad where Günter had arranged to meet his HVA courier. While Pierre practiced a fox-trot with his mother on the dance floor of the hotel restaurant, Guillaume sat down next to the courier at the bar and passed him his room key. In a matter of minutes the documents were photographed, and the courier drove off to catch a ferry bound for the GDR.

Back in Bonn, Christel's surveillance was resumed, heavy-footed as before. Her suspicion aroused, she broke off a *treff* with her courier in a supermarket, walking past the cosmetics stand where the transfer of information was to have taken place. Afterward a car tailed her on her way home. Günter was able to confirm the surveillance but believed it was part of a routine security check, since Christel had applied for a job in the Defense Ministry. The couple decided, nonetheless, to suspend espionage activities and contacts for the time being.

Chancellor Brandt was planning another vacation, this time in southern France in October, and Guillaume's sagging morale was given a badly needed boost when he learned that he was again slated to accompany the chancellor. He resumed contacts with Arno and arranged for a complicated but more secure method of passing information to him. Arno called Guillaume in his office in the federal chancellory, asking for a "Fräulein Ines." This was the password. Fifteen minutes later Guillaume arrived at a bus stop they had already agreed on. Lying on a bench at the bus stop was a magazine someone had apparently forgotten. Inside the magazine, next to a caption, was a scrawled code word for their actual meeting place. Shortly afterward Guillaume entered a small restaurant where Arno sat drinking beer and eating. Arno passed on an urgent warning to him from Wolf: at the first sign of surveillance by the BfV, Guillaume was to immediately return to East Berlin. Guillaume was not ready to leave. When he accompanied Chancellor Brandt to the south of France, the BfV obliged him once again by failing to observe him. Again, he made full use of his excellent personal contacts with the BND communications officials.

When the Guillaumes looked out the window on a dismal day in December 1973, they saw a camping van parked on an empty lot opposite their apartment house in Ubierstrasse. The BfV surveillance officials who were crammed inside the van made no secret of their presence. Guillaume remarked later that he and Christel were left with no doubt that the "hunters" had arrived for the kill. Still the BfV failed to snap shut the trap. Was it sheer incompetence, Guillaume asked himself, or was their blundering designed to lull him into lowering his guard?

In February 1974 Guillaume took Pierre along for a *treff* with Arno in Holland. Pierre still did not have the least suspicion that his parents were engaged in espionage, a considerable feat on their part over so many years. The young Guillaume was now seventeen and a member of the Jusos, the youth wing of the SPD, and was politically well to the left of his "conservative" parents. At the bar of their Dutch hotel, father and son drank too much. When Pierre had gone to his room, Guillaume signaled to Arno, who was seated nearby, that all was clear for a *treff*—he was not being followed.

Guillaume decided to take a few days off during the long 1974 Easter holiday and drive to southern France on his own. Just before leaving he had another *treff* with Arno in Cologne, where he was able to pass several choice documents to him: a confidential paper written by Henry Kissinger on tactical changes in U.S. security policy; a report on Brandt's views on inter-German relations, and those of his aides, as well as differences within the SPD leadership; an account of Brandt's meeting with the labor unions; and the role of Helmut Schmidt as the SPD's strong man. Little did Guillaume imagine that his espionage activities would help Schmidt to become the next German chancellor.

Heading toward France on the Autobahn, Guillaume glanced in the rearview mirror and saw that he was being followed. He abruptly veered off the highway at the next gas station; his pursuers sped past. But they were waiting for him further down the Autobahn and remained close behind him as he drove through Belgium and into France, where a car belonging to the Service de Documentation Extérieure et Contre-Espionage (SDECE), French intelligence and counterespionage, took up the chase. Guillaume accelerated to more than ninety miles an hour, repeatedly trying to lose his tail on the ring road around Paris. Guillaume's observers kept their distance as he lay exhausted in the sunshine in Saint Maxime. The next day, during an excursion by car, he managed to shake off his pursuers on the winding roads. This was his last chance to try to make his way undetected back to the GDR, a step his controller had told him to take as soon as he was sure that he had come under observation. But he resisted the temptation. He could not leave Christel and Pierre in the lurch.

The morning after his return to Bonn, at 6:32 A.M. on April 24, 1974, the buzzer in the Guillaume apartment rang shrilly. Thinking it might be the milkman, Günter put on his bathrobe and pressed the button to let the caller in. Opening the door, he heard many pairs of feet pounding up the stairs. He instantly knew it was all over.

"It wasn't one milkman. It was twelve of them," he later cracked.

"Are you Herr Guillaume?" one of the men asked that morning.

"Yes, what do you want?" he replied.

The man said he had an arrest warrant and pushed Guillaume backward into the vestibule.

"I am a citizen and officer of the GDR. Respect that!" he blurted out. It was an absurd, uncalled for remark and, worse yet, as he realized as soon as he had spoken, an admission of partial guilt. What would Wolf think of him now? What would happen to Arno and Nora, their two couriers who at this moment were still in the West?

Pierre opened his bedroom door a crack and saw the hand-cuffs being slipped on his father and mother. Guillaume assured his son that everything would be all right. But the boy suffered severely under the barrage of media stories about his "traitorous" parents, and a few months later he was allowed to join relatives in the GDR, where he led a privileged and sheltered life.

Twelve days after the Guillaumes were arrested, Willy Brandt resigned as chancellor. Ostensibly, he was forced to step down because Günter Guillaume knew all about the frequent "interviews" Brandt gave to female journalists in the sleeping compartment of his government train. Guillaume was in an ideal position to blackmail the chancellor. Increasingly, though, the main West German protagonists in the drama became ensnared in conflicting statements as to why Guillaume was allowed to remain Brandt's aide for eleven months after he was first suspected of espionage. A conspiracy theory — that the authorities allowed Guillaume to remain in order to harm Brandt — was never proved. But it was clear that for some time the Free Democratic Party's Hans-Dietrich Genscher and Herbert Wehner, the SPD's "kingmaker," had wanted to replace the lackadaisical Brandt with Helmut Schmidt, the forceful finance and economics minister. Schmidt, in fact, succeeded Brandt as chancellor; Genscher, in turn, was rewarded with the foreign minister's post in the center-left coalition.

Thanks to Guillaume, both Wolf's and Mielke's stars rose to new heights. Mielke advanced from candidate member of the Politbüro in 1971 to full membership in 1976. Freshly decorated with the GDR's highest award, the Karl Marx medal, which he received in January 1974, Wolf was at the peak of his career. The supermole in the chancellor's office also served to greatly enhance Wolf's value to Mielke, who left his spymaster alone to conduct espionage with a minimum of interference. Erich Honecker, the new GDR leader, assured Mielke that while he would publicly claim to have had no knowledge of the mole in the chancellor's office, Mielke should know that the HVA's excellent work was appreciated by him personally and by the entire Politbüro.

Paradoxically, the discovery of Guillaume sent morale

among Wolf's officers, agents in the field, and informers higher
than ever before. Wolf had made West German counterespionage
look farcical and had proven to everyone that his HVA ranked
among the world's most effective intelligence services.

Ordinary East Germans, however, were far from elated.
They were afraid that Brandt's resignation over an East German
spy would lead to a hardening in Bonn's relations with the GDR,
thus ending their dream of one day being allowed to visit the West.
The Stasi registered a spate of spontaneous protests: On May 8,
1974, "unknown perpetrators" renamed a street in Neustrelitz
after Willy Brandt. Anonymous postcards were found condemning "GDR spying" against Brandt. And, in a town near Erfurt,
where Brandt had been jubilantly welcomed in 1970 on his first
visit to the GDR, protesters had scrawled a huge slogan in chalk
on the railroad station at night: "SED [Socialist Unity Party]
betrayed Brandt." In Leipzig, Stasi informers reported that hand-
written slogans had been found accusing the GDR of collaborat-
ing with the conservative opposition CDU in West Germany. The
post office in Güstrow informed the local Stasi that three young
women had tried to send a telegram to Brandt saying that they and
"like-minded people" in the GDR had been deeply upset by his
resignation. "We hope that your successor will bring to a conclusion the undertaking that you began," they wrote in the telegram,
which was never sent.

Günter Guillaume was sentenced to thirteen years in prison
for treason and violation of official secrets; Christel was given
eight years for aiding and abetting the crime. Although far from
draconian compared with the life terms spies often got in America
or Britain, the sentences were harsh for West Germany, where
spying was far more widespread, and Eastern agents were seldom
given long prison terms.

Ironically, Guillaume had provided East Berlin with highly
confidential information on West Germany's *Ostpolitik* that, in
the final analysis, only served to convince the Communists that
Bonn's motives were genuine. He provided the HVA, and thus the
KGB, with top secret communications from the White House and
the West German chancellor's office that merely reinforced what
the Soviet leadership already knew about NATO's preparedness

from studying thousands of Western publications and collecting its own intelligence. But Wolf, Mielke, and Honecker had developed an insatiable appetite for confidential documents and the lip-smacking exclusives on the West German leadership that Guillaume was providing. As with so much espionage material, Guillaume's information had served largely to boost the ego and the budget of the intelligence agency, the HVA.

Wolf, years later, publicly regretted that his mole had provoked Brandt's fall, and he admitted that much of Guillaume's information had been overrated. Brandt's resignation had been a "self-goal, a very bad one," he conceded. Although the GDR remained officially silent about the arrest and sentencing of the Guillaumes, the HVA radioed a musical greeting to its top spy, who was languishing in Rheinbach prison near Bonn:

> Greetings to Captain G. in Bonn, tra-la, tra-la
> We've got lots more like him, tra-la, tra-la.

Captain G. was released nearly six years later, six months after Christel, in one of the periodic East-West spy swaps. The Guillaumes were given a hero's welcome in East Berlin where at a special ceremony Mielke praised their courage, loyalty, and personal sacrifices, which, he said, should be an example for all members of the State Security Ministry and the "many spies on the invisible front." Wolf received his top mole, now heavily bearded, the day after his return to East Berlin: "Günter," he exclaimed, embracing Guillaume. "Mischa," Guillaume responded. Contrary to what Guillaume expected, Wolf failed to criticize him for having admitted upon arrest that he was an officer of the HVA. Years later, though, Wolf accused Guillaume of having violated orders by not escaping to the GDR after he realized he was under observation. Stung by the rebuke, Guillaume heatedly denied that he had been given any such orders.

Günter and Christel Guillaume's marriage, despite strains, had survived the enormous pressures of decades of espionage. The HVA could take a good deal of the credit. Wolf knew that nothing threatened the work of an agent more than marital discord. A broken marriage invariably meant a disgruntled ex-wife who could easily turn against her former husband. Over the years, Kurt Gailat, Guillaume's controlling officer, did everything he could to make sure that Christel felt that she was as important a mole as her husband and that she was being treated equally by the HVA.

But the moment West German security officials told Christel about Günter's extramarital affairs, the marriage was doomed. It was annulled after their release from prison. Both of them were handsomely rewarded with lifelong pensions by the MfS. Günter, now suffering with a heart ailment, was given a lakeside house outside Berlin. For a time he gave lectures to the HVA on working as a "spy for peace" and was befriended by East German Army and intelligence officers. After Mikhail Gorbachev's rise to power in Moscow, Guillaume railed against the Soviet reformer as a gravedigger of socialism. Christel got a new apartment. Their son, Pierre, disillusioned by the GDR and his father's Stalinism, returned to West Germany in 1988, a year before the fall of the Berlin Wall. Guillaume died of cancer in April 1995. Wolf paid his respects at the burial by throwing a single red rose into the grave.

The tragedy of the Guillaumes was a very German one, but it did not trouble Markus Wolf. Adopting the doublespeak of a senior Party official, he heaped praise on Mielke, a man he inwardly despised but with whom he had reached an accommodation over the years. Typical was his tribute to Mielke at a January 1986 Party conference of cheering HVA officers in their headquarters:

> The clear application of the policies of the Party leadership to our Ministry, especially to our tasks in intelligence, by Comrade Erich Mielke, member of the Politbüro of our Party and minister, is always important and valuable for our orientation. Each day we witness the critical and demanding nature of our minister. But we have always had his help and support in using the great resources of our ministry as well as in some recent, rather costly, but necessary projects.

For this we give you our very heartfelt thank-you, Comrade Minister. We do so by fulfilling the obligations we have pledged in our report to the Party.

The pledge was to boost the number of world-class spies. Wolf had previously suggested that it might be better to concentrate on a few top intelligence sources rather than conduct blanket espionage, but this idea had been summarily rejected by Mielke.

Wolf consoled himself by submerging himself even more totally in the world of espionage. Like a surgeon, he perfected the imperceptibly delicate insertion of his instruments into the enemy's vital political, military, and economic organs and the silent, undetected removal of their secrets through nearly invisible conduits. It had become the most fascinating work imaginable: developing a strategy that even his sworn enemies would soon acknowledge made the HVA Europe's most potent espionage agency, deploying his highly trained agents, caring for them and monitoring their progress. Wolf also displayed a healthy dose of bravado. He delighted in occasional forays to neutral Austria, Yugoslavia, Sweden, and Cyprus for meetings with his top moles. In doing so he was exposing himself to unnecessary danger, but he wanted to prove that he was no pencil-pushing spy chief and could perform as expertly in the field as any of his moles.

As for the ethics of serving in a profession in which one used treason while pursuing and killing traitors, he, like his fellow espionage chiefs, was scarcely aware of a moral dilemma. Nor was he very discriminating about the company he kept if it served the interests of the HVA.

One of Wolf's closest associates was Alexander Schalck-Golodkowski, a murky figure who served as a state secretary in the Foreign Trade Ministry, but who, in fact, was East Germany's chief financial wizard. The first time I saw the heavy-jowled Schalck-Golodkowski was during an East German reception for West German industrialists and bankers I attended at the Leipzig Fair. He had a beaming countenance that radiated self-assurance, and initially I thought he was West German. A massive man, he pumped hands, patted backs, and cracked jokes at the expense of the high-ranking East German flunkies who stood near him. I soon discovered that he was the superior of every East German in the room. When I spoke with him briefly, an aide whispered something in his ear, and he barked to me that he had nothing against journalists as long as they minded their own business. With that he guffawed loudly and turned his attention to the West Germans, who clearly were the only people he considered worthy of his attention.

Only later did I learn that Schalck was head of KoKo (Commercial Coordination), a vast conglomerate responsible only to the Party leader, Erich Honecker, that earned dollars, deutsche marks, Swiss francs, and a dozen other hard currencies for the GDR. KoKo became a state within a state, employing more than three thousand people. Schalck was also a colonel in the Stasi, an elite OibE (officer in special service) who enjoyed the confidence of Erich Mielke and Honecker as well as Wolf. KoKo operated at home and in the West with the goal of maximizing the hard currency intake of the Party and the Stasi. Schalck's organization provided Honecker with a slush fund he used to import Western products for the leadership and to finance the West German Communist Party. The Stasi used the hard currency Schalck earned to buy embargoed Western technology for its clandestine operations at home and abroad.

Schalck was the man who obtained the hard currency that Wolf needed to pay for his increasingly expensive espionage activities in the West. East German factory directors fought tooth and nail to get permission to import vital Western-made machinery for hard currency but were routinely turned down by the central planners; whereas as GDR intelligence spread its net ever wider, Wolf was fortunate to be able to rely on Schalck for the deutsche marks and dollars the HVA needed. In return, Wolf provided Schalck with his own expertise and that of his officers and agents in the field. In short, theirs was a mutually advantageous partnership.

Only by employing capitalist methods, Schalck was convinced, could the socialist countries hasten the downfall of the West. To boost KoKo's hard currency intake, Schalck carried out risky stock market deals, speculative gold and silver trading, as well as arms sales. After the Soviet invasion of Afghanistan, he moved precious metals back and forth on East German freighters between Rostock and London. He was afraid the West would impound the East German assets if they were left in London bank vaults.

The leading purveyors of hard currency for KoKo were disreputable characters, including a few Jewish survivors of the Holocaust. In the chaos of postwar Germany, they were attracted by the black market that thrived amidst the ruins. Running afoul of the law in both East and West Germany, they quickly aroused the attention of the Stasi and Schalck, who set them up in the business of raking in hard currency for the GDR; Mielke and Wolf provided the cover for their obscure international dealings. Perversely, two of the most prominent Jewish operators conformed to a traditional anti-Semitic German image of the Jew: sharp as a knife and willing to profit from the misfortunes of their fellow men.

Polish-born Michael Wischnewski, alias Horst Libermann, headed a KoKo subsidy, F. C. Gerlach, that smuggled embargoed goods into the GDR. Wischnewski made his first money in the postwar black market and was henceforth on the wanted list of the police in Eastern and Western Europe. He found refuge in the Stasi during the 1950s, and he proved a gifted agent. Wolf was much indebted to Wischnewski for his intelligence information as well as the hard currency he brought in.

One of Wischnewski's closest friends, apart from Schalck, was Simon Goldenberg, who headed another KoKo company, G. Simon, which represented leading Western companies such as IBM, British Petroleum, and Daimler-Benz in East Berlin. After the war Goldenberg smuggled East German alcohol to the West, and had a police record in the West that was an arm long. The Stasi was impressed by his business acumen and was not disappointed in him. He earned millions in hard currency for the GDR and was a major supplier of embargoed COCOM products for Mielke and Wolf.

Wolf tacitly approved of Schalck's KoKo machinations, just as he did the selling of prisoners to West Germany. This was another source of hard currency for the regime. Each person released to the West brought in an average of DM 40,000. The prisoners the GDR sold were East Germans convicted of opposing the state or attempted escape. West Germany would present a list of the people it wanted released to Wolfgang Vogel, the East Berlin lawyer responsible for humanitarian questions. Vogel then passed the list to his Stasi contact officer, Heinz Volpert, who gave it to Mielke and his aides. They crossed off the names of prisoners the Stasi was not willing to release, sometimes adding names of common criminals the regime was happy to get rid of. The list was then returned via Vogel to the West Germans.

Admittedly, it was hard to imagine Wolf having scruples about the sale of prisoners if the West German government itself had none. But Wolf was not blind to the moral corrosiveness such deals had on his own, allegedly socialist society.

Wolf's closest links with Schalck were in the field of high-tech espionage, which was the domain of the HVA's science and technology department. Schalck needed Wolf's agents to obtain access to the advanced Western hardware and software that was on the COCOM list of embargoed high-tech goods. With the help of the HVA, suppliers were found in the West who were willing to sell microprocessors, IBM computers, and even bombing sights for jet fighters to the GDR at the right price — usually double or triple the market price.

Ironically, it was with the help of Goldenberg and Wischnewski that Schalck was able to obtain a DM 1 billion loan in 1983 from West German banks that helped the heavily indebted GDR to survive. Goldenberg was a business partner of the März brothers in Bavaria, one of the two leading Bavarian meat packers who bought great quantities of East German meat. The other meat packer was Alexander Moksel, who as a Jew had suffered for five years in Nazi concentration camps. Moksel paid his commission into a Swiss bank account of one Günther Forgber, a shady East German who dealt largely for the Stasi.

The März brothers were close friends of the late Franz-Josef Strauss, Bavaria's colorful prime minister and head of the Bavarian wing of the ruling Christian Democrats. Schalck used the März brothers' influence with Strauss to get West German banks to loan the DM 1 billion, which boosted the GDR's credit rating and enabled the state to borrow even more money from the

West. In return, East Germany's Erich Honecker agreed to dismantle the thousands of self-firing shrapnel guns mounted on the final border fence to West Germany. In his frequent meetings with Strauss, Schalck pumped information out of the Bavarian leader, reporting back to Mielke what Strauss had to say about his political friends and enemies. Strauss had his use for Schalck, too; he used this line of communication to the East Berlin leadership to outflank his conservative rival, Chancellor Helmut Kohl. Later, however, Kohl would use Schalck as his own contact with the East Berlin leadership.

Although Schalck was one of Wolf's most unscrupulous companions, the spymaster had several other strange bedfellows, including some of the most dangerous international terrorists. By the early 1970s, Wolf and Mielke had concluded that the best way to obtain firsthand information on the tactics used by West German and international terrorists was to enter into a closely controlled, clandestine cooperation with the terrorists. By doing so the East Germans hoped to weaken the West while warding off potential harm to themselves. But the Stasi's at first limited cooperation with the Red Army Faction (RAF) and the Fatah, as well as its Middle Eastern allies in Syria, Libya, and Iran, soon took on an extraordinary life of its own.

Mielke ordered the Stasi to closely monitor the RAF's struggle to overthrow German capitalism while making sure that the terrorists were kept away from the GDR. The Stasi's Department 22, antiterrorism, was set up to "detect, prevent, and combat acts of terror and violence" by right-wing and left-wing extremist organizations against the GDR and its citizens. At the same time the GDR sympathized strongly with Third World liberation movements including Yasir Arafat's Fatah wing of the Palestine Liberation Organization, which had a quasi-diplomatic status in East Berlin. The Stasi was fully aware that Fatah's then sworn enemy was Israel and that Fatah was also helping to train German RAF comrades at camps in the Middle East. Wolf's officers instructed Fatah members in basic intelligence work, and Fatah guerrillas and the infamous Abu Nidal group were trained with Soviet weapons by East German Army instructors. Only a few months after attending a course in rocket launchers given in 1985, members of Abu Nidal launched projectiles at Vienna and Rome airports, killing twenty people.

The world's most wanted terrorist, Ilyich Ramírez Sánchez, alias Carlos, was regularly booked into an East Berlin luxury hotel together with other hard currency guests. The Venezuelan boasted that he was responsible for the bomb blast in West Berlin in August 1983 that wrecked the French Consulate, killing 1 person and injuring 22. Carlos directed his terrorism against targets in Western Europe from the GDR and Hungary but was finally ordered to leave when the secret police feared implication in his blood-soaked attacks.

Subsequently it was learned that in August of 1983, Lt. Col. Helmut Voigt of Department 22 had ordered 24 kilograms of Nitropenta explosives, which had been confiscated earlier by GDR customs, released to one Johannes Weinrich, care of the Syrian Embassy in East Berlin. Weinrich was the fanatic young German right-hand man of Carlos, who had earlier carried out attacks on El Al airliners in Paris and on Radio Free Europe in Munich. He was given asylum in Damascus. A Syrian and a Lebanese member of the "Carlos" group planted the explosives in the French Consulate in West Berlin, and in the aftermath of the explosion the terrorists returned to safety in East Berlin. Mielke later, not very convincingly, claimed that he had known nothing of the bombing beforehand. Lieutenant Colonel Voigt, who was left holding the smoking gun, was given a four-year prison sentence in 1994 for complicity in murder and terrorism.

Voigt was an old hand at dealing with terrorists, having arranged for prominent members of the RAF in West Germany to make clandestine visits to the GDR. Four of the top RAF terrorists — Christian Klar, Helmut Pohl, Adelheid Schulz, and Inge Viett — were trained in the use of explosives and other weapons, including Soviet antitank grenade launchers, at special Stasi camps. Two women RAF terrorists, Schulz and Viett, were later given "asylum" in the GDR, along with six other West German terrorists whom the RAF leadership released from service. Mielke and Honecker saw them as victims of capitalist society who were ready to be taught what real socialism was. The ex-terrorists were given false identities as well as jobs and apartments in various East German cities. They raised children, grappled with shortages, and lived humdrum East German lives until the day the Wall fell. Then they were betrayed.

Stasi connivance with terrorists also led to its complicity in the deaths of two American soldiers and a Turkish woman on April 5, 1986, at the West Berlin La Belle discotheque, which was a popular hangout of American servicemen. More than 200 people, including 50 Americans, were injured. Washington charged that the bombing was directed by diplomats in the Libyan mission in East Berlin. Nine days later, U.S. warplanes retaliated by swooping down on "terrorist centers" and military bases in Libya.

Erich Honecker indignantly rejected Western suggestions of an East German role in the bombing. But one of Wolf's supermoles, planted deep within West German counterespionage, had learned otherwise. Stasi defectors to the West had told him that Mielke and Wolf knew who smuggled the explosives into the GDR. He said the Stasi was told that the terrorists had three possible targets: the kindergarten of the German-American John F. Kennedy School in West Berlin, one of the U.S. Army school buses used by the school, and La Belle discotheque. Mielke could have prevented the attack that took place but did not.

Stasi support for terrorists may have even played a role in the downing on December 21, 1988, of the PanAm jumbo airliner over Lockerbie, Scotland, and the deaths of 270 people. British and American intelligence officials obtained evidence of an East German connection in the terrorist bombing of the airliner. Stasi officers were said to have sold the Swiss-made electronic timing device to the two Libyans who were accused of responsibility for the bombing.

Markus Wolf, who by 1986 had relinquished control of East German espionage, washed his hands of any involvement with terrorist groups. Regardless of all the evidence to the contrary, he said that the only knowledge he had of terrorism came from reading Mielke's reports on the subject.

CHAPTER
5

Although sex has been used to gather intelligence since ancient times, it was Wolf who resurrected the much-neglected Romeo agent, a twist on the female spy who seduced her victim to obtain secrets. In his quest for innovative espionage that would satisfy the leadership's enormous appetite for political, military, and economic secrets, he turned the Romeo agent into a highly effective intelligence weapon.

Early in his espionage career Wolf realized that it was not enough to infiltrate East German agents into the West. His agency, the HVA (Central Intelligence Administration), would have to concentrate on recruiting West Germans with access to top-level secrets. Experience showed that it was usually much simpler for his agents to recruit the secretary of a high-ranking Western official than the official himself. Moreover, secretaries often had the same access to confidential information as their bosses. Wolf unleashed his Romeo agents onto thousands of unsuspecting female secretaries in Bonn government offices and NATO headquarters in Brussels. All the women had one weakness that made them susceptible to the wooing of the HVA agents: they were lonely. Many of them had developed a deep-seated fear of spending still another weekend or vacation alone. They often took to inventing stories to tell in the office on Monday mornings about the exciting weekends they had experienced with fictitious male suitors.

Maria, the forty-year-old divorced secretary of a high-level

West German Defense Ministry official, was one of them. After a brief marriage she had to pay off the debts that she and her ex-husband had accumulated. Wolf's network of informers in the West German registry offices and banks alerted East Berlin head-quarters of her predicament. She was conscientious and devoted to her boss — her job was all she had left. Not unattractive, Maria nonetheless had few opportunities to meet men, and occasionally she sent her name to the lonely hearts agencies. Here, too, East German intelligence had its informants.

Early one evening, the doorbell rang, and, believing it to be her neighbor, Maria opened the door to find a man of her own age holding a large bouquet of flowers and smiling shyly. He apologized for disturbing her and said he was looking for a certain young lady whose name he mentioned. Maria said she knew of no such person in the building. He explained that he had recently met the young woman and wanted to give her the flowers as a sign of his affection. But it appeared that she had intentionally given him the wrong address, he claimed.

Maria was touched by this sympathetic man who was in such obvious distress. Blushing, he handed her the flowers, saying that at least she might get some pleasure from them. She took the flowers and spontaneously decided to ask the man in for a cup of coffee. The interlude lengthened into dinner, at his invitation, and the beginning of a liaison that Maria soon believed was genuine love. At work, she could no longer wait to get home to her lover.

Maria began telling him about her work at the Defense Ministry, and he showed interest. When he asked her to get some information for his "research project," she photocopied it for him. Soon she photocopied everything he wanted, and before she realized it she had become an espionage "source" for East Berlin.

Dagmar Kahlig-Scheffler, a divorced twenty-seven-year-old West German secretary, was hooked by Wolf's Romeo bait during her vacation in Bulgaria. Lolling at the beach, the slender young blonde met a handsome young East German who introduced himself as Herbert Richter, an engineer. Instead of the expected brief flirtation, she fell in love. They were wed in East Berlin in a ceremony that East German intelligence chillingly referred to as an "operative fictional marriage." HVA officers played the role of best man and registrar, and the bride suspected nothing.

Kahlig-Scheffler did whatever Richter told her to out of her boundless affection for him. He instructed her to send her daughter to a boarding school in Switzerland (Wolf agreed that the HVA would pay half the costs) and to apply for a job at the West German Foreign Ministry. Failing to obtain that position, she succeeded in getting a job in the federal chancellory in December of 1975. Using a Minox camera, she photographed everything of interest that she came across, passing the film to couriers in Geneva and Vienna. Wolf was treated to highly confidential communications between Chancellor Helmut Schmidt and President Jimmy Carter and learned how Bonn was preparing itself for the follow-up Conference on European Security in Belgrade.

Whenever she protested to her couriers that she could no longer continue working for the HVA, a reunion was quickly arranged with her "husband" Herbert in East Berlin to "stabilize" their relationship. She was whisked past the border controls at Friedrichstrasse station in East Berlin, and Herbert, summoning all his virility and persuasive talents, managed to convince her to continue spying. After her arrest in 1976, she learned that Herbert had previously entered into a fictional marriage with another secretary in the West German Foreign Ministry. Emotionally scarred for a lifetime by her experience, Kahlig-Scheffler was sentenced to four years and five months imprisonment for espionage.

Wolf regretted losing her, but over the years he had developed the ability to shake off such inevitable setbacks. After a good night's sleep, he plunged into perfecting the HVA's techniques and its ever expanding network of agents. The optimism he exuded was contagious, and his officers developed a pride in their work and an esprit de corps that contrasted sharply with the impersonal, demotivating atmosphere at West Germany's BND (Federal Intelligence Agency). Morale in the ranks of the highly bureaucratized BfV (West Germany's counterintelligence agency) was also at rock bottom, and successes against Wolf's agents were rare events.

Aware that many Westerners would balk at spying for a

Communist intelligence service, Wolf's Romeo agents would sometimes operate under a false flag, convincing their secretarial prey that they were agents of Britain's Secret Intelligence Service (SIS), the French Service de Documentation Extérieure et Contre-Espionage (SDECE) intelligence branch, or even Dutch intelligence. One handsome young HVA officer was given the identity of Peter Krause, a South African, and was sent to Bonn to seek out a lonely secretary who worked for the Foreign Ministry. He soon scored a success with Helge Berger, newly arrived in Bonn and very lonesome until he spoke to her one early spring day in 1966 on the street.

After winning Berger's affections, the HVA officer proposed to his buxom dark-haired new girlfriend that they spend a brief vacation in Italy. Once they were comfortably settled in, he disclosed to her that he was a British intelligence agent and that she was to tell no one. Leaving nothing to chance, the HVA had sent an informer to Italy to make sure Krause was not being observed by Italian counterintelligence and to find an escape route for him in the event that Berger refused to cooperate.

In fact, Helge Berger was relieved when her lover said he was an agent of Her Majesty's Government and not a Russian or East German spy. She readily agreed to keep his secret. Although she had little of interest to report, she willingly provided information to her "British" agent-lover and was code-named Nova by the HVA. Shortly before she was transferred to her new job at the West German Trade Mission in Warsaw, Berger was introduced to Krause's alleged superior at British intelligence in the suite of a first-class hotel in Frankfurt. He was ideal for the part; although he was East German, he seemed to her to be a very English-looking gentleman, and as a former Wehrmacht prisoner of war in Britain, he spoke fluent English.

At the Trade Mission in Warsaw, Berger slipped out documents for Krause in a plain plastic bag covered only by her knitting. The information gave Wolf an inside track on the West German negotiations with Poland that were a crucial element in Willy Brandt's *Ostpolitik*. Because the HVA rented a flat from Polish intelligence for Krause to use for his trysts with Berger, Wolf personally decided that Polish intelligence was to receive a copy of the information she gave to Krause in order to simplify his activities in Poland.

Heinrich Böx, the head of the West German Trade Mission who subsequently became Bonn's first postwar ambassador to Poland, also thought highly of Helge Berger (alias Nova). He asked her to become his personal secretary as well as his mistress. Distraught, she told Krause about her dilemma. He immediately consulted with his headquarters in East Berlin, which quickly dispatched Krause's bogus "superior at British intelligence" to Warsaw to sort out the problem. He managed to convince Berger that it was vital that she cultivate a relationship with Böx.

Krause's "superior" frequently visited Warsaw to assure Berger of how important her information was to London. He even awarded her a certificate of commendation from London headquarters, which, he assured her, would entitle her to a number of privileges in Britain once her services were completed.

Yet Berger wondered why she had been told to flee to an address in East Berlin if an emergency arose. She was plagued by growing suspicions that she might actually be working for a Communist espionage service. But she suppressed her fears, unable to bear the thought that she might have been duped by Krause.

Polish intelligence was mainly interested in the personal affairs of the other members of the West German Trade Mission, because the Poles wanted to blackmail West Germans into spying for Poland. One of the West German diplomats had several Polish girlfriends, all informers for Polish intelligence, who saw to it that he was recruited by a Polish agent. But the diplomat immediately confessed to Böx that he was being blackmailed by Polish intelligence. When Böx asked Berger to type up a confidential report on the diplomat for the Foreign Ministry in Bonn, as always, she kept one copy for Krause. Wolf then took it upon himself to personally inform his Polish counterpart that the Poles had been duped by the West German diplomat.

Early one wintry morning, a man, his face partly buried in a scarf, walked up to the West German Trade Mission, silently handed a letter to the caretaker, and vanished. The letter was addressed to the president of West Germany's BND. The writer said he was an employee of Polish security and had information that Polish intelligence had recruited a member of the Trade Mission. He demanded $20,000 for further information, as well as a pledge that he would be given asylum in West Germany.

Berger immediately informed Krause about the incident. Wolf ordered Nova's controlling officer and another officer to go to Warsaw for consultations with Polish intelligence. The Poles were convinced that the letter had come from someone within their own intelligence ranks, and they ordered that the Trade Mission be placed under observation day and night. But the writer of the letter learned about the surveillance order, and, in order to circumvent it, he hit upon an elaborate stratagem. He ordered a bouquet of flowers at a local florist to be sent to one of the German diplomats. But instead of sending it directly to the West German Trade Mission, he gave the address of a Polish family who lived in an adjoining house and attached a letter. As planned, the flowers were delivered to the Polish family, who promptly delivered them to the West German Trade Mission without being intercepted. But once again the letter fell into Berger's hands. When the writer of the letter found out that Polish intelligence had once again been alerted, he angrily accused the Trade Mission of having failed to keep the contents of his previous letter from reaching the ears of the Poles.

Unable to locate the letter-writer this time, the Polish intelligence agency called on Wolf for help. He was to have his officers get a description of the man who had bought the bouquet from the Warsaw florist. Wolf sent three of his officers to Warsaw, one of whom was fluent in Polish. They brazenly identified themselves to the owner of the flower shop as officials of the West German intelligence agency and demanded that he give them an accurate description of the man who sent the flowers. The store owner, a patriotic Pole, grew angry at such impudence, screaming back at the East Germans that he could give no such description. Besides, he said, he had already told what he knew to the "others" who had questioned him. Thus the HVA learned that BND agents from Munich had already interviewed the florist.

The angry florist promptly alerted the Polish police about the insolent Germans, and a nationwide search for Wolf's three bogus BND agents was ready to be set in motion. It took the head of Polish intelligence to delay the manhunt until the three HVA officers had safely crossed the Polish border into the GDR.

Berger informed Krause that she was being transferred back home in September 1970 and would begin work as a secretary in the office of Sigismund von Braun (brother of the German-American rocket scientist Wernher von Braun), an undersecretary in the West German Foreign Ministry who was famed for his female conquests.

Sensing one more opportunity to plant a mole inside the Bonn establishment, the HVA ordered Peter Krause to move as close as possible to Berger in order to motivate her with his amorous favors. Krause took an apartment using the identity of an East German named Klaus Wöhler who had emigrated to Australia. Frustrated at work where she had little access to secrets, Berger was buoyed only by Krause's affirmations of his undying love.

Impressed by her skills, intelligence, and modesty, Berger's superiors at the Foreign Ministry promoted her to secretary to the head of the section dealing with nuclear energy, space research, and arms exports in the European Community. As before, Berger removed copies of secret documents from her office in a plastic bag covered by her knitting.

When Berger was told that she was to be transferred to the NATO mission in Washington, East Berlin considered putting its contacts with her on ice. The danger seemed too great that she would run afoul of the expected stringent security checks for the Washington assignment.

Although she repeatedly told herself that she was working for British intelligence, Berger was not really surprised upon learning that her colleagues at work had been questioned about her by West German counterintelligence (the BfV). Heinrich Böx, her former boss, was also questioned. He lavishly praised his ex-secretary, and he testified that she was so trustworthy that she had even typed up the report on the West German diplomat who had been unsuccessfully recruited by Polish intelligence. The BfV's normally dormant curiosity was aroused. The agency asked Herr Böx to give some additional details about Berger.

East German intelligence found out about the deepening

BfV investigation of Berger and ordered Krause to tell her to abort all espionage activities. While driving her one evening to the train for Bonn after they had spent the day in each other's arms in his apartment, Krause caught sight of the brake lights of a nearby parked car blinking twice. He suspected that it was a signal to a surveillance team that was following them. Assuming that Berger's telephone was bugged, Krause said he would call her neighbor if he had to contact her.

The following day, Krause managed to shake off his surveillants and immediately escaped to the GDR, leaving Berger behind. Only hours later, she was called to the telephone by her neighbor. It was Krause. He used a prearranged code word that was meant to warn her that she was in danger of arrest and should flee to the GDR. But Berger balked. The HVA's elaborate intelligence charade had served its purpose, but Krause had left behind a dazed and immobilized Helge Berger. When she was arrested shortly afterward, Berger, alias Nova, insisted that her espionage employer was the SIS in London, and that she had been used to control the "unreliable" Germans. Although the evidence against her was overwhelming, the court ruled mitigating circumstances, judging that she had been drawn into espionage against her convictions by the unscrupulous practices of East German intelligence. She was sentenced to four years and six months in prison.

In the wake of her arrest Wolf was concerned lest his other agents in the West begin questioning the reliability of his agency after they learned the sordid details of the case from the media. He succeeded in establishing contact with Berger and offered the GDR's help to gain her release. But she never responded. She was so deeply embittered after learning that Krause had feigned his love for her that she wanted nothing to do with the GDR.

Helge Berger was released after serving three and a half years of her sentence, on condition that she pay a fine of DM 20,000 and an additional DM 48,000 in legal expenses. She married not long after her release and tried to forget the past.

All intelligence agencies used "Romeo" agents, Wolf later argued. It was perfectly true. But nowhere was this cynical practice developed to such perfection and used so extensively as by his HVA. The investment in terms of manpower, time, and money was enormous, but the rewards were sometimes dazzling. Wolf's top mole in the West German Defense Ministry in the 1970s was a Romeo, Lothar Erwin Lutze, a West German who had been recruited by the HVA while still a young man serving in the Luftwaffe. In September 1972 Lothar married Renate, a homely looking, raven-haired secretary in the Defense Ministry. Out of love for him, she agreed to work for East Berlin, and she helped him get a job in the Defense Ministry, where he eventually landed in the armaments section. Together they photographed and passed to the HVA nearly a thousand documents on the state of readiness of the West German Army and NATO. These included plans for a new German-British battle tank as well as top secret information revealing what NATO's military response would be to a Soviet attempt to take over West Berlin. The KGB and the Soviet Army High Command were jubilant over acquiring these secrets.

The end of the Lutzes' career came in the early morning hours of June 2, 1976, when Lothar and Renate were hauled out of bed and arrested in their apartment near Bonn. West German security officials found all the evidence they needed to convict them of espionage: Minox camera photographs of secret defense papers, stolen confidential documents that had not yet been photographed, and copies of keys to Defense Ministry safes. Lothar Lutze was sentenced to twelve years in prison, and his wife got six years. After serving the greater part of their prison terms, they were exchanged in spy swaps with East Berlin.

Wolf regarded lonely secretaries and their Romeos as valuable assets in the waging of the cold war. Like a GDR sports trainer who devoted all his skills to his top athletes so that they would set world records for the glory of the GDR, Wolf saw his agents as pieces of human machinery that, if correctly serviced and maintained, would perform outstandingly for the GDR. When, after the cold war had ended, I asked Wolf about the morality of misusing the emotions and trust of vulnerable women, he reminded me that his intelligence service did not act by the rules and regulations of either a "girls' school or the Salvation Army."

Not all of Wolf's Romeos latched onto hapless secretaries.

Gabriele Gast was a demure student of political science at the Technical University in Aachen. Fair-haired and angular, she was nervous in the presence of young men of her age. In 1968, at a time when West German youth were in ferment, she was a member of the conservative Christian Democratic student organization.

Professor Klaus Mehnert, a leading West German kremlinologist, chose her to be his assistant. He enthusiastically backed her idea to write her doctoral thesis on the political role of East German women, and he suggested that she try to do her research in the GDR. Gast wrote her relatives in Karl-Marx-Stadt (formerly Chemnitz) who obtained permission for her to visit them in the spring of 1968. The regional office of the Stasi was also eagerly awaiting her arrival.

She encountered surprisingly few problems in the GDR and was taken by car to her interviews with East German women who were active in politics and the state labor union. Over a beer one evening in the Kosmos bar, she and the driver of the car got to know each other better. He was a friendly man with a crew cut and a beer belly who said his name was Karl-Heinz Schmidt and that he was a technician. He looked like someone's kindly uncle, was considerably older than Gast, and spoke in a cozy Saxon dialect. Gast had always preferred older men, and, at the age of twenty-five, had seldom had a date. They arranged to meet again.

Gast was back again in Karl-Marx-Stadt in the late summer of 1968 and saw Schmidt often during her two-week stay. Before she knew it she had fallen in love with him and nicknamed him Karliczek. His real name was Karl-Heinz Schneider. He was an officer of regional Department 25 of the State Security Ministry (MfS), the section responsible for espionage in Karl-Marx-Stadt. Schneider told his superior, Gotthard Schramm, about the affair, and Gast was invited to East Berlin, where the three of them met in the Hotel Unter den Linden. Schneider, alias Schmidt, introduced Schramm to her as his "friend," Gotthard Schiefer.

After informing Gast that they were from the MfS, Schiefer bluntly told her that State Security suspected her of being a Western agent who had been sent to spy on Schmidt. Her relationship with him would have to be terminated, Schiefer said, unless, of course, she helped them by obtaining some information about her professors.

Gast was staggered. Schmidt was no longer a kindly uncle but her lover. Because she could not bear the thought of losing him, she agreed to cooperate with them, informally, without signing anything. She told them she wanted no money for her work. Once she had overcome her first reservations about her recruitment, the rest followed automatically. She was given her new code name, Gisela, a forged passport, and a handbag with a secret compartment. She was directed to come to East Berlin every three months. Her frequent visits were designed to "intensify" her relationship to Schmidt, who accompanied her to Karl-Marx-Stadt. Here she was given an introductory course in the tools of espionage: She learned to use invisible ink, to photograph documents, and to monitor coded radio messages. She was also taught how to conduct herself at conspirational *treffs* with her controller.

Back in Aachen, she tuned in her shortwave radio at the same time every Tuesday evening and wrote down the columns of numbers read off by a woman in a monotone voice. The numbers she decrypted were messages from Schmidt. In April 1970 she was engaged to Schmidt in a guesthouse of the MfS near Plauen. He made her promise never to reveal that he was her fiancé.

Gast obtained her doctorate and completed her dissertation on the political role of women in the GDR. Her conclusion: their role was minimal. She criticized the Vietnam War and West Germany's lapdog relationship with the United States. Although critical of her own Christian Democratic Party, she joined an ultraconservative think tank that dealt with security problems. She photographed everything of possible interest to the HVA, which sent a courier to pick up the film. Gast continued to refuse all payment for her services, since she told herself she was working in the interest of peace.

Replying to an ad placed by the West German Foreign Ministry, she was surprised by being contacted by a man who said he was from the Federal Intelligence Agency (BND). But she showed interest, and he gave her an application form. In a letter written in invisible ink, she proudly informed Schmidt of this promising development. Gast was hired by the BND after passing a less-than-stringent security check, and, on November 1, 1973, she moved into her new office at BND headquarters in Pullach, near Munich. She was given her West German code name, "Frau Dr. Leinfelder," and was assigned to the section of the analysis department that dealt with the Soviet Union. Here she photographed confidential documents that the BND prepared for the use of the West German government and Parliament, passing on the films to her courier. Her controller never had to tell her what East Berlin was interested in, trusting her to know.

Gast, alias Frau Dr. Leinfelder, alias Gisela, lived for the times when she could be with her lover, Schmidt, in Austria or northern Italy. She was informed about the rendezvous by coded message from East Berlin. The couple would dine in cozy restaurants, dance, and go to the opera in Vienna. Gast's controlling officer in East Berlin was careful to protect the intimate, private nature of her relationship with Schmidt.

Wolf quickly realized that he had struck gold with his mole inside the BND. Her information from the BND's Soviet section was of particular interest to the KGB, which continued to get copies from East German intelligence of everything that was of even the remotest interest to Moscow. Wolf set up an illegal residence in West Germany that was responsible exclusively for Gast and consisted of an East German couple who had entered West Germany from Britain. The woman met Gast every few weeks in a ladies' room, where they swapped hollow deodorant spray cans containing miniature films.

Wolf used one of East Berlin's favorite means of transporting espionage material: the smoke-belching Reichsbahn railroad, a rolling safe drop. The courier slipped containers with exposed film from Gast behind a panel underneath the washbasin of the regular train between West Germany and East Berlin, leaving a chalk mark at the spot. In East Germany, one of Wolf's officers entered the train and searched for a chalk mark designating concealed espionage material.

Wolf was anxious to get to know his prize BND mole, so he arranged to meet her in September 1975 at the secluded resort of Rabac on the Slovenian coast of Yugoslavia. Traveling under a false identity, he arrived by car together with an aide at the seaside bungalow where Gast and Schmidt were staying. The handsome, casually dressed man who strode toward her was totally at odds with the mental picture she had of the head of East German intelligence.

"*Guten Tag*, I am so glad to meet you," Wolf said, smiling warmly and offering his hand. "Please call me Mischa as my friends do," he urged.

"Gabrielle, but call me Gaby," Gast said, peering into the dark sunglasses that covered his eyes.

She had expected a stilted, baggy-faced Communist functionary, but instead standing opposite her was a tall, slender, youthful-looking man in his mid-fifties with a soothing timbre in his voice and an accent that betrayed his southwest German origin.

They swam in the warm blue-green Adriatic, sipped wine on the terrace of their bungalow, and looked like two ordinary vacationers. Wolf was impressed by his mole's intelligence and analytical powers. They discussed *Ostpolitik* (Eastern policy) and the problems of the Soviet Union and its allies. Wolf was undogmatic, freely admitting that the Communist countries had a long way to go before they could profit from socialism's inherent advantages.

Before she had a chance to do so, he raised the subject of the arrest of the Guillaumes more than a year earlier. He had an uncanny ability to predict the questions that others were likely to ask him. His disarming frankness gave him an aura of complete honesty. Although the West German media viewed the Guillaume case as proof of the superiority of East German intelligence, Wolf said that the uncovering of the Guillaumes had also brought to light defects in the HVA's work that had since been corrected. He assured her that the safety of his agents was of paramount importance to him.

As to her own security, it was assured by the fact that no one in the HVA, apart from Schneider and three other officers, including himself, knew of her existence. But if the West Germans should ever discover that she was working for the GDR before she was able to escape, he wanted her to know one thing: the State Security Ministry and the leadership of the GDR would do everything in their power to gain her release. Gast was grateful for his sincerity and felt honored by this pledge. At night, Gast and the good-natured Karl-Heinz Schmidt, who addressed Wolf with the obligatory "Comrade Minister," retired to their bungalow. After making love to her, he whispered that they would always remain together.

While Wolf was conversing with his espionage jewel over glasses of dry white wine by the glistening Adriatic Sea, Western intelligence services were unable to turn up so much as a recent photo of him. The latest picture they had was a faded image of Wolf in his thirties.

West German intelligence promoted Gast to government councilor in 1976, a considerable achievement for a woman in the male-dominated German civil service. Her concise analyses of internal developments in the Soviet Union and its allies was distributed to all West German government ministries.

Gast would pass a total of forty-nine lengthy intelligence reports to the HVA from inside the BND, where she rose to the position of deputy head of the Soviet section. The report topics ranged from internal economic problems to analyses of Soviet politics and the Soviet space program as well as the summit meeting between Presidents Reagan and Gorbachev. Equally important, she gave Wolf everything she knew about the organization of the BND and the real names of its officials, its codes and agents, and code names of all its resident agents abroad.

Wolf, too, was delighted by her steady progress in the BND hierarchy. The higher she rose, the greater was her value to him. His pulse quickened and his mind grew giddy at the mere thought of the top secret documents she could obtain for him. Enhanced by the rich diet of Gast's material, his reputation with the KGB would soar to even higher peaks.

Wolf met Gast again the following year near Split, Yugoslavia, where she and Schmidt spent an unforgettable week together. This time Wolf spoke of his youth in the Soviet Union, his father's plays and books, and his brother's films. Gast felt privileged to know this man who seemed to embody all that was noble and worthwhile in socialism. In 1978 Wolf, accompanied by Colonel Lorenz, met Gast and Schneider for several days in Hercegnovi, south of Dubrovnik, Yugoslavia, where they discussed her work, the international political situation, and, once again, his father and brother. They took trips by car to Kotor and other sights, just like any of the hundreds of thousands of Western tourists who visited Yugoslavia.

In 1979 Gast traveled to Göteborg, Sweden, where she met Schmidt, who gave her a GDR diplomatic passport. They then took the ferry to Sassnitz, East Germany, and were driven to East Berlin. Wolf received his mole Gisela and together they went sailing on Müggelsee, the large lake in East Berlin, on an HVA boat. In the evening Wolf fulfilled a promise he had made her in Yugoslavia, that when she came to East Berlin he would prepare one of his favorite Russian dishes.

It was all second nature to him, the recipe for *pelmeni* that he had learned as a boy in Moscow from his mother. *Pelmeni* is the Russian noodle dough specialty filled with ground beef, pork, and lamb, well-spiced, boiled in water, and doused with sour cream and freshly ground pepper. They drank Russian vodka with the meal, and Wolf regaled his guests — Gast, Schmidt, and other officers of the HVA — with humorous accounts of life in the Soviet Union. Gast laughed until tears came to her eyes. How different this all was from the "Soviet threat" she constantly read about in the BND documents that crossed her desk, she reflected.

Wolf met with his supermole three more times in East Germany, in 1981, 1984, and 1986 at the HVA guesthouse in Dresden and at a mountain resort. Unlike her colleague Alfred Spuhler, a captain in the BND who with his courier brother collected nearly half a million deutsche marks from Wolf's HVA for betraying computer lists with the names of Western agents,

Gast continued to refuse all payment for her services to the GDR. She spied out of love for Karl-Heinz and her conviction that she was helping to maintain peace. She felt certain that the bonds between Karl-Heinz and herself had ripened into a relationship that went far beyond most marriages. But the sheer mental strain of her double life between the BND and the HVA had become unbearable. The next time she met Schmidt in January 1980 in Innsbruck, Austria, she told him that she would have to curtail her work for East Berlin. She was going to take over the care of a spastic child. The following September, when Gast was in East Germany, Schmidt's superior, Colonel Lorenz, asked her whether she realized that any reduction in her commitment to the HVA would mean that Karl-Heinz would not be allowed to see her. Her throat constricted and went dry. She could not bear the thought of not seeing her lover again and told Colonel Lorenz she would try her best.

In 1985 Gast and Schmidt spent their winter vacations together with the spastic child in Bad Gastein, Austria, and once again she told him that she had to end her work for the HVA, because the child needed her full attention. Schmidt once more alerted his superior, and Colonel Lorenz arranged for a *treff* with Gast in December in Zell am See, Austria. The Colonel made it crystal clear to her that if she stopped working for East Berlin, her friendship with Karl-Heinz would be endangered. It was only then that the truth fully dawned on her. She had been totally dependent on the HVA from the moment she fell in love with Karliczek.

During the time that she was assigned to work in the federal chancellory in Bonn, Gast was responsible for putting together the special BND report for Chancellor Helmut Kohl. Only days later, Wolf, too, was able to read it. Mielke, for his part, especially appreciated the BND's annual intelligence report. He knew that the KGB was eager to obtain West Germany's analysis of the Soviet Union's military, political, and economic strengths and weaknesses.

Each anniversary of the founding of the Cheka (the forerunner of the NKVD and the KGB) was an occasion to present a gift to the KGB. It was always a highly confidential document, sometimes a new NATO report on the readiness of the Atlantic Alliance or a set of cruise-missile blueprints. This time, in the early 1980s, the document had been obtained by Gisela, Wolf's mole in the BND. The Stasi did not reveal her real name, Dr. Gast, to the KGB. East Berlin could not be careful enough, because if a Western mole had managed to penetrate the KGB, he would be in a position to betray Gast to the West.

At the ceremony Mielke proudly handed a flat red leather-covered box to the head of the KGB rezidentura in Berlin-Karlshorst. The assembled officers of the State Security Ministry rose to their feet and bellowed, "Long live the glorious Chekists. Hurrah! Hurrah! Hurrah!" The box, embossed with the shield of State Security, contained a copy of the BND's secret annual intelligence report. Wolf sat beaming in the front row of the MfS auditorium, looking splendid in his white lieutenant general's uniform with the gold braid.

Medals were exchanged, and Mielke droned on about the eternal "fraternity of arms" between the KGB and the MfS. The relationship had long since ceased to be one of senior and junior partners since Wolf's HVA was a prime source of intelligence for the KGB. The HVA, with 2,500 staff officers in the mid-1980s, was exceeded in manpower within the Warsaw Pact countries only by the KGB's foreign intelligence arm, but the East German agency was second to none in its dedication and skill.

Yet all the while Gast had been suffering from the strain of her dual existence. She had grown increasingly worried about what would happen to the disabled child in her care if she were caught. She repeatedly tried to summon up the courage to tell Wolf that she wanted to stop spying, but she did not wish to show ingratitude toward him. He had taken time from his busy schedule to receive her a total of seven times. He had personally awarded her the Fatherland Order of Merit for her services to the socialist German state. Alone as she was in Munich with the spastic child, constantly having to conceal her true identity, her meetings with Wolf had always been an enormous boost to her depressed spirits. He had told her so often how invaluable she was to the HVA and the cause of détente. She was determined not to disappoint him. Although Gast would continue spying for East

Berlin until her betrayal, the discovery that her beloved Karliczek had been merely a device to ensnare her was the most bitter blow of all.

In Bonn, about 347 miles northwest of Munich, a woman wholly unlike Gabrielle Gast and the hapless secretaries who landed in the clutches of Wolf's Romeo agents was working overtime in the headquarters of the Free Democratic Party. She was the kind of person one instinctively liked. Her friendly, open face and direct manner inspired trust. Sonja Lüneburg, by dint of her hard work and dedication, had risen to the upper echelons of German politics. She did not need a man to boost her self-confidence.

Often Lüneburg sat in her apartment in the evening listening to the shortwave radio. She held a pencil in her hand, and a piece of paper lay on the table in front of her while a monotone voice read off numbers. When she heard her code name she suddenly began writing down the numbers. It was a message from her controlling officer in East Berlin. Sonja Lüneburg was, in fact, Johanna Charlotte Olbrich, formerly a respected teacher and employee of the National Education Ministry in East Berlin. At the age of thirty-eight she had been approached by an officer of the HVA who asked if she would like to work for "socialism and peace on the invisible front" — that is, in the West.

Her reasons for signing on as a spy for the HVA were varied, she told me years later. Coercion was not among them, but guilt for the crimes committed by the Nazis was. During the Second World War she attended a school for teachers in Lower Silesia, now Poland, that was located near a branch of Auschwitz death camp. After the Nazi surrender, she saw the half-naked, emaciated survivors and said she could never forget the sight. By working for the HVA she believed that she could help prevent a future war and another rise of Nazism in West Germany. But, she readily admitted, there was also an element of romantic adventurism in her decision to spy for East Germany.

After choosing the code name Anna and being trained in the routine techniques of espionage, Olbrich was told in late 1966 that she was about to become a totally new person. She was to adopt the identity of Sonja Lüneburg, who by this time was a badly deranged woman. Lüneburg was an East Berliner who had married a West Berliner before the Berlin Wall was built. After divorcing him, she returned to East Berlin in 1966, where the Stasi interviewed her and discovered that she had a severe nervous disorder. Diagnosed as schizophrenic and given drugs, she was placed in a mental institution. The way was clear to transfer her identity to Olbrich.

First, though, Olbrich was dispatched to Lüneburg's former apartment in the Koloniestrasse in West Berlin. She told the caretaker there that she was a friend of Lüneburg's from the West. She paid off Lüneburg's debts to a court in West Berlin and was given a suitcase filled with Lüneburg's belongings, which had been left with an acquaintance. Among the items was Lüneburg's identity card and a school report card.

Following the HVA's carefully hatched out plan, in 1967 Olbrich, alias Lüneburg, proceeded to Colmar in eastern France. From there she wrote to the West Berlin office responsible for registering citizens and their current addresses that she was moving to France and wished to deregister. From Colmar she moved to Offenbach, West Germany, where she returned Sonja Lüneburg's old identity card to the authorities and obtained a new one with her own photo on it. She now had the coveted "genuine" identity of a citizen of the Federal Republic of Germany.

Her first job in the West was with an insurance company in Frankfurt and Hamburg, where she gained valuable experience. But she also discovered how difficult it was to pretend at being Sonja Lüneburg, a person of little formal schooling. She told her controller about this dilemma, and in no time HVA forgers had produced the Abitur certificate, which was given to students who completed the rigorous German high-school academic program. In 1969 she was told by East Berlin to advertise in newspapers in the Bonn area for a secretarial job. She was hired by William Borm, a prominent Free Democratic Party (FDP) member of Parliament, who in his younger years had been thrown into prison in East Germany on political grounds. He was on the important foreign relations and inner-German relations committees and was a leading advocate of rapprochement with the GDR and the Soviet Union.

Borm was also one of Wolf's most highly prized West German informers. Wolf and Borm met frequently in an HVA villa in East Berlin to discuss the future of divided Germany. Neither Borm nor his caring secretary, Frau Olbrich, suspected that the other worked for the same genial boss in East Berlin. Only years later did Olbrich learn that two other employees of Borm also informed on him for the HVA. By this time Wolf's voracious appetite for secrets about the West German leadership was tying down a growing part of his human and material resources. Some of the political secrets that he gave to Mielke and the rest of the Politbüro turned out to be little more than the personal peccadilloes of overstressed West German politicians.

Olbrich was Borm's trusted secretary until 1973, and she passed on everything even remotely important to East Berlin. She hid the films with photographed information in a specially prepared can of hair spray that she handed to a courier. He concealed the can in the HVA's main logistical support, the interzonal Reichsbahn train from Aachen to East Berlin. But this method had to be abandoned when Olbrich broke too many of the spray cans. She was later assigned a resident intelligence agent who was responsible for logistics.

Repeatedly, Olbrich was subjected to routine security checks by West German counterintelligence (BfV), but she always emerged lily-white. It never occurred to the West Germans to check whether Lüneburg's graduation certificate had actually been issued by a West Berlin school. When Borm left the Bundestag in 1973, Olbrich was employed by Karl Hermann Flach, the new general secretary of the FDP. After he died, she served his successor, and then Martin Bangemann, who was the head of the liberal Free Democratic Party, the junior coalition partner of Chancellor Helmut Schmidt. Olbrich served as his chief secretary for four years, during which she virtually became a member of the family, watering the flowers in his Bonn apartment when he was away and addressing him and his wife with the familiar "*Du*" form that few German secretaries dared use. She was to follow Bangemann to the European Parliament in Brussels.

Twice a year she traveled to Scandinavia on a false passport and entered the GDR for meetings with Maj. Theodor Schönfelder, her East Berlin controller. She glowed with pride in 1975 when she was told that the "boss" wished to meet her personally. The occasion was the tenth anniversary of her signing on with the HVA. She was told to address Wolf as "Herr Colonel General" and to use the formal "*Sie*." She was even told the topics of their meeting, so she fully expected the aloof stiffness of an East German ritual ceremony.

To reach the meeting place, Olbrich first drove to Copenhagen and then took the train and ferry from Gedser to Warnemünde in the GDR. She scarcely noticed a group of East Germans standing at quayside and looking wistfully at the ferry that they were not allowed to board. She was driven to an HVA guesthouse furnished with glossy cabinets and overstuffed chairs. But upon meeting Wolf, Olbrich was pleasantly surprised to find that he was wholly unlike the remote individual she had been led to expect.

Wolf listened attentively as she told him about her general impressions of life in West Germany. He wore a light blue shirt and a tailored suit that accentuated his athletic build. She sensed genuine concern in his voice as he asked about her daily life and how the HVA could help with her problems. He praised her for serving the cause of peace but said they would not speak in detail about her work, that this was a matter for her controller, Major Schönfelder, who listened, awestruck, to the conversation. Olbrich felt a warm glow as she realized that all the reports she had delivered on politicians in the West had actually helped to maintain peace and strengthen socialism. Wolf convinced her that he, too, favored an understanding between the two German states. They continued their conversation over drinks before dinner. She spoke about the younger politicians in West Germany who wanted to reform industrial life and widen worker participation in companies, and he asked probing questions.

Wolf grew increasingly animated as he spoke about his birthplace in the Swabian hills of Württemberg, now West Germany, and about his father and brother. He gave her his favorite Russian cooking recipes and hinted that he would enjoy nothing more than to prepare a dish of *pelmeni* for her at their next meeting. Olbrich was captivated by him. He had made her feel that she belonged to his inner circle of elite agents, and she was determined, more than ever, to do her best for this man. Although a master of his profession, he had remained a compassionate, sincere, and utterly charming gentleman, Olbrich felt.

Olbrich remained with Martin Bangemann after he became West Germany's Economics Minister, working as his secretary and then as a full-fledged official of the ministry. On learning that Günter Guillaume had been arrested in Bonn, she made a conscious effort to resist oncoming panic. An officer of the HVA phoned her from West Berlin and told her in coded language that she was to be extremely careful. She lay low for nearly four months, not photographing so much as a single document until she was absolutely certain that the West German authorities did not suspect her.

Olbrich was as conscientious a spy as she had been a teacher and administrator in East Germany's National Education Ministry. She often personally brought the miniature rolls of film she had shot to the interzonal train in Cologne. She attached the film rolls with small magnets under the washstand of the toilet and made a mark with her ballpoint pen to indicate whether the washstand contained one or two packets. Once the train entered East Germany, an officer of the HVA went through the entire train, checking in the toilets for the "present" from Wolf's mole.

Not for a moment could Olbrich forget her double existence or relax because her daily life was a high-wire act. She knew that she was always in danger of being detected since she could never be entirely like the real Lüneburg. Once a girlfriend who knew that Lüneburg had been a ladies' hairdresser, asked Olbrich to help set her hair. Olbrich, who always wore her hair in the same plain bob, had to quickly think up an excuse. But was it wholly credible, she wondered?

Her mother and sister still lived in Poland, and sometimes she visited them using her real identity, Olbrich. Occasionally, they visited the GDR, spending vacations with her in Stasi guesthouses in Dresden and the Harz Mountains. The family was told that the guesthouses belonged to the GDR Foreign Ministry and that Olbrich worked as a GDR diplomat in North Korea. Once she was allowed to attend the theater in East Berlin, shielded from the rest of the audience in a reserved private box. Returning to the West from a brief respite in the GDR was the most difficult transition of all. On one such occasion, back in Bonn, she momentarily forgot that she was Lüneburg and signed a check as Olbrich, catching herself just in time to tear it up. Sometimes, when she was asked something about her past, she paused a moment to reflect—which past?—then worried that she had hesitated too long before replying.

Throughout her espionage career in West Germany she was paid 700 GDR Marks a month by the HVA, and the money went into an account in East Berlin. At the peak of her career as a secretary to Herr Bangemann in Brussels, she earned a net of DM 6,500 per month. But money, she insisted, was always unimportant to her. Her ideals were paramount. She never asked what had happened to the real Sonja Lüneburg, assuming that she had died. But, in truth, she did not wish to know.

Over the course of her service Olbrich was awarded ten medals, including the highest decoration the GDR had to bestow, the Fatherland Order of Merit in Gold, personally given to her by Wolf along with 10,000 GDR Marks. With her controlling officers she was a self-assured, independent-minded woman, filled with a Germanic pride in her work, whether as a secretary in Bonn and Brussels or as one of Wolf's elite moles. She proved her organizational talents and her loyalty to her employers—in the East and the West. Both had profited equally from her work, she decided.

In July 1985 after a *treff* with her controller in the GDR, she embarked on the roundabout route back to Bonn. She had told her employer in Bonn that she was vacationing in Greece, so on the first leg of her return trip she flew from East Berlin to Athens using the forged passport of a fictitious West Berliner. From Athens she flew to Rome, where she had been told to remain for a few days. She carefully stowed away her identity papers, in the name of Sonja Lüneburg, in her baggage. At Rome airport, she hailed a taxi and, struggling with too many bags, put down her handbag on the floor of the cab. It contained the forged Western passport as well as DM 5,000. Only minutes after arriving at her hotel, she noticed, horror-stricken, that she had forgotten her handbag in the taxi. Her fear was that the passport would be turned in to the Italian police, who would hand it over to the West German authorities. Although it was an excellent forgery, the officials would discover soon enough that it did not match any registered West German citizen.

Olbrich informed her controller by coded message about her mishap, and a few days later she received a reply. She was to proceed to Lübeck in the northern part of West Germany for a *treff* with two HVA instructors who would guide her back to the GDR. They met on August 3, a sweltering day, and began hiking eastward through thick woods toward the frontier. After several hours they reached an inlet on the Bay of Lübeck and a rowboat the officers had hidden in dense reeds. The boat was to take them back to the opposite bank and the safety of the GDR. But a fisherman had taken up position only a few yards from the row-boat and sat holding his line. A thunderstorm broke, and the two men and Olbrich huddled under an umbrella, hoping the rain would persuade the fisherman to row home. When the shower was over, however, he curled up in his boat and dozed off.

Several hours passed before the man awoke, hauled in his line, and rowed away. Olbrich and her companions hurried to their boat and swiftly rowed the several hundred yards to the GDR side of the inlet. The two men led the way through heavy under-brush to a large metal gate in the border fence. They rang a bell. A border guard appeared, opened the gate, and welcomed them to the GDR. Olbrich and the two men were given guard uniforms to wear as they crossed the next few hundred yards of open ground, which was in clear view of the West German Border Defense troops on the other side. The East Germans took every precaution to prevent the West from discovering where the HVA smuggled its agents across the 835-mile-long green border between East and West Germany.

In the car on the way back to East Berlin, Olbrich learned from her controller that her mission as Sonja Lüneburg was over and that she would not be returning to the West. "*Der Chef*" (the boss), Wolf himself, had decided this, Olbrich's controller told her. But how would the HVA continue to get information from the highest level of the Free Democratic Party and the Eco-nomics Ministry she asked? Her controlling officer looked at her, smiled, but said nothing. She knew that Wolf's decision was irreversible.

After a heroine's welcome by Wolf in East Berlin, Olbrich was given a pension and a choice modern flat in Bernau, just outside Berlin. She furnished the apartment with tasteful antiques bought with the considerable back pay she had accumulated. Charlotte Olbrich had been homesick for East Germany during all those years in the West, and now she was home, back in the GDR among her own people. But after eighteen years in the West, she was surprised to see how dissatisfied East Germans were. They grumbled over the poor supplies of fresh fruits and vegetables, the "extortionist" prices for better-quality goods, and their inability to travel to the West. She, too, had changed. At first she walked into East German shops and told baffled-looking salesgirls what she wanted, just as she had done in the West. Invariably, whatever it was, it was unavailable. When she asked to taste the liverwurst in her local Kaufhalle supermarket, just as she had done in Bonn and Brussels, the salesgirl snickered. No one ever asked to sample the liverwurst in the GDR. It tasted exactly the same everywhere.

Charlotte Olbrich, in retirement, traveled widely in the Communist world, enjoyed going to the theater and concerts in East Berlin without having to conceal herself, and never told anyone about her previous life as Sonja Lüneburg. Apart from Wolf himself, only her former controllers knew about her past. If she could not trust them, who could she trust? she asked herself.

6

E rich Mielke had laid down an iron rule that officers of State Security were to lead unblemished, morally irreproachable lives as befitted those who wielded the sword and shield of the Party. Above all, they were not to have extramarital affairs, and were warned that a divorce would be detrimental to their careers. Yet Mielke was forced to make an exception, his deputy, Markus Wolf, who grew even more handsome in middle age.

During the 1970s Wolf's inspection trips took him increasingly often to the Karl-Marx-Stadt (KMS) branch of East German intelligence. KMS, the former industrial city of Chemnitz situated in the district of the same name in the southeast of the GDR, was one of Wolf's most active regional espionage centers. State Security in KMS district was also a superb organizer of the hunting trips that Wolf had come to enjoy. But KMS held another attraction: Christa, his willowy young mistress.

Christa Heinrich was twenty years his junior, tall and blonde, and passionately in love with him. She and Wolf had met in January 1971 at a State Security party in KMS district during one of Wolf's hunting trips. Christa had been brought to the party by a girlfriend who she later suspected had arranged the rendezvous with Wolf. When she first met him, Christa thought that the urbane Wolf had to be an HVA agent. She was captivated by his mellifluous voice and sincere manner and fell in love with him that very evening. From that time on they met secretly on Wolf's frequent visits to KMS.

Christa was flabbergasted when Wolf told her that he was head of the HVA and deputy minister of State Security. She confided in him about her closest girlfriend, Andrea Stingl, from her hometown of Lauter in Saxony. Andrea had been taken into custody by the Stasi in 1968 for attempting to escape from Romania to the West with her boyfriend. After confessing her guilt, Andrea was told by the Stasi officer who interrogated her that her boyfriend had another woman. With the help of Wolfgang Vogel, the enigmatic East Berlin lawyer who was authorized by the Stasi to represent imprisoned East Germans, Andrea was released after four months in prison. Andrea looked back with such revulsion on her imprisonment that she was unable to speak about it. She married and had a daughter, Claudia, who was Christa's godchild.

Mielke was infuriated when he found out about Wolf's relationship with Christa, and he demanded that his deputy end the affair. Any other State Security officer would have been immediately dismissed by the prudish Mielke. But Wolf was, after all, head of the espionage corps whose successes Mielke never tired of boasting of to his fellow Politbüro members. Faced with Wolf's refusal to give up Christa, Mielke consented to Wolf's getting a divorce. In March 1976, after thirty-two years of marriage, Markus and Emmi Wolf were divorced. The Stasi saw to it that Emmi was given a comfortable apartment, since it was essential that Wolf's ex-wife not be embittered by her treatment. Disgruntled ex-wives of spies and spymasters were potential prey for Western intelligence services. But Emmi remained loyal to Wolf and the Party. She immersed herself in her work as custodian of the Friedrich Wolf archives.

The Wolf children were long since grown up and out of the house. Michael, the oldest at age thirty, was a chemist. Tatjana, twenty-seven, who had brought the seditious pop records to school, was a journalist for a Party newspaper. She often spoke with her father about the injustices she witnessed daily. He would nod knowingly and remark that as long as the old guard clung to power in Moscow there could be no reforms. Tatjana was married to Bernd Trögel, an HVA officer in Department 9, which spied on West Germany's counterintelligence service (the BfV). The Stasi encouraged intermarriage among MfS personnel and their families, because it was believed that such alliances reduced security problems and enhanced the feeling of being one big harmonious family. Wolf's youngest son, Franz, who was twenty-three, served as a GDR diplomat.

Only three months after his divorce, Wolf married Christa, and the following year their son, Alexander, was born. The birth of Sascha, as he was soon known, jolted Wolf, at fifty-four, into an awareness of his health. He stopped smoking and began eating yogurt and honey, lots of vegetables, and little meat. He performed yoga, bicycled, and swam, and was determined to remain as virile and youthful as possible for his attractive young wife. Markus was charming and tender toward Christa, and like most men who are considerably older than their wives, he began searching in the mirror for signs of age. Once, for no apparent reason, he told Christa that a gypsy had read his palm when he was a youth in Russia and had predicted that he would marry three times. At the time Christa thought he was joking.

The Wolfs lived in a spacious apartment atop a tall new building at 2 Fischerinsel in the heart of East Berlin. He and Emmi had moved to the apartment a few years earlier after they decided that the house was too much work and that contact with ordinary people would do them good. Mielke, who lived in a large, well-guarded mansion, balked at the idea of his deputy residing at such close quarters with regular citizens, people who were not employees of the MfS. But he finally relented. Wolf's Western counterparts would not have dreamed of living in an apartment house — the security problems would have appeared overwhelming — but Wolf felt unassailable among hundreds of fellow tenants. Fiete, his driver, picked him up and dropped him off at the front door, and Christa and Markus celebrated their birthdays and New Year's Eve with new friends — an architect, a secretary, and a journalist — who lived in the building. Many of them knew how Wolf earned his living but asked no questions. Wolf, on the other hand, was interested to learn what people outside the narrow confines of the MfS were thinking. Through talking to neighbors his suspicions that the Party was increasingly out of touch with reality were confirmed, and he saw that East

Germans were deeply frustrated by their isolation behind the Berlin Wall.

Shortly after their marriage, Markus bought a dacha, a week-end house, in Prenden near Berlin. The steep-roofed cottage, surrounded by trees and near a lake, was conveniently close to one of the Stasi's guest villas. Christa would never forget the dacha, because it would later be the scene of a passionate affair involving Markus and another woman that would undo their marriage.

Spring 1976 marked a setback for a new method Wolf had found for infiltrating his agents into West Germany. HVA in-formers had been sent out to comb through cemeteries in Argen-tina and Chile to find the names of deceased Germans. Wolf's agents then assumed those identities, posing as German em-igrants returning from Canada, Australia, and South America. Under Brandt's successor as chancellor, Helmut Schmidt, the counterintelligence agency, the BfV, was finally unleashed to track down these GDR agents. Setting its new computers to work on the official records of newly registered Germans who had returned from abroad, the BfV was able to filter out the names of suspects. Nearly thirty HVA agents were arrested, and more than a hundred others fled to the GDR to avoid arrest. This time the reaction of East German spies to the arrest of their comrades was the opposite of their response to the discovery of Guillaume in the federal chancellory. Wolf's agents in the West suffered a loss of confidence in the HVA, and without warning several of them stopped their espionage activities. Even Wolf's top moles in the West became unnerved and began bombarding their controlling officers with doubts about their security. Wolf and his men worked overtime to reassure agents and moles and to map out costly, time-consuming new ways of infiltrating agents into West Germany.

In the summer of 1978 Wolf made plans to take Christa along on a very special trip during which he was going to meet one of his more promising West German "sources," Dr. Friedrich Cremer, a Social Democratic member of the Bavarian parlia-ment. Cremer was one of a select number of Stasi agents and informers who had not been asked to sign a cooperation pledge.

The clandestine meeting with Cremer was to take place in July in neutral Sweden, after the Wolfs visited Helsinki and sailed across the Baltic to Stockholm. Christa would get a taste of the forbidden West that was denied to her fellow East Germans. Markus was especially looking forward to the intoxicating experience of traveling to the West under an assumed identity.

He handed his GDR diplomatic passport, identifying him as Dr. Kurt Werner, to the Swedish immigration official at the Stockholm ferry port. The official glanced at the passport, whacked an entry stamp onto it, and handed the document back to Wolf with a nod. Christa gave him her passport as Frau Dr. Werner. The official thumbed the pages, reflecting that there were not many East German couples of their age who were allowed to travel together to the West. Normally one person was left behind as a hostage. He noted down their names and, when the Werners had left, told his superior about the well-dressed Herr Dr. Werner and his attractive wife.

The chief espionage officer at the GDR Embassy had arranged to have Wolf and Christa stay in an apartment that the embassy rented in a suburb of Stockholm. Wolf should have known that Swedish counterintelligence suspected that the apartment was used for espionage *treffs*. Whoever entered or left the building was observed by plainclothes Swedish counterespionage officials.

Christa was in the apartment with Wolf on July 1 when he met Dr. Cremer, a thickset Bavarian who had left behind a young girlfriend in his hotel. One of Wolf's aides introduced Wolf to Cremer as a "good friend" from East Berlin, a subterfuge Wolf had decided was necessary in order to soothe Cremer's conscience. When Cremer was later sentenced by a Bavarian court to two years and six months in prison for spying, in May 1980, he swore that he had never seen Wolf.

On that summer day in 1978, outside the apartment building Swedish counterintelligence was lurking. Cameras clicked as Cremer emerged from the building followed by the mysterious Dr. Werner, wearing sunglasses, and his wife. Another series of photos was taken as the Wolfs sipped coffee in a Stockholm café. A couple at an adjoining table, who happened to be from Czechoslovakia, turned to the Wolfs and asked whether they had noticed that they had just been photographed. Wolf instantly knew that he and Christa were under observation, but it was too late. For the remainder of their stay, the Wolfs acted like ordinary tourists, visiting art galleries and even a porno shop.

Swedish intelligence still had no clue to the real identity of Dr. Werner, although the photos taken of Wolf were excellent. He was suspected of being an important East German agent, but since he had done nothing to violate Swedish laws during his stay, he could not be detained. The photos were circulated to West Germany's BfV in Cologne for possible identification, but here, too, the elegantly dressed gentleman wearing sunglasses drew a blank. Only someone from the HVA who knew Wolf would be able to identify him. That someone was preparing to make his move.

First Lieutenant Werner Stiller of Department 13, scientific and technical espionage, busily took notes as Major General Markus Wolf spoke at the meeting of Communist Party officials of the Central Intelligence Administration, the HVA. Stiller, at thirty-one, had just been elected the Party's first secretary in his department, an honor bestowed only on the most trustworthy officers. It was January 17, 1979, the day before Stiller planned to defect to the West.

Wolf's words rang in Stiller's ears: "Comrades, do not forget that the worst thing that could happen to us would be for the enemy to break into our ranks."

For a split second Stiller thought that Wolf had glanced accusingly at him. But up to this day neither Wolf nor any of his subordinates suspected that Stiller was a mole of West Germany's Federal Intelligence Agency, the BND. Stiller had performed brilliantly as a controlling officer of East German agents inside the West German nuclear and scientific establishments. Stiller, like Wolf, was fascinated by espionage with all its duplicity. His marriage to Erzsébet, a curvaceous Hungarian, seemed harmonious to his superiors, but it was a marriage in name only. Beneath the protective facade of Stiller's zealous Communist ideology, and in spite of his Stasi privileges, he was deeply discontented.

Stiller earned nearly 2,000 GDR Marks a month, more than

double the East German average. He had a new apa
enjoyed superior medical treatment in the special Sta.
hospital. He had also been able to buy a used Wartburg ca.
the Stasi. But he was sick of leading a highly controlled life, in
which he was always required to inform the HVA of his whereabouts, and was on call twenty-four hours a day. Unlike other
junior officers who frowned on the corruption among some senior
Stasi officers, especially those with contacts to Schalck's KoKo
empire, Stiller longed for freedom and the better things in life,
which he knew only the West could offer.

Stiller offered himself as a mole to the BND in early 1978, a
move that triggered immediate suspicion in Pullach. But he satisfied the doubts of the West Germans by agreeing to disclose the
names of his own agents operating in the West. The West Germans in turn promised not to arrest the agents until Stiller was
safely settled in the West. If the agents were rounded up any
sooner, Stiller, their controller, would be the Stasi's prime suspect. Stiller and the other HVA officers had been warned often
enough that the penalty for treason against the GDR was the
death sentence.

One of Stiller's most productive agents was Gerhard Arnold,
alias Sturm (Storm), an East German electrical engineer who had
been sent to West Berlin with an S-Bahn ticket courtesy of the
MfS. Arnold had risen swiftly in the ranks of IBM Deutschland,
where he got hold of batches of IBM publications and passed
them on to East Berlin. Although readily available to specialists in
the West, the publications fell under the Western COCOM (Coordinating Committee for East-West Trade Policy) ban on exports
of strategic information and goods to Communist countries.

At one point Stiller quipped that Arnold was one of the
"fathers" of East Germany's belated computer age. The GDR
computer company Robotron grew as dependent as a junkie on
Arnold's IBM information. State firms like Robotron paid the
HVA a fixed sum of money for every item of stolen information
they received. The amount depended on what it would otherwise
have cost to purchase the information in the West and illegally
smuggle it to the GDR. In the long run this industrial and economic espionage actually undermined research and development

in the GDR, and Wolf suspected as much. But he could hardly criticize a practice that enhanced the prestige of his intelligence service.

Gerhard Arnold was another of Wolf's agents who refused to accept payment. Arnold spied for the GDR not out of sympathy for the Communist system, which he realized was inferior, but because of his attachment to his former homeland and his gratitude for the free higher education it had given him. In 1973 he quit IBM and went into business for himself, while continuing to supply IBM publications to East Berlin.

Stiller was most impressed by his agent R. Paul Fuelle, cover name Klaus, who while working as an accountant in West Germany's nuclear fuel reprocessing center at Karlsruhe dispatched enormous quantities of confidential material to East Berlin. Stasi chief Mielke and his Politbüro colleagues were convinced that West Germany was working feverishly to produce nuclear weapons, and agent Klaus was responsible for obtaining the evidence.

Once he had betrayed his agents, Stiller worked out a deal with the BND under which he would provide the agency with information about the inner workings of Wolf's intelligence network. In return the West Germans would pay him a handsome sum of money. No one at the HVA thought it unusual that Stiller, the workaholic, was often the first officer to arrive in the morning at his fifth-floor office in the recently completed HVA headquarters. All the while he was using those early-morning hours to photograph secret HVA documents for the BND.

Stiller had made his approach to the BND with the help of his East German girlfriend, Helga, a waitress at Hotel Panorama whom he had met in the winter resort of Oberhof. A widow with a teenage son, she was deeply in love with Stiller and agreed to work with him for the West. Helga's brother who lived in West Germany, served as Stiller's messenger to the BND. She and Stiller accomplished virtuoso feats virtually from within the lion's den. Stiller, with chutzpah worthy of his mentor, Wolf, had introduced her to the HVA safe apartment that he regularly used for *treffs* with his agents. The apartment, which they dubbed the "castle," was located in a crumbling tenement building in the Marienburger

Strasse. At the "castle" the faithful Helga deciphered radio instructions from the BND and mailed messages in invisible ink to the BND's cover addresses in West Germany. Stiller used the place to hide microfilmed documents that he was preparing to smuggle out to the West.

In late summer of 1978, East German counterespionage, in a routine screening of mail bound for West Germany, found a letter from the "castle" that set alarm bells ringing. It was addressed to an all too frequently used cover address of the BND and contained a coded message from Stiller in invisible ink. Although the Stasi was unable to crack the code, Lt. Gen. Günther Kratsch, the pudgy head of GDR counterespionage, ordered that the unknown sender of the message be tracked down. For months platoons of Stasi officers sought to pinpoint the suspected traitor the next time he messaged the BND. They sifted through sacks of outgoing letters arranged according to the city districts and mailboxes where they had been collected. Despite twenty-four-hour surveillance of a suspected mailbox, the culprit could not be found. The circle narrowed, however, in late November 1978, when Helga sent a hand-written telegram to one of the BND cover addresses saying that she had not been able to "fulfill your wish." This meant that she had not succeeded, as previously arranged, in hiding Stiller's rolls of microfilm in a dead drop, the toilet of the interzonal train to West Germany, where they would be picked up by the BND. West German intelligence, like the Stasi, had discovered the convenience of transporting espionage material by rail.

Instead of being routinely forwarded to the BND in Pullach, Helga's telegram was returned to East Germany as "undeliverable." The BND had forgotten to inform the local post office, which served as a cover address, that telegrams were to be automatically forwarded to Pullach. The telegram landed on the desk of East German counterintelligence, which now had another handwriting sample from the culprit. This time the agency determined that the telegram was written by a woman, whom it presumed was the wife of the suspected spy.

A week later, Helga succeeded in depositing the rolls of microfilm in the toilet of a train traveling from Leipzig to West

Germany, and she sent another telegram to the BND cover address — from a post office in Marienburger Strasse, only a few hundred yards from the "castle." This telegram, too, was returned as "undeliverable" and landed with Stasi counterintelligence. Lieutenant General Kratsch was now brimming with confidence that the espionage couple would soon be trapped.

When Helga learned that Erzsébet had just given birth to her second child — Stiller had conveniently forgotten to tell her — he summoned up all his talents to convince Helga that he loved only her. But instinct told him that with Erzsébet threatening to divorce him and inform the Stasi about his affair with Helga, his days were numbered. He asked the BND to arrange for him, Helga, and her son to escape to West Germany.

An attempted escape in mid-December was called off because the BND had made mistakes in the passports it smuggled to them. Around the same time the Stasi achieved a breakthrough in its pursuit of the unknown espionage couple. Stasi postal snoopers had found several parcel post ticket stubs with what it believed was the same handwriting as on the telegrams. The parcels had been sent by Helga to her brother and contained her prized glassware. Her full name and address in Oberhof were on the stubs.

Lieutenant General Kratsch wanted to be absolutely certain, so he sent the handwriting samples to a Stasi expert. Like most institutions in East Germany, the Stasi virtually shut down during the long Christmas holidays. It took two weeks before the report confirming a positive match came back from the handwriting expert. An officer was to be dispatched to Oberhof to find out more about Helga, but by this time it was early January, and the GDR was in the grips of its worst enemy: severe cold and heavy snows that triggered serious energy shortages. The Stasi had orders to radically reduce official car trips, and officers were reluctant to travel by train.

It was nearly the second week in January before one of Kratsch's officers ventured out to Oberhof in Thuringia. But the Panorama Hotel, where Helga worked, had been forced to close down for several weeks because of the extreme cold. The Stasi officer did learn that Helga was in Berlin and that her boyfriend owned a Lada car. After deliberating these and other findings,

Stasi counterintelligence decided that Helga's partner was the likely spy, and that he lived somewhere in Marienburger Strasse. Orders were given to investigate all owners of Lada cars in that area and to observe the express trains leaving Berlin for Thuringia, since Helga was expected to return shortly to Oberhof. Perhaps she would be seen off at the station by the treacherous agent himself.

By this time Helga and her son were already on a train, but they were traveling eastward to Warsaw, and not south to Thuringia, on the first leg of their escape. Stiller drove his car — a Wartburg, and not a Lada as the Stasi believed — to the safe apartment in the Marienburger Strasse, and thus slipped through the net thrown by his own Stasi. He was preparing to escape to West Germany by train the day after he attended Wolf's speech. Using a new passport from the BND (West Germany's Federal Intelligence Agency) that one of its couriers had left in a dead drop in East Berlin, Stiller was to take the interzonal train from Halle to Hannover, West Germany, where the BND would be awaiting him.

Before leaving he had some business to attend to. Waiting until after office hours that last evening, Stiller, carrying a large attaché case, went to the fifth floor of his department in HVA headquarters and removed a key that hung in a key box on the wall. He opened the door to the office of the head of his department, Günter Jauck, and went over to the heavy steel cabinet that contained the names of all the agents his department had deployed in the West. Fervently hoping that the guard downstairs would not hear the noise, he took out a hammer and chisel to pry open the cabinet. But it failed to yield in spite of his most powerful blows.

Leaving behind the tools, Stiller dashed from the office into the anteroom, where he caught sight of another steel cabinet. He was familiar with this type of cabinet and its structural weakness. Delivering a few sharp blows, he tipped the cabinet sharply. The doors sprang open, revealing a treasure beyond credibility: files on HVA agents and other sources, secret directives to agents, three years' worth of material from the analysis section, a telephone directory of the department with names of all the officers and their photographs. He swept the contents into his attaché case.

As he was about to leave a stack of forms attracted his attention. He had used them in the past to enter the hermetically sealed-off "West side" of Friedrichstrasse railroad station. That part of the station served Western subway and S-Bahn passengers who switched trains at this juncture for northern and southern parts of West Berlin without being subjected to the rigid East German passport and customs controls. East German intelligence agents entering East Berlin routinely left their bags containing espionage material in luggage lockers on the "West side" of the station, where they were picked up by their HVA controllers. The moment he caught sight of the forms, intuition told Stiller to change his escape route to the West. He pocketed several of the forms and made his way out of the building, exchanging a few words with the guard downstairs, who was not permitted to inspect the belongings of operative officers. At the main gate, Stiller wished a *Gute Nacht* to the guard, a member of the Stasi's elite Felix Dzerzhinsky unit, who returned the greeting.

After driving his Wartburg to the Marienburger Strasse, Stiller filled out a form in his safe apartment. He grabbed two suitcases crammed with rolls of microfilm and documents he had collected in recent months, and closed the door behind him for the last time. After parking his car near Friedrichstrasse station, he entered the station through a side door innocuously labeled "Service entrance, access only for German Reichsbahn employees."

Stiller fingered his pistol before ringing a bell next to a curtained window. He had decided that if he were caught he would use the gun on himself, since the alternative was the death sentence. The curtain was shoved aside. Stiller held his MfS identity card to the window, and the Stasi duty officer behind it nodded and pressed a buzzer. A door opened, and Stiller handed the officer his papers. The officer's gaze lingered on the stolen form. Something was missing, he said. Stiller, his stomach sinking, displayed no emotion. The duty officer asked Stiller whether he was unaware that since the first of the month he was required to write the words "baggage run" in the space after "purpose of mission." Without hesitating, Stiller replied that the secretary had simply forgotten to inform him. The officer gazed at Stiller and the suitcases. It was obvious that this colleague from the HVA was only bringing an agent's baggage to the lockers. He pressed a buzzer, and Stiller walked through the door to the "Western" side of the station.

From this point on Stiller entered the field of vision of Hungarian Videoton security cameras, whose images were monitored by the Stasi inside the station. Carrying his briefcase and suitcase, Stiller approached the baggage deposit boxes. This was a critical moment, because he was supposed to check in the luggage and return to the "Eastern" side of the station. If the Stasi monitoring officer detected any abnormal behavior he only had to press a button for guards to swarm out from all sides and grab Stiller.

Cold sweat trickled down his back. He reached the stairs that led to the underground S-Bahn line. Together with subway line number 6, it cut through central East Berlin and then back into West Berlin. Friedrichstrasse was the only stop the S-Bahn line made in the East, and Western passengers were permitted to enter and leave East Berlin at this stop after being subjected to minute border controls. Stiller reckoned that if he was detected at the last minute it would be more difficult for the East Germans to stop the subway, which was under West Berlin control. So he headed for the subway to West Berlin, which was reached by passing along a pedestrian tunnel from the downstairs S-Bahn platform.

It was shortly before nine at night when he stepped onto the nearly deserted subway platform. He glanced at the illuminated sign giving the train's destination: Tegel, in West Berlin. It might as well have been Los Angeles. More TV cameras surveyed the subway platform. He stared into the tunnel, desperately hoping to see the dim headlights of an approaching subway train. But there was only blackness. Then, ever so faintly, the light of an approaching train flickered on the walls of the tunnel. The yellow cars glided into the station and came to a halt. Stiller walked with measured steps toward one of the closed doors and, yanking it open, entered the brightly lit car. The subway train would not exit East Berlin for another three stations.

He remained rigid in his seat as the train slowed down each time it passed, without halting, through three dark and abandoned East Berlin stations and then emerged into the first station in West Berlin, Reinickendorfer Strasse. When his feet touched the grimy concrete platform it felt like a cloud, so softly did he bound toward the exit. Outside, he saw Western neon advertisements that told him, incontestably, that he was safely in West Berlin. Only at this point did he savor the moment. He hailed a taxi and told the driver to take him to Tegel airport.

"I am an officer of the GDR State Security Ministry, and I have just defected from East Berlin," he told a West Berlin policeman at Tegel airport in the French sector of West Berlin. "Please contact the BND in Pullach." Chaos reigned as West German, French, and American intelligence officials tried to make contact with the BND, which had expected its double agent to arrive in Hannover by train from Halle.

Günter Jauck, the head of Stiller's department, was staggered by what he saw when he entered his office on the morning of January 19, 1979. His secretary's steel cabinet was wide open and plundered. A chisel and hammer lay next to his own steel cabinet, which the burglar had tried to pry open. Within hours it became certain that the perpetrator was Werner Stiller, the hardworking, likable thirty-one-year-old first lieutenant who had just been elected Party secretary of his section.

Helga and her son were unable to escape by plane from Warsaw until four days after Stiller's escape, because the BND had provided them with incorrectly forged Polish entry stamps in their new West German passports. All the while the Stasi, in an uproar over Stiller's defection, was desperately trying to track Helga down. But she was hidden in the West German Embassy in Warsaw until new BND-forged passports could be sent by courier from Pullach.

Stiller was flown out to Munich the day after his escape and welcomed at Riem airport by the BND. The intelligence agency officials were momentarily speechless when they saw the material the double agent had brought with him: two suitcases filled with HVA documents and rolls of microfilm, some twenty thousand pages in all. That same day he was flown to the Cologne head-

Else and Friedrich Wolf
with Markus Johannes,
in front of their house
in Hechingen, summer
of 1923.

Markus dousing his
father, Friedrich, with
cold water; from
Friedrich's book Nature
as Healer and Helper.

Else Wolf with Markus, 1925.

Markus with his father, Friedrich, in Hechingen, 1926.

Else Wolf (center), Markus (left), and Konrad (known as Koni, right), in Moscow, 1934.

Markus between Konrad (Koni) and Friedrich Wolf, Moscow, 1935.

Markus, rear, next to Emmi carrying their daughter, Tatjana. On the far left is Emmi's sister. Friedrich Wolf is in foreground beside Else with their grandson Michael on lap. Photo taken in Prerow, 1950.

Wolf with Christa, his second wife, and their son Alexander (Sascha), together with Raúl Castro, Cuban Defense Minister, during a visit to Cuba, 1985.

Ex-HVA colonels on trial in Düsseldorf, April 15, 1994. Standing in front of courtroom A01, from left to right: Gerhard Behnke, Dr. Kurt Gailat, Günther Neefe, and Werner Groth.

Armin as witness in April 1994.

Photo by Leslie Colitt

Ex-Colonel Gerhard
Behnke, Armin's old
HVA controller, at
Behnke's trial where
Armin appeared as a
witness, April 20, 1994.

Photo by Leslie Colitt

Armin at home in Rheinbreitbach, April 1994.

Wolf, his son Alexander (Sascha) next to him, Christa, his second wife, and Wolf's son Franz, holding his son, Robert, on lap. Photo taken circa 1980.

Wolf in the living room of his duplex during a meeting with the author in 1993.

Photo by Leslie Colitt

quarters of West Germany's counterintelligence agency, the BfV, where he was questioned by its president, Heribert Hellenbroich, and senior officials of the BND, the Federal Criminal Office, and federal attorneys. Stiller, relaxed and confident, told of his recent past as if he were describing the life of another person.

Shortly afterward West German counterintelligence officials from several cities fanned out to the known addresses of Stiller's HVA agents and took seventeen of them into custody. It was the worst blow the HVA had ever suffered. Most serious of all was the damage done to the confidence of Wolf's other agents in the field.

Wolf was at home when he got the news of Stiller's defection over the telephone. He called Werner Grossmann, his deputy, who lived in the two-family house they then shared. The first thing to do, they agreed, was to warn Stiller's agents in the West so that as many of them as possible could evade arrest and escape to the GDR. More than thirty of them managed to flee.

R. Paul Fuelle, alias Klaus, who was Stiller's top nuclear spy, was among the agents who were taken into custody. But Fuelle managed a spectacular escape when his guards slipped on ice while walking him to the federal attorney's office. He fled to the Soviet Military Mission accredited to (that is, operated with the consent of) the Western Allies in Baden-Baden. The Russians hid him in a crate and smuggled him across the border to East Germany. The adventurous accountant soon wearied of "existing socialism" and secretly established a contact to West Germany's BfV, which smuggled him back out again. But he was not spared a trial for espionage, and in 1984 he was sentenced to six years imprisonment.

By contrast, Gerhard Arnold, alias Storm, was arrested and sentenced to a comparatively mild two and a half years in prison. Much to the chagrin of the HVA, the West German court found that over the nineteen years that Arnold had worked at IBM, the information that he supplied to East Germany amounted to more "quantity than quality" and had not "concretely harmed" West Germany.

Normally, Wolf was greeted in the morning at HVA headquarters by Lt. Col. Horst Wittke of the duty detachment, who would report that there had been no "special occurrences" overnight. But the mood was grim when Wolf showed up the day after Stiller's escape. Belated controls had been ordered for every MfS (Stasi) employee entering and leaving headquarters, their brief-cases, and packages. Each HVA officer was shown a photo of Stiller and asked whether he or she had recently had any contact with him.

Everyone was a potential accomplice, and morale in the HVA plummeted. Even the private telephones of HVA officers were tapped in the attempt to track down other "traitors." Stiller's immediate superior at the HVA was in the greatest danger of being accused of aiding the defector, but he managed to prove his innocence. He survived the crisis with a reprimand and was transferred to another department.

Mielke exploded with rage when he was told about Stiller's defection. A Communist Party Congress was to be held in the near future at which he had planned to report that the MfS had attained new heights of "Chekist vigilance." And now a double agent had been discovered in his midst. At a crisis meeting in Mielke's office, he lashed out at Wolf for shoddy HVA security and for allowing the "traitor" to virtually help himself to state secrets. Mielke was particularly angry that Stiller had absconded with several of the Stasi chief's signed directives.

Lieutenant General Kratsch, who was also present, came in for even more biting criticism. His face red and his veins bulging, Mielke screamed at his head of counterintelligence for "twiddling his thumbs" while the spy and his girlfriend prepared their coup. Kratsch had allowed them to escape through his fingers by decid-ing that it was late in the day and time to go home for supper, Mielke said mockingly.

Although Mielke was ultimately responsible for the remark-ably lax security at the intelligence service, he sought to deflect the blame for Stiller's defection with a withering attack on Wolf and his "intelligence dummies." Wolf's brilliant career appeared to be close to ruins. But Mielke knew fully well that he and Wolf were in the same boat. He had allowed Wolf and his fellow intelligence officers to believe that they were an elite group within State Security, immune to the regulations that bound the others. He would show them their place, Mielke vowed.

Erzsébet Stiller was interrogated for hours before being told that her husband had defected. Her first thought before fainting was that her husband's escape meant that her seven-year-old daughter and eleven-month-old son would be taken from her. She was moved with her children to Wandlitz near Berlin, interrogated for months, and not permitted to use a telephone, listen to the radio, or watch TV. All of her photos of her husband were taken from her, and she was told that he would be put to death when they caught him.

Stiller's defection exposed some elementary gaps in HVA security. The guard detachment that was on duty on the evening that Stiller fled had failed to detect his entry into his superior's room. Equally serious, there were no controls on operative officers leaving headquarters. Although Wolf had succeeded in ruthlessly exploiting the critical weaknesses of his Western opponents, he had a curious blind spot when it came to the gaping holes in the HVA's internal security. Wolf had inherently trusted his subordinates, because they had sworn their loyalty to socialism and the GDR.

Mielke ordered that the entire HVA building be electronically secured by Robotron electronics in Dresden, whose specialists wired the office doors of all fifteen hundred rooms. Monitors on the desk of the duty detachment registered whenever a door to an unoccupied room was opened. But as with so much high-tech equipment in the GDR, the system worked imperfectly. False alarms were frequent on windy days, when the doors constantly vibrated. Wolf himself had a buzzer installed under his desk by which he could call a guard in the event of an emergency.

During the series of crisis meetings on Stiller, Wolf spent much of the time holed up in his new ninth-floor office. But despite the enormous tension, he took Stiller's defection philosophically. While his wife, Christa, fumed and cursed at Stiller's "cold-bloodedness," he reminded her that defections were in the nature of his business. At night he was still able to sleep like a man without a care in the world.

Klaus Kinkel, the new head of West German intelligence, savored the afterglow of the BND's coup with Stiller. In a remarkable coincidence, Kinkel came from Hechingen, the small town in southwestern Germany where Wolf had been born. Kinkel's father had also been a physician there and had known the "dissident" Dr. Friedrich Wolf. The sons were now sworn adversaries in the cold war's covert struggle of espionage services.

During his debriefing, Stiller was shown a sheaf of photos taken by Swedish counterintelligence of a handsome East German couple who had entered Sweden as Dr. Werner and wife. Stiller smiled. The man was none other than his former boss, Markus Wolf, of this he was dead certain. Stiller told the West Germans that he had attended a lecture by Wolf to Party delegates only a day before he defected.

Shortly afterward the West German news magazine *Der Spiegel* triumphantly published a cover photo of Wolf in Stockholm. Wolf studied the cover of the March 5, 1979, issue and told Christa when and where the photo had been taken. The publication of Wolf's photo was a serious blow to the spymaster who had brazenly met his agents in Sweden, Yugoslavia, and Austria. He was demasked and had lost his cover. Above all else, though, he ceased to be the "man without a face" to his Western opponents; he had sustained the first significant chink in his armor. From that time on, it would be impossible for him to physically leave the Communist bloc.

Stiller, as had been promised, was amply rewarded by the BND for the masses of information he had provided. He and Helga were given false identities and were guarded around the clock against potential Stasi killers. Stiller's affections toward Helga cooled markedly, though, and she soon realized that he had used her as a means to an end.

On one of Stiller's outings with his West German bodyguards he managed to break away and engage in a brief but torrid affair with a young woman. The BND realized it could not guarantee Stiller's safety in Europe and arranged, with the help of the CIA, to have him and Helga sent to the United States, where they would live separately under assumed names. Stiller took the name of Peter Fischer and studied business administration in Saint Louis, after which he got a job on Wall Street and remarried. His money-making talents were discovered by a leading American investment banker, which sent him to London and then Frankfurt. Helga was happily married to an American but still felt a lingering resentment toward her dashing former boy-friend.

Even after the collapse of the Stasi and East Germany, the mere mention of Stiller's name sufficed to bring an ex-HVA officer's blood to boil. Stiller was a common traitor who had sold himself to the highest bidder, one officer told me. But what about the agents the HVA had recruited in the West? Had they not committed treason? No, the same officer replied, they were different. They had spied out of sympathy for socialism and the GDR.

The photograph of Wolf in the Western media made ordinary East Germans, who were habitually glued to West German TV, aware of him for the first time. One of them, an East Berliner named Willi Meisner, stared incredulously at his television set as the West German channel displayed the photo of General Markus Wolf secretly taken in Stockholm. Willi nudged his wife, Lise, and excitedly blurted out that he was certain that he had seen Wolf only recently in the flesh. His wife laughed in disbelief, but he insisted. He said he had been out walking in the nearby Fischerinsel area when Wolf walked past him with a woman. Can you imagine, he told Lise, the man who planted Günter Guillaume in Willy Brandt's office was strolling with his wife only a few streets from where they lived?

The Meisners had made their peace with the German Democratic Republic and were loyal but critical citizens, like most of the other tenants in their apartment house in Berlin-Mitte. Neither they nor their friends had ever had more than the briefest contact with the Stasi. Once, Willi had been called in to his department head, who introduced him to a man who said he was a detective. Willi suspected the visitor was Stasi when he asked about a colleague who had escaped to the West.

When the Berlin Wall went up, Willi was living in Bernauer Strasse, smack on the border to West Berlin, where he often went to the movies. He could have easily escaped to the West in the first days after the barbed wire was rolled out. But after much soul-searching, he decided that he could not abandon his parents in the East and leave his workmates in the lurch.

Soon after the Meisners and the other families moved into their newly finished, prefab building in 1972 they became friends and together celebrated birthdays, weddings, and the socialist coming-of-age of their children. The Meisners and their neighbors stuck together in times of need. They minded each other's children, consoled each other after divorces, and shared scarce bananas. They laughed together, argued, and made up over schnapps and beer.

Willy was a chemical engineer, his neighbor to one side worked for the Reichsbahn railroad, and the other neighbor managed a Kaufhalle supermarket. At noontime you could ring every doorbell in the house and no one would be home. Nearly all the women worked and left their small children at a nearby state nursery.

Social differences mattered little in Willi's world. There was also little envy. There was no reason for it, since hardly anyone in the building earned more than 1,200 GDR Marks a month, whether they were blue-collar or white-collar workers, academics or Party members. In fact, the blue-collar workers earned the most, as befitted a Workers' and Peasants' State. The engineers, doctors, and other professionals were the worst off, considering how long they had studied. But, then again, as Willi would say, no one worked himself to death under socialism. They all paid nearly the same rent, 110 GDR Marks (less than $50) a month for a three-room apartment, including heat, electricity, and water.

When the families moved into the building, hardly anyone had a car. But by the mid-1980s, their fifteen-year waiting periods for a ridiculously expensive two-stroke Wartburg or Trabant were up, and a number of the families took delivery of their new status symbols. The money the wives earned then went mainly toward keeping the cars repaired and filled with gasoline.

Willi and Lise never forgot the western half of Berlin, even long after GDR maps showed West Berlin only as a blank white space, a place that their children had never seen. But if they had lost hope of seeing the West before reaching retirement age, the Meisners still looked forward to vacationing in the mountains of Czechoslovakia and lolling at the Black Sea beaches of Bulgaria and Romania.

Willi and Lise, like most other East Germans, had, in spite of everything, grown used to the GDR. Mielke may have wanted to control the lives of every adult citizen of the GDR, but in practice things looked quite different. By the mid-1980s the Party no longer meddled overtly in the private lives of citizens as long as they mouthed the right words in public.

Not that Willi or Lise said very much in public. They kept their views to themselves, and the Party was content. Willi knew several middle-ranking Party members who made critical remarks about the system. Everyone did. But as Willi would say, you couldn't change the system even if you wanted to.

Marcus Wolf, if he had known Willi, would have secretly sympathized with him. He, too, shared Willi's critical views about the Communist system, as well as his fatalism. And, like Willi, he was careful not to let anyone, apart from his closest family and friends, know what he thought.

CHAPTER

7

When I began working as a correspondent in Berlin and Eastern Europe, I decided not to allow the secret police, its surveillants and informers, to become a phobia with me. After all, I reasoned, I enjoyed a degree of protection as an American. If the Stasi and its "fraternal" State Security services in Eastern Europe did not like what I was doing, they could not ride roughshod over me as they did their own defenseless citizens. They would simply make me leave the country, I told myself. But I would have been a good deal less sanguine had I known about the seriousness of the case that the Stasi was building against me.

In September 1978, during one of my regular reporting visits to the biannual Leipzig Fair, I realized, for the first time, that I was under overt surveillance. It was absurd. Whenever I looked at the two men who kept bobbing up near me in the crowded streetcar, they turned away, burying their faces in a newspaper or looking intently out the window. I had first noticed them only minutes earlier as I waited at the streetcar stop on windswept Karl-Marx-Platz.

A few stops later, an attractive, well-dressed woman who was unable to reach the ticket-canceling machine next to me passed her ticket to me with the help of her fellow passengers. I inserted the 20-pfenning (8-cent) ticket, banged the canceling button, and handed back the ticket. *"Danke schön,"* she called out with a broad Saxon accent. At that moment, one of the men looked in my direction, but when our gazes met for a split second, he quickly glanced away, pretending to be absorbed in an advertisement exhorting citizens to take out fire insurance.

I got off the streetcar at the main gate of the technical fairgrounds. The two men were still on my heels. I stopped abruptly in front of building 1, which housed exhibits of Western and Eastern chemical companies, and began leafing through my appointment book. My pursuers also stopped and waited, carefully averting my gaze. I walked on, so did my two surveillants, joining me in a line of fairgoers at a stand selling grilled Thuringian sausages. One of the men, young, fat-faced, and wearing a shiny blue nylon jacket, stood at my elbow; the other, in a brown leather jacket, was directly behind me. When it was my turn to be served, on an impulse I turned to the fat young man at my side and asked if he and his friend would care for a sausage. He stared rigidly past me without moving a muscle. I walked on to building 16, where I asked an official at the British information stand about a scheduled press conference. My two shadows waited patiently near the stand, wheeling into motion when I emerged. At the men's room they waited outside until I emerged. I stopped to talk with the Austrian manager of the IBM exhibit and turned to point out my two Stasi observers. But they had melted into the crowd, only to reappear as I walked to building 6.

2:02 P.M. Caesar visited collective stand of USA, stand 220
in building 6.

This was the entry my observers made in their report on me dated September 6, 1978. Thirteen years would pass before I saw my surveillance report and discovered that the Stasi had pursued me for more than two decades. It was all there in a bulging MfS file between yellowing cardboard covers with my code name, Caesar, scrawled on the top. The dossier on Caesar was stored, along with nearly six million other secret files, in a top security section at Stasi headquarters in Berlin-Lichtenberg.

In 1978 my observers, part of a surveillance task force of the Leipzig branch of the Stasi, had been given orders to tail me everywhere, clandestinely, and report on every move I made, as was standard procedure in the Stasi rule book. Obviously, though, something had gone amiss. My shadowers could not have been more obtrusive. Perhaps, I speculated at the time, they had been miffed at being assigned to someone under "operative personal control" like myself who, instead of riding around in a car, traveled around Leipzig by streetcar, by urban railroad, and, worst of all, on foot. They had probably gotten soft and were used to following their victims in the relative comfort of a Lada car.

On the other hand, I pondered, my overt surveillance might also have been a shot across the bow, a warning to me to refrain from contacts with certain East Germans. Only later did I learn that during the Leipzig Fair, when the city was filled with West Germans and other Westerners and swarming with Stasi officers from East Berlin and the regional bureaus, the Stasi had strict orders not to attempt to recruit or otherwise take overt actions against Westerners. Nothing could be more damaging than a Westerner, miffed about being approached by the Stasi, staging a press conference and exposing the Stasi's methods. For them to breach their regulations, they must have suspected that I was up to something rather serious.

The surveillance continued, minute by excruciating minute:

2:16 P.M. He left the above-named stand and walked to the snack stands next to the Fiat exhibit. Caesar bought broiled chicken, which he placed in his shoulder bag. He returned to hall 16 where at . . .

2:34 P.M. he again visited the British trade information stand.

3:10 P.M. Caesar emerged with a male person — code name Windsor. . . .

The choice of Windsor as the code name for the British official revealed that even the Stasi was not entirely humorless. The agency even chose Nero as the code name for a newspaper colleague of Caesar's, Tony Robinson, who visited me in Leipzig and East Berlin.

The surveillance report on me was typical of the mountains of trivia that piled up on the desks of MfS (Stasi) officers, clogging the files of State Security and making a mockery of Wolf's precept that quality and not quantity were paramount in the gathering of intelligence.

The final evaluation of Caesar by Lieutenant Colonel Gittner, head of the surveillance task force, included a disconcertingly flattering remark about me: Gittner observed that I was "properly attired and well-groomed." He also revealed that Caesar had used his window-shopping in Leipzig to "control his surroundings." In other words, suspecting that he was being followed, Caesar had glanced in shop windows as a countersurveillance measure. Lieutenant Colonel Gittner went on to note: "This was further substantiated by Caesar's abrupt habit of suddenly stopping and going back the way he had come. During the entire observation time, it was noticed that his facial expression remained unchanged and indifferent."

These observations were all the more remarkable because back in 1978 at the Leipzig Fair I felt highly agitated and considered all the possible reasons I was being followed, even the interviews I had done years earlier for the CIA when I was a student in Berlin. I wondered whether the escape of my wife, Ingrid, from East Berlin after the wall was built in 1961 might be grounds for the surveillance. I decided, however, that this was unlikely as East Germans who had escaped were periodically amnestied by the GDR and allowed to visit their former homeland. Ingrid fell into this category of former Easterners. Unbeknownst to me, I was suspected by the Stasi of "hostile and subversive activities in obtaining information," of "influencing the political underground" in the GDR and Eastern Europe, and of "other forms of state crimes." The Stasi had also determined that my reporting on the GDR and Eastern Europe for the *Financial Times* in London was "negative-defamatory." But far more seriously, I was suspected of being a spy for an "imperialist" intelligence agency. Unknowingly, I stood accused of enough antisocialist crimes to land me behind bars in the GDR for years.

In fact, by giving publicity to the "political underground" — civil rights campaigners such as Andrei Sakharov in Moscow or Václav Havel and Jiří Dienstbier in Prague — Western correspondents afforded them at least some protection from persecution by the secret police. State Security forces in the Communist countries found themselves increasingly reined in by their leaders after the 1979 Helsinki Declaration, which stated that respect for human rights was an essential condition for improved relations between East and West.

In September 1979 I again registered with the authorities at the press center in Leipzig, received a police stamp in my passport, and picked up a registration card from the office that provided private accommodations to visitors. Printed on the paper was the name and address of the person who was renting out a room for the duration of the fair. I took the streetcar to the stop closest to the address and walked the rest of the way.

The apartment door was opened by a young woman holding a dripping scouring cloth. She had been on her knees scrubbing the hallway of the apartment. She looked at me, scowling through her tousled auburn hair. "What do you want?" she said irritably as she wrung out her cloth and eyed my overnight bag. She was one of the loveliest women I had ever seen in Saxony, a region renowned for its beautiful Fräuleins.

I gave her the registration card and told her I needed a room for a few days. She told me to leave my bag and to come back later when the corridor was dry enough for me to enter my room. Rising to the challenge, I took off my shoes and padded across the moist corridor floor to the room at the rear of the apartment. A few minutes later she heaved my bag into the room without a word.

Her mood improved measurably during the next few days as we talked in her spacious living room. Beate was divorced and had a lively, angelic-looking three-year-old son. Her large prewar apartment had belonged to her father, a professor of classical languages, and she was anxious to keep it in the face of pressure from the authorities to move into a smaller flat. She had studied Greek and Latin and was a translator of Russian and other Slavic languages.

On the last evening of my stay Beate took out a bottle of Hungarian wine as we sat in the living room. She lit a candle and, in the flickering light, gracefully shed her sweater and skirt. Even if I had wanted to I would have been unable to resist her charms.

Years later I discovered that Beate had been an "unofficial collaborator" of the Stasi, an IM, and that she had reported virtually every detail of what I told her to her controlling officer in Department 2, Section 6, of the Leipzig district headquarters of the Stasi. Thirteen years after that trip to Leipzig I pored through her reports in the voluminous file the Stasi had kept on me:

> **Leipzig, Oct. 3, 1979**
>
> L. Colitt was of the opinion that no one listens to the long, droning speeches by Erich Honecker [the GDR leader]. He said that politics in the GDR are forced down the throats of ordinary people who are under continuous ideological influence. . . . The leaders of the GDR had special shops, medical facilities, and other privileges of which the ordinary working man could only dream, he said. . . .

Beate had given a remarkably accurate report of what I told her. This made her a reliable informer for the Stasi, who had no use for distorted reports. Informers who dressed up their information or told outright lies to the Stasi were usually discovered before long and their services terminated. Yet even the most accurate information from informers was often doctored while being evaluated and rendered more palatable for the cynical eyes of senior Stasi department heads and the Communist leadership.

But what had made Beate, who was deeply skeptical about the Communist system, become an informer in the first place? Perhaps Beate had agreed to inform in order to hold on to her apartment, I thought. Or was there something else that she had desperately wanted and that only the Stasi could provide? Many East Germans who were approached by the Stasi to inform on their fellow citizens, even relatives and close family, refused without suffering retaliation.

In the months following that trip to Leipzig I almost forgot about being under surveillance. My attention was diverted from East Germany by the wave of strikes that swept across Poland in 1980. In the late summer an unemployed electrician, Lech Wałęsa, leaped over a fence of the Lenin shipyard to lead a strike, the result of which was Eastern Europe's first independent labor union, Solidarity.

During the strike Markus and Christa Wolf were soaking up the sun at the Black Sea resort run by the Bulgarian secret police. They did not have an inkling that the drama being acted out in Poland would radically alter their lives and those of every East European in the not so distant future. Officers from the security services of the Warsaw Pact countries who were vacationing at the Bulgarian resort were ordered to return home for emergency meetings on the Polish crisis. But Wolf turned to Christa and remarked that a strike like the one in Gdańsk (Danzig) would not be possible in the GDR. What made Wolf so certain that an eruption such as the one in Poland could never happen next door in his GDR?

After all, his superior, General Mielke, arrived at quite a different conclusion. He ordered that security forces be put on heightened alert in the face of the class enemy's counterrevolution, which he believed was sweeping toward East Germany from Poland.

Wolf was convinced that he knew his fellow East Germans and their innermost fears better than Mielke did. He believed that they yearned for nothing more than stability and order, and that they deeply mistrusted whatever the "fraternal" Polish people did. He was right. Each time I returned to Berlin from Poland in 1980 and 1981, I was confronted with the same question from the disciplined East Germans: "When are the Poles going to stop striking and go back to work?" Faced with a choice between freedom and order, the East Germans chose order.

After the uplifting experience of covering developments in Poland, I did not return to Leipzig until the spring of 1981. Again, I stayed with Beate. I told her how confident I was that Lech Wałęsa and his movement would totally alter the face of Poland in years to come. She listened, nodded in apparent agreement, and took my hand. We went to the Falstaff restaurant, ate dinner, and, as she dutifully reported to her Stasi control officer three days later, remained "from 7:30 P.M. until 11:30 P.M." Her taped and transcribed account of what I had told her was scrupulously accurate. My code name, Caesar, had been inserted in the transcription by the Stasi, because Beate was unaware of it. She dictated:

> Caesar has contacts in Poland to the Solidarity union and had several interviews with Wałęsa, his advisors, and many members of the intelligentsia including students of Warsaw University. Furthermore, he had contacts to the union in several large unnamed factories. Caesar said that the union was to be taken very seriously and that most of the population was now involved. He found it highly interesting that an increasing number of Party members have joined the union. According to Caesar, Poland at the moment is like a free country. Almost every Pole believes that it is only a question of time before the old order collapses.

I could not have put it more succinctly. She also dutifully reported what Caesar had done during the three days he was in Leipzig, as well as his planned movements. Yet she never once betrayed her emotions toward Caesar to the Stasi. For that I am grateful to her.

Beate was only the most attractive in a long line of Stasi informers and officers who had shown an interest in me. The bulging file kept on me by the Stasi revealed that I had been enveloped by MfS "unofficial collaborators," or informers. My file showed that two of Wolf's staffers from his science and technology section, colleagues of Werner Stiller, had contacted me in March 1972 at the Leipzig Fair, introducing themselves as officials of the state trade union. They reported back to headquarters that Caesar showed possibilities of being of use in "intelligence activities."

The informers soon realized their mistake, however, and considered using Caesar as a conduit for disinformation, or the spreading of bogus information. This last bit was fabricated by Department 10 of the HVA, a department in which Wolf took a special interest. Again, the agents misjudged me, because I shied away from further contacts with them.

As I pored through Caesar's MfS file, the gaunt, dark-suited figure of Bodo reentered my life. I met him for the first time in the autumn of 1974 in the restaurant of the Leipzig Fair press center where Western correspondents whiled away the hours. He translated for British and American journalists who had been invited to the fair, and he often sat with me and other Western correspondents at a table in the press center restaurant. He seldom spoke, but he listened attentively. Once he confided to me that he originally came from West Germany.

At the restaurant Western correspondents were fed morsels of disinformation by "unofficial collaborators" of the Stasi while they eyed the attractive young waitresses who waited on tables as part of an apprenticeship at Leipzig's hotel school. The waitresses were warned against having close contacts with Westerners, but some succumbed, only to be hauled in by the Stasi for interrogation and threatened with expulsion from school. Some gave in and agreed to become informers.

West German TV correspondents flocked to Leipzig during the trade fair, when the standing official ban on interviewing East Germans was lifted. GDR officials were terrified by the impact of the West German TV news, which was widely viewed in East Germany. The East Germans idolized the correspondents, so much that one evening in Leipzig a West German TV correspondent got a call in his hotel from a local doctor who had just seen his TV report from the city. "You sounded as if you have the flu," the doctor said. The correspondent admitted he did. In less than half an hour the doctor arrived at the hotel room, administered shots and pills, and refused any payment.

Bodo was a Stasi IMV, an informer with a "confidential relationship" to his victim, as I was to discover in my Stasi file. Bodo, whose code name was Bertram, was initially assigned to see whether Caesar could be used for an "unofficial activity," that is, espionage, as well as "planting image-building" articles about the GDR in the Western news media. But as the Stasi's suspicions about Caesar grew, it changed tack and ordered Bodo to find out as much about him as possible. What Bodo did not know was that the Stasi also suspected him of possible links with Western intelligence. Such paranoia was second nature to the Stasi — its chief, Mielke, regarded virtually every East German as a potential Western agent.

Bodo encountered several obstacles in dealing with Caesar that were unique to Communist countries. For one thing, as he complained to the Stasi, despite all his efforts, he still had no telephone at home. Furthermore, it took an average of six days for mail from Leipzig to reach Caesar in West Berlin. But Bodo had an even greater problem that he did not dare mention to the Stasi: I had become deeply suspicious of him and would make wide detours to avoid him.

In Bodo's lengthy reports on Caesar to his Stasi controller, he claimed to have gained his quarry's confidence while obtaining important information from him. Bodo bragged that he was the first GDR citizen in Leipzig to learn about the "resignation of Harold Wilson, nearly two hours before the official announcement" carried by the East German news agency.

Buried deep inside an evaluation of Bodo's informing activities by his Stasi controller lay the clue to why he had agreed to become an informer. He had hoped, with the help of the MfS, to be allowed to work again as a journalist, as he had done before coming to the GDR. His hopes, however, were badly misplaced. The Stasi saw through Bodo's claims to having a confidential relationship with Caesar, and by late 1976 his credibility as an informer had been destroyed. His controlling officer decided that for subjective and objective reasons, Bodo had failed to fulfill the instructions he had been given. Even worse he had tried to "deceive" the MfS for personal reasons. On those grounds the "cooperation" between the MfS and Bodo would be terminated. "Since Caesar avoided contacts with Bertram [Bodo] in the last phase of the cooperation, it cannot be excluded that Caesar knows about Bertram's unofficial work or suspects it," the controller concluded, accurately.

Bodo vanished out of my life as abruptly as he had entered it. Several years later, though, we met accidentally in a streetcar in Leipzig. His eyes more deeply set than ever, Bertram told me that he had applied to the authorities for him and his family to leave the GDR for West Germany.

My Stasi file revealed that the GDR's stepped-up surveillance of me in Leipzig between 1978 and 1979 had, in fact, been triggered by a previous assignment in Czechoslovakia. I had gone to Prague in January 1977 to report on the creation of the Charter 77 human rights movement by Václav Havel, later president of

Czechoslovakia, and his fellow dissidents. I spent two weeks in Czechoslovakia, interviewing Havel and the spokesman of Charter 77, the ailing Professor Jan Patočka, who shortly afterward died of heart failure after repeated interrogations by the Státní Tajna Bezpečnost (the StB), or Czechoslovakia's secret police. My nightly interviews with him took place in his home, which was being closely watched by StB agents in cars parked outside. I assumed that the StB already had a file on me dating from my reporting from Czechoslovakia during and after the Warsaw Pact invasion in August 1968.

On the night train that lurched toward East Berlin from Prague on February 3, 1977, I was searched by Czechoslovak border controllers before the train entered the GDR. All my notebooks and two tapes were confiscated, one of them containing an appeal to the West for help by Pavel Kohout, the Czech playwright, a tape that I had rather foolishly agreed to take with me. I was hauled off the train in Dresden's main station, where the Czechoslovaks turned me over to an East German border guard who directed me to a table in the shabby Mitropa railroad restaurant. There I was told to wait until the next train for Berlin arrived in five hours' time.

Interrupted only by occasional patrols of Soviet military policemen who were on the lookout for deserters, I managed to reconstruct the most important of the more than ninety pages of confiscated notes on Charter 77. My detainment by the Czechoslovak authorities led to a protest by the State Department in Washington, which was widely reported in the media and duly registered by the Stasi. The East Germans' previous suspicions about my nefarious activities in Eastern Europe were confirmed.

The Stasi, aided by the Czechoslovak and Hungarian secret police, suspected me of a "hostile intelligence connection," either American or British, according to my file. On February 4, 1977, immediately after I returned to West Berlin from Prague, the Stasi issued search order number 222959 for me. I was to be followed each time I entered East Berlin and East Germany. I suspected nothing on this scale at the time, or I would have been a good deal more unnerved. Shortly afterward, the Stasi's blanket surveillance of my comings and goings in Leipzig and East Berlin began in earnest. Stasi suspicions that I was a Western spy reached fever pitch on March 16, 1978, the fourth day I was under observation during the Spring Leipzig Fair. But the spy hunt got bogged down in the mind-boggling minutiae of my pursuers and their stopwatches.

11:44 A.M. Caesar bought a package of biscuits from a cart and returned to platform 11.

11:47 A.M. He entered car number 34 of the Kraków to Eisenach express train and took a seat at 11:47 A.M. in a nonsmoker compartment in car number 38.

11:52 A.M. Caesar departed in the train for Erfurt.

2:09 P.M. He got off the train at Erfurt main station and walked toward the exit. On his way, he threw away the plastic bag he had with him into a paper basket and walked on. After approximately 15 meters he turned around, walked back to the paper basket, and retrieved the plastic bag he had previously discarded. Caesar then walked over to the train schedule at the exit and made notes.

Caesar's behavior was highly suspicious. Lieutenant Colonel Gittner, who evaluated the report submitted by his surveillants, concluded that Caesar had carried out "unmotivated actions suggesting a control" of his surroundings. The "observing side" judged that Caesar's throwing away then retrieving the plastic bag, as well as his frequent note-taking at posted train schedules, indicated "control" of his surroundings.

Actually, indecisive as always, I had retrieved the plastic bag after deciding not to throw it away in a country where bags were reused to the point of disintegration. My frequent writing down of train schedules was another distortion: I merely wanted to find out how often trains left Erfurt for Leipzig. My surveillants followed me into Erfurt on what, for me, was a sentimental return. It was here in March 1970 that I had witnessed the tumultuous welcome East Germans gave to Willy Brandt on his first visit to the GDR. During my visit to Erfurt they recorded the following observations:

2:25 P.M. Caesar asked a question of a male pedestrian who pointed toward Bahnhofstrasse. He entered. . . .

2:28 P.M. Bürgerhof restaurant, where, despite the empty tables, he walked out and at . . .

2:30 P.M. went to the Winzerkeller restaurant diagonally across the street, which, at . . .

2:32 P.M. Caesar entered. He checked his coat in the vestibule and sat down at one of the empty tables. Caesar ordered a Margonwasser [soda water] without flavor and one portion of chicken hearts from the waiter.

Apart from the chicken hearts, almost everything else on the menu had been crossed off. Suddenly, at this point, the surveillance record took an unexpectedly dramatic turn. The blood in the veins of my observers must have begun to race as they registered what appeared to be a classic spy *treff*:

2:50 P.M. A lieutenant of the NVA, Air Defense, approached the table of Caesar and asked if he could sit down. The lieutenant — he is codenamed Himmel [sky] — sat down next to Caesar, and both began to talk. Their conversation became increasingly animated and intense. In the course of their meeting they drank several cognacs; while Himmel also drank a number of beers. The following snatches of their conversation could be overheard: "Political instruction, delivery slip, show exit slip at gate . . ."

The report was pure fabrication, but Caesar's observer, who claimed to have overheard the conversation, probably envisioned himself nailing a couple of spies and earning a promotion.

The officer mentioned in the report was in his late twenties, tall, and with close-cropped blonde hair. He was not allowed to speak with Westerners but did not realize that I was one until well into our conversation. His tongue loosened, and he told me about the Wartburg car he had on order for 20,000 GDR Marks with a twenty-year delivery time. He explained that he earned enough money and had considerable responsibilities. "I'm in air defense, and if one of them ever got through . . . ," he blurted out in an apparent reference to a plane or missile, while looking at me with glazed eyes. I inquired no further.

He downed a brandy. "You know, we Germans, East and West, work hard. Both our countries show that," he boasted. The Poles, on the other hand, were lazy, and the Italians were cowards, in his opinion. His father had served with the Wehrmacht in Italy and had told him so. Suddenly he exclaimed that the recent "criminal" Israeli invasion of Lebanon and "extermination" of the Palestinians showed that the Jews were doing "exactly what Hitler did to them." He ordered another round of brandy and beer and leaned toward me. Did I know that the Jews had been "bunched together" in camps in Warsaw and other places during the Second World War, making it difficult for the German Army to "deal with them"?

I stared dumbfounded at the two gold stars on the shoulder boards of his gray-green uniform, which so strongly resembled the one his father had worn. I abruptly took leave of him, and at this point the Stasi task force shifted its full attention to Himmel.

4:24 P.M. Himmel bought a ticket to Dresden-Neustadt and proceeded to platform 1, where he went to the toilet located there. After leaving the toilet he walked to the luggage lockers in the upper glass-roofed hall and removed a suitcase from one of them. Himmel then proceeded to platform 1, where he entered the express train to Frankfurt/ Oder via Leipzig and Cottbus at . . .

4:30 P.M. and took a seat in a compartment.

4:34 P.M. Himmel departed in the express train bound for Leipzig. During the trip Himmel bought four bottles of Wernersgrüner pilsener, drank one of them along with liquor that he took from his travel bag. He carried on a lively conversation with the other passengers in the compartment.

Himmel's observers got out of the train with him at Leipzig's main station. There he went to the Neues Restaurant, left his coat and hat in the cloakroom, and sat down at the bar and consumed more brandy. Afterward he sat at a table where, at

8:10 P.M. he greeted two female persons of between twenty-four and twenty-seven years of age who sat down at his table.

Himmel and the two women drank heavily. After buying a bottle of Sekt (sparkling wine) and a box of chocolates at the bar, Himmel and his female companions left the restaurant at 11:55 P.M. and went to the taxi stand in front of the main station, where at

12:05 A.M. Himmel and the two female persons drove off in a taxi toward the Hotel Astoria.
12:10 A.M. The observation of Himmel was terminated.

I first learned the identity of Himmel from reading my Stasi file. He was born July 16, 1954, in Magdeburg and lived, remarkably enough, in the same apartment building where Markus Wolf had, 2 Fischerinsel. He was single and a member of the Communist Party.

Lieutenant Colonel Gittner's evaluation of Caesar's meeting with Himmel brought to a white heat previous suspicions that Caesar was a spy. Gittner suggested that by asking directions of a passerby in Erfurt, Caesar had purposefully made his way to the Winzerkeller restaurant. His *treff* there was "no accident," as shown by the fact that both Caesar and Himmel conversed animatedly, "whereby they also spoke of official matters. In this connection, Himmel answered Caesar's questions in great detail."

Gittner found it particularly noteworthy that Caesar, on arriving in Erfurt, had inquired about the 4:34 P.M. express train to Leipzig but did not return to Leipzig on this train. "Instead, it was Himmel who took this train," he noted ominously.

Stasi counterintelligence headed by Lt. Gen. Günther Kratsch, concluded in a report on April 5, 1978, that Caesar and

Himmel were to be regarded as guilty until proven otherwise. A full-scale security investigation of suspect Himmel was launched by a general in military counterintelligence. Himmel's background in missiles, including the latest Soviet types employed by the East German and Soviet air forces in the GDR, was laid out in exhaustive detail. These were unquestionably the top military secrets that Caesar was so eager to obtain from Himmel.

Himmel, despite repeated lengthy interrogations about his alleged espionage contacts with Caesar, steadfastly denied any previous knowledge of me. Unable to make any headway, the officers finally closed the investigation of Himmel with the words: "It was determined that his meeting with Caesar was unplanned and, with virtual certainty, that there was no connection between [Himmel] and the foreigner."

A cloud of suspicion, however, remained over Himmel, who was kept under close scrutiny by military counterintelligence. His chances of promotion were blocked, and his military career effectively ended. As for Caesar, the Stasi, in spite of its temporary setback, was more determined than ever to confirm its earlier suspicion that he was guilty of espionage.

Gisela Münzenberger was one of my favorite landladies in Leipzig during the Fair: a red-cheeked middle-aged schoolteacher who shared her ascetic-looking husband's passion for astronomy and hiking. I stayed with them in March 1982 and several following years. Both Münzenbergers were extremely dedicated science teachers. Their impressive collection of books lining the living room wall was their only luxury. They paid 63 GDR Marks a month rent for their three-room, prewar apartment, which was heated by tiled coal ovens. The solidly built prewar building was still pockmarked with bullet holes from the last days of the Second World War when the Americans took Leipzig only to hand it over to the Russians three months later. Over the portal was the inscription The Lord protect this house and all who enter and leave it.

I felt comfortable with the Münzenbergers, and returning to their apartment in the evening was a bit like coming home. They were a well-informed couple, critical of the regime's orthodoxy, which caused children and adults alike to present a public face approving the regime while in private they scorned it.

At the crest of the wave of applications to leave the GDR in the 1980s, when tens of thousands of Leipzigers sought to emigrate to West Germany, I asked Gisela Münzenberger whether she and her husband had ever considered leaving. No, she said, her husband was offered a job in West Germany in the 1950s, but they chose to remain in the GDR even though they would have been considerably better off in the West. Their reason for staying had nothing to do with sympathy for the Communist regime, though. She explained that they felt a moral obligation to stay with their pupils.

There were many East Germans like the Münzenbergers, upright and dedicated people who worked long hours for little pay out of a sense of duty to their fellow citizens. But where did such people draw the line between doing their duty and silently obeying a totalitarian rule?

The answer was, that despite her high moral standards, Gisela Münzenberger was one of my informers, as evidenced by this report:

> Mr. Colitt told my husband at breakfast that he had spoken with young people at a performance of the Akademixer cabaret. He asked them what détente had brought them personally, and they were unable to think of anything. One of them said they still could not travel where they wanted to, but another said that at least world peace had been kept. On March 14 and 15, 1982, he got three phone calls from the stand of WMW in Hall 20 of the technical fairgrounds to confirm an appointment and got several calls from London.

Unlike the "unofficial collaborators," Gisela had not signed a pledge to work for the Stasi. She was a "social collaborator of security," a GMS, a status she shared with many East Germans who were not full-time informers. Her neighbor was employed by the Interior Department, which worked closely with the Stasi. Every Western visitor to Leipzig (or to anywhere else in the GDR) had to sign a "house log" if he or she was staying with private people or relatives, and Gisela's neighbor asked her to report on her foreign guests during the Leipzig Fair. Gisela had a deeper reason for agreeing to talk with her neighbor about her guests. She told me later that her son had been expelled from the army and was in prison. She hoped he would benefit from her cooperation with the Stasi.

As with the other GMSs, Gisela Münzenberger had no idea that the Stasi had given her a code name, Münze, and regarded her as one of its regular "sources." She appeared shocked to learn this when she met me again years later.

Strangely, when I discovered who my informers had been from their reports on me in the Stasi file, I felt scarcely any emotion, neither revulsion nor sadness. It was as if I had expected them to act as they had done.

Although the Stasi collected a vast amount of material on me, it had virtually nothing on my wife, Ingrid, although she was a former East German. She and I had assumed that her escape from East Berlin shortly after the building of the Berlin Wall had attracted the Stasi's attention.

When Ingrid crossed in September 1961, the border posts to the West were still manned by inexperienced young guards from the provinces who had been pressed into service. She had dyed her hair to match the photo in my sister's passport and sat holding the passport tightly as she waited for me in a café in Friedrichstrasse. We downed two vodkas, rehearsing the phrases I had taught her in English in case she was asked questions at the border.

Our fears dampened by the alcohol, we left the café and walked up Friedrichstrasse toward the border. Passing an empty lot, we flung our remaining East German marks into the night air. In the distance we could make out a lone border guard standing under a dim streetlight. Around the corner from him was West Berlin.

We approached the very young looking guard. I showed him my passport, and then Ingrid took out my sister's passport from her handbag. But trembling, she dropped it, and all three of us dove to the sidewalk to retrieve it. The incident served to break the tension. The guard only glanced at the photo in the passport then murmured his approval, wishing us a pleasant *Gute Nacht*. We walked on as if in a trance, turning the corner and walking across the freshly painted white borderline, soon to be known as Checkpoint Charlie, and into West Berlin. We were so drained of emotion that we were unable to celebrate Ingrid's escape.

Ingrid did not dare reenter the GDR until nearly ten years later, after her crime of "flight from the Republic" was absolved under one of the periodic East German amnesties. By that time she was an American citizen. Her father was questioned by the Stasi after her escape and demoted at work, although it was evident that he had known nothing of her plans.

My file showed that the Stasi in June 1982 attempted to recruit the husband of one of Ingrid's girlfriends in East Berlin to inform on me as an "unofficial collaborator." Ingrid had written her girlfriend the previous Christmas, but the letter was intercepted by the Stasi and steamed open at the main post office. The Stasi's plan was to have the husband encourage his wife to invite Ingrid to East Berlin, and he then would report to the Stasi about me. This, of course, would have turned him into an informer on his own wife. The plan collapsed when he wisely told the Stasi officer that he would be unable to conceal his contacts with State Security from his wife. Since the Stasi feared nothing more than breaches of the secrecy surrounding its clandestine network of informers, it backed away from recruiting him.

His refusal to inform on his wife proved that the Stasi could be resisted by citizens who had no fear of reprisals or hopes of favors. The tragedy of one prominent dissident, Vera Wollenberger, whose husband informed on her for the Stasi, was not inevitable even in a police state. He could have rejected the blandishments of the Stasi but did not.

It took courage to resist the Stasi, and not many Germans displayed that quality, either during the twelve years of Nazi rule or the forty-four years under the Communists. One East German who did, Heidemarie Fischer, fought a steadfast twenty-six-year battle with the Stasi, which she ended up winning through her fearlessness and candor. She told me of her ordeal in 1993, after it was over.

In 1963, two years after the Berlin Wall went up, someone in the East Berlin TV plant where Heidemarie worked as a technical draftswoman had hurled hundreds of leaflets from a stairwell to the main entrance below. The leaflets had been produced using a child's printing set, and they carried an incendiary message:

> We call for a neutral Germany
> For a nuclear-free zone
> For withdrawal from the military pacts
> For peace and understanding
> For the right to travel between East and West
> For tolerance and against agitation
> For national policies . . .

Shortly afterward an envelope containing five hundred of the leaflets, which had been mailed to a West Berlin address, was intercepted by the Stasi. One of the employees in the TV plant, a draftsperson, was suspected of being the perpetrator. The Stasi's Central Department 8, headed by one of its most unsavory officers, Maj. Gen. Dr. Karli Coburger, singled out Heidemarie Fischer as the prime suspect. She was twenty years old at the time. Coburger's department was in charge of observing everyone suspected of dissident activities in connection with the West, searching their homes, and taking "measures" against them. Ferreting out such illegal activities was a growth industry, and by 1989 he would have fifteen hundred staff members and tens of thousands of informers.

Department 8 set up an "operational base" in an apartment next to the one where Heidemarie lived with her mother in East Berlin. She was observed day and night and informed on by unofficial collaborators. Heidemarie was a regular churchgoer, and one of her informers was a student of theology who worked for the Stasi in the hope of advancing his career. He was told by his controlling officer to invite her to a café, where he was to obtain a saliva sample from her glass and search her handbag while she went to the ladies' room.

The Stasi had a fixation about collecting saliva and odor samples from persons under operative control. Unofficial collaborators spent much of their time taking saliva samples from drinking glasses and maneuvering their victims onto bits of cloth that picked up body odor. Tens of thousands of these samples were preserved in airtight containers against the time when police dogs might be needed to track down the suspects.

Heidemarie foiled the Stasi's plans by rejecting the theology student's invitation. Mischa Wolf might have told the operatives that one did not snare an attractive woman with a gangly, offputting theology student. But at this point the domestic Stasi did not interfere in his affairs, and he kept largely out of Mielke's.

Apart from a few attempts to walk Heidemarie home, the student informer got no further with her. His lack of success did not deter him from composing lengthy, imaginative reports about her for his controlling officer. They read like those Bodo wrote about Caesar. Such reports were attached to her Stasi file, which mushroomed to nearly fifteen hundred pages. Eventually, the controller saw through the lies, and the student informer was ignominiously withdrawn from service. Undeterred, the chameleonlike young man went on to become a respected Lutheran pastor. As a clergyman he played an active role in the Christian Democratic Union (CDU) of the GDR, one of the muzzled "block" parties that supported the Communists. After the collapse of the GDR and with German unification, he found himself, to his relief, on the victorious side — in Chancellor Kohl's All-German CDU.

Much to Heidemarie's surprise and to the consternation of the Stasi investigators, the culprit responsible for the inflammatory leaflets turned out to be a disgruntled member of the Socialist Unity (Communist) Party (SED) of the GDR. But even so, the Stasi did not give up surveilling her. Reading her Stasi file years afterward, Heidemarie discovered a slew of other informers, including members of her church congregation. Heidemarie Fischer became Heidemarie Brauer upon marrying a talented researcher who had been given the GDR's prestigious National Prize in 1972 for his work in liquid crystals. A year after their wedding, a man came to the house they had built in Fürstenwalde near Berlin and asked to speak with Herr Brauer. The caller identified himself as a police detective, but it was clear to the

Brauers that he was "Stasi," because its members shied from disclosing their true employer to the public. The Stasi detective said that the police suspected that a recent production problem at Herr Brauer's place of work had been caused by "sabotage," and that he was expected to cooperate by naming the criminals. Brauer replied without a moment's hesitation that far from being an act of sabotage, the mishap was the result of "homegrown GDR sloppiness."

At this point the detective shed his cover and urged Brauer to work as an unofficial collaborator (IM) for the State Security Ministry. Herr Brauer refused.

"I would think it over," the Stasi officer said.

"I don't have to," Brauer replied.

"In that case, I will have to report your remarks. I must inform you that under no circumstances are you to tell your wife about this conversation," the man said sternly.

"My wife is in the adjoining room and has overheard every word you said," Brauer replied curtly.

The Stasi officer, his face flushed, turned on his heel and scurried away without even an *"Auf Wiedersehen."* He retreated, knowing that Herr Brauer was one citizen who recognized that the secret police had to remain secret in order to retain its fearsome reputation.

In Heidemarie's experience, officers on the domestic side of the Stasi — she had no experience with Wolf's elite HVA — as well as informers, tended to resemble stereotypical dim-witted cops. Typically, they would go about discovering the simplest facts in the most complicated manner. It took weeks for the Stasi to find out her husband's occupation, even though this had long since been established in previous investigations. One report in her file stated that since her husband had shown considerable skill in repairing a TV set, it could be surmised that he was a "person with a technical profession."

On January 3, 1988, the Brauers joined the ranks of the hundreds of thousands of East Germans who had officially applied to emigrate to the West. After a few days, a letter came back from the GDR's Internal Affairs Department. They were informed that they had no reason to leave and would have to sell their house if they did. But the Brauers renewed their application each following month. Their telephone was tapped, their mail often disappeared, and a policeman was posted in front of their house on May Day to prevent them from staging an antigovernment demonstration. Heidemarie's husband had problems at work because of his application to leave, but unlike most East Germans who had applied to emigrate, he did not lose his job. His work was too valuable to the GDR.

The Brauers refused to join the growing number of East Germans who reacted to their rejected emigration applications by openly provoking arrest and imprisonment—either through half-hearted attempts to escape or by openly insulting the regime. After serving a year or eighteen months in prison, these East German detainees would be bought free by the West German government. In 1985 alone, Bonn paid more than DM 300 million to the GDR to gain the release of 2,700 political prisoners—most of them East Germans who had been refused exit permits—as well as 17,300 East Germans who were allowed to join their families in West Germany. This cynical sale of human beings for hard currency was an important factor in helping to undermine Communist rule.

In December 1988 Heidemarie Brauer received a letter telling her to make an appointment with the mayor of the town. When the Brauers met with the mayor he was all smiles and said that he could help them get out of the GDR quickly if they gave the government the right to buy their house before anyone else. Heidemarie said she already had a buyer who would be acceptable to the mayor. That evening, for the first time, she came close to a nervous breakdown. At the Brauers' next meeting with the mayor, Herr Brauer informed him that under GDR law the authorities had no right to buy a dwelling before anyone else.

The Brauers won out, selling their house cheaply to a family who promised to allow Heidemarie's elderly mother to keep her room, since she did not want to go to the West. In late December, they were finally told by the authorities that they "had to depart from the GDR" within a few days after proving that they had no debts and renouncing their citizenship. The Brauers began life anew in a cramped apartment in West Berlin, never imagining that in less than a year the Berlin Wall would come down.

The rarity of civil courage in the GDR accounted for the ease with which Mielke and his henchmen were able to cow the population. Frau Brauer's Stasi file revealed that a total of thirteen informers had been attached to her and her husband. Not one of them had been coerced into becoming informers, but all had agreed to work for the Stasi because of the benefits, large and small, that were promised.

In the Stasi's mania to record every remark that seemed even remotely to threaten the Party's rule, it paid special attention to the Protestant churches, the sole institutions, along with the Catholic Church, not controlled by the authorities. The largest Protestant church, the Evangelical [Lutheran] Church was crawling with informers, and any pastor looking out on his congregation on a Sunday morning could be certain that several of the most devout churchgoers were working for State Security.

Wolf was repelled by Mielke's paranoiac need to learn about every bishop's foibles and the activities of the still ineffective Church-backed peace movement. He suspected that the vast flow of information from hundreds of church informers produced little benefit for socialism. But these were heretical thoughts that he did not voice openly.

One clergyman in particular, Pastor Reiner Eppelmann of the Church of the Good Samaritan in the East Berlin borough of Lichtenberg, was more closely watched than any other. This fearless, outspoken man was a leading figure in the unofficial GDR peace movement, which numbered nearly five thousand people and operated under the protection of the Evangelical Church. "Peace movement," was a euphemism for "human rights movement," used by the always cautious opposition.

Eppelmann, who bore an uncanny resemblance to Lenin, down to his pointed beard, was one of the small number of GDR churchmen who could not be muzzled. The evening peace group sessions the pastor held with young people in the parish hall were invariably attended by several informers. Yet Eppelmann made no attempt to minimize the gap between the Church leadership and the so-called Church from Below. The grassroots peace movement he was a part of criticized the militarization of education in the GDR, demanded an alternative to military service, and called for an end to the disastrous pollution of the environment as well as demoralizing travel restrictions.

Although the authorities had a long-standing dialogue with the Church, they refused to speak with Eppelmann. Instead, they dealt with senior Church officials such as the eloquent and well-connected Manfred Stolpe, the leading Church layman in the Berlin-Brandenburg diocese. They complained to him about Eppelmann, and Stolpe would relay the complaint to the obstreperous pastor.

Eppelmann once told me that Stolpe had pointedly reminded him that the peace movement was only one of many "cups in our cupboard." "False," Eppelmann replied. "The peace movement was all that was in the cupboard." He meant that the Church, stripped of the peace movement, held little appeal, especially to younger East Germans. Eppelmann believed that if the Church approached the young people using religious language it would "bite on granite." His analysis was accurate, as the nearly deserted Protestant churches of post-Communist eastern Germany later proved.

At a meeting I attended in 1982 in the parish hall of his church, Pastor Eppelmann told a group of young supporters that East Germans had been satisfied to lead the life of snails. If the people did not tell the leadership what was best for it, then the leadership would decide "what was best." It took seven more years before the East German opposition summoned up enough courage to openly challenge the country's rigged elections.

The GDR's man in charge of combating all forms of opposition, real and imagined, was Lieutenant General Paul Kienberg, head of the Stasi's Central Department 20. Born in 1926, he was an officially recognized "Combatant against Fascism," like Wolf, and as a Jew he had been persecuted by the Nazis. Kienberg's department was in charge of preventing, detecting, and combating PID and PUT—the acronyms for "political-ideological subversion" and "political underground activities." In practice, his department placed everyone under surveillance, from writers and doctors to university professors and athletes. Section 4 of his department controlled the Protestant and Catholic churches, recruiting informers from among pastors and churchgoers alike. Some senior churchmen were given preferential treatment because of their lofty functions and did not have to sign pledges to cooperate with the MfS. In some cases they did not even know that they were unofficial collaborators but only that they were regular "conversational partners" of the Stasi. Manfred Stolpe was one of them.

Stolpe, a man of moral rectitude, had a gift of speech and persuasion that was rare among the reticent East Germans. As a young man in the GDR, his talents were discovered by the Protestant Church, which sent him for legal training to West Berlin. He returned to the East before the Berlin Wall was built, and began a career as a Church lawyer. But the Church was not the only organization that had its eye on Stolpe. The Stasi also recognized the young man's talents. Approached in 1964 by a Stasi officer using a false identity, Stolpe agreed to talk about questions of mutual interest. The Stasi opened a file on him labeled "Preliminary unofficial collaborator." Six years later he was promoted to unofficial collaborator, assigned a controlling officer, and given the cover name Secretary, all without ever being asked to sign the loyalty pledge that was required of ordinary informers. By this time, he was head of the Secretariat of the Federation of Evangelical (Protestant) Churches in the GDR.

One thing appeared certain to Manfred Stolpe. The Communist regime would last as long as he lived, backed as it was by the armed might of the Soviet Union. So cooperating with the powers that be, just as Martin Luther had once urged on his followers, was the right thing to do. Stolpe told himself that what he was doing was quite different from the Church's collaboration with the Nazis. The Communists were misled but not evil, and did they not, after all, preach the same goals of brotherhood as the Church?

Stolpe was determined to avoid conflicts between Church and State by drawing as close to his confidants in the regime as possible without being swallowed in the process. It was a delicate tightrope act, but he was certain that he was skillful enough to carry it off. Stolpe told Church officials of his highly confidential and beneficial contacts with the "state organs," without, however, mentioning the Stasi, and they were impressed. Here was a man who could conduct a confidential dialogue with the rulers on "special humanitarian cases" without compromising the Church. Humanitarian cases consisted of everything from obtaining the release of a Church member detained by the authorities to getting permission for the Church to import Western equipment for its hospitals and mental institutions. Despite the humanitarian role he played, Stolpe could not conceal his driving ambition to succeed at the fascinating Church job that brought him into contact with the high and mighty in the East and the West.

He had no difficulty honoring the Stasi's demand that he maintain absolute secrecy about the meetings with his controller, Lt. Col. Klaus Rossberg, which took place in a safe apartment. Stolpe secretly passed documents of the Church Federation to Rossberg and informed him about the politically relevant themes discussed by the federation. This information was given to the East German leadership.

Pastor Eppelmann had considered Stolpe to be a committed servant of the Church ever since Stolpe had helped him when he refused to do military service; Eppelmann had served in a construction battalion instead. Stolpe also had spoken in support of the peace groups that were forming under the umbrella of the Church. The headstrong pastor felt bitterly betrayed when he later learned from his Stasi file that Stolpe, alias Secretary, had informed on his private life in a manner designed to make him appear to be sexually driven. Worse, he said, Stolpe had pretended to fight for the young people of the peace movement when he was betraying them to the Stasi.

Stolpe knew that he was a conduit being used by both sides. For all this he earned only a modest salary from his Church employers and got a few presents from the Stasi. But money could not buy much in the GDR anyway. Knowing the right people was far more important. Always well-informed, Stolpe bought an imposing brick house in Potsdam cheaply from an elderly man who was about to move to West Germany.

Stolpe was a world away from the ordinary Evangelical Church informer of the Stasi. Pastor Jürgen Kapiske was more typical. As editor of a Church newspaper in Mecklenburg, he reported to the Stasi as a Church informer for nearly eighteen years. He was a diligent informer, penning some three thousand pages of reports on his colleagues, dissidents, and Western correspondents. He was paid for his efforts and given a medal by Erich Mielke.

Detlef Haupt, a student pastor from Erfurt, had clandestine contacts with the Stasi for decades, in order, as he put it, to help overcome confrontation between State and Church. He claimed that he had wanted to help correct the Stasi's erroneous views about the Church's grassroots movement. Actually, he helped the Stasi play one churchman against the other.

Manfred Stolpe had no need for payment or medals, although he was awarded the GDR Order of Merit, a medal he almost forgot about until it was discovered after the demise of the Stasi. Stolpe was one of two prominent East Germans who were implicitly trusted by Western politicians. Wolfgang Vogel, the fastidious, deeply religious East Berlin lawyer who served the regime, was the other. Vogel represented the GDR and the Soviet Union in their negotiations with the West on spy swaps and the sale of East German prisoners. Stolpe and Vogel knew each other and trusted each other. Stolpe provided the Stasi with valuable information on the Church and on prominent Westerners, without any formal commitment. Vogel, who performed many a service for Bonn and Washington, was directly controlled by the Stasi. The difference between them was one of degree.

After the collapse of the GDR, Stolpe became the object of massive allegations that he had been a Stasi informer. But East Germans rallied to his defense. In 1990 he was nominated by the Social Democratic Party (SPD) and elected prime minister of the state of Brandenburg, becoming by far the most popular politician in the former GDR. His supporters, who recalled the compromises, large and small, that they themselves had made with the Communists, were in no mood to moralize.

Another East German who rose prominence in 1990, Gregor Gysi, the Woody Allen look-alike who headed the post

Communist PDS (Party of Democratic Socialism), was also confronted with damaging evidence that as a lawyer representing
several dissidents, Gysi had kept the Stasi informed about his
clients.

As for Caesar, the Stasi continued its "operative measures" against
him as a suspected spy until October 1985, although MfS counterintelligence was getting nowhere on the case. But to give up
after all that time would have meant to concede defeat, an intoler-
able admission for the secret police. If something convincing
could be nailed on him, all the years of informing and observation
would be proven worthwhile.

CHAPTER

8

Wolf had top moles who spied mainly out of conviction — such as Guillaume, Olbrich, and Gast. There were others whose motives reeked of avarice: the lure of deutsche marks and U.S. dollars attracted some of Wolf's most successful Western spies.

Wolf was sitting in his office in the early autumn of 1981 when an aide handed him a remarkable letter. It was sealed inside two envelopes and had only recently been dropped in the mailbox of the GDR's Permanent Mission in Bonn. The letter was addressed simply to the "Head of the HVA." The anonymous writer identified himself as an official of the Bundesamt für Verfassungsschutz (BfV), or West German counterintelligence, in Cologne and said he was willing to cooperate with East German intelligence under "certain conditions." He proposed a *treff* in Brussels with one of Wolf's representatives to discuss those conditions. He enclosed a DM 10 bill, which was to be used as identification by the person who met him in Brussels. He also provided a code that would allow the HVA to contact him by radio message. No doubt, Wolf decided, this was a highly skilled operator.

Western intelligence agents who offered their services to East Berlin were treated with the utmost caution. Wolf was skeptical of the offer, sensing that it could well be a trap. After conferring with his top officers responsible for the West German intelligence services, Wolf ordered that a message be sent to the anonymous BfV official giving a time and place for a *treff* in

Brussels. Wary of a trap, Wolf's agent did not approach the un-named West German but observed him for some time and then reported back to East Berlin.

Major Stefan Engelmann of the HVA followed up by con-tacting the mysterious letter writer and calling on him to provide "material" that would prove his sincerity. No, the BfV official replied cagily, first the HVA would have to agree to meet a series of his conditions. Engelmann consulted with his superiors and re-plied that the terms were, in principle, acceptable. The shadowy BfV official responded by disclosing the code name East Berlin had given one of its agents who had subsequently been turned into a double agent by West German counterintelligence. Wolf promised that the HVA would not arrest the double agent, thus protecting the anonymous Western contact.

The West German who was about to land in Wolf's waiting arms was Klaus Kuron, a senior BfV official whose job was to "turn" East German and Soviet agents, to get them to work for the BfV as double agents. He made sure that his double agents continued to convince East Berlin and Moscow that they were trustworthy spies. They were fed deceptive information designed to mislead the enemy as well as to discover his plans. Anyone engaged in work as devious as Kuron's needed to be closely watched.

Kuron had piled up debts building a house and preparing to send his four children through college, all on his relatively modest civil service salary of DM 48,000 a year. He was frustrated at not being able to advance beyond his present grade merely because he lacked a university degree. Kuron regarded himself as one of the few professionals among the many incompetent bureaucrats in the BfV. Over the years that he worked for West German counterintelligence, he grew more and more impressed by the skills of his superb adversary, Markus Wolf. To work for Wolf would be the pinnacle of his career; he might also double his income if he played it right.

The double agent Kuron betrayed to Wolf had been given the code name Wolfgang by the HVA. The young East German translator had first been sent by the HVA to Britain under a false identity. Later he was assigned to Argentina and Brazil and given the macabre task of combing cemeteries for the names of deceased ethnic Germans on tombstones. Future HVA agents in West Germany would take on those identities. When Wolfgang defected and converted to a double agent, Kuron's reputation within the BfV soared. Kuron rationalized his sacrifice of Wolfgang to the HVA by telling himself that he had done it for his own self-protection. Everyone knew that double agents were capable of turning against their controllers and becoming lethal triple agents.

In June 1982 Kuron met Gunther Nehls, an HVA section head, at a prearranged *treff* in Vienna. Kuron told Nehls about his work at the BfV and about several of its operations against the HVA. That summer a meeting was arranged between Kuron and Wolf in the GDR.

On October 12 Kuron traveled to Vienna, where Nehls handed him a GDR diplomatic passport issued under a fictitious name. Kuron was then driven in an East German Embassy car to an airport in nearby Bratislava, Czechoslovakia, where Major Engelmann was waiting. Here they boarded an Interflug plane for a special flight to Dresden. Lt. Col. Bernd Trögel, Wolf's son-in-law, met the men with a car at Dresden airport. During a brief sightseeing tour of Dresden, Kuron was appalled by the hideous new slab-concrete buildings that had been erected over the ruins of this once majestic city. But he said nothing. He was taken to a Stasi mansion in the wooded Weisser Hirsch suburb of Dresden, and Wolf joined him there later in the afternoon, accompanied by Colonel Karl-Christoph Grossmann, a zealous HVA officer who was then deputy head of Department 9. Headed by Major General Harry Schütt, it was responsible for penetrating the West German intelligence services as well as bugging official telephones in Bonn and West Berlin. It was Wolf's largest department, encompassing thirty-two sections, and Wolf acknowledged its importance by acting as its Party secretary. As second in command, Grossmann had access to the names of the HVA's senior moles in the West German security services. Like Kuron, he was also capable of betraying his own grandmother to the enemy if the price was right.

Wolf introduced himself to Kuron with the standard opening line he employed to put his top agents at ease: "Friends call me Mischa." He sized up his prospective new mole, a beefy man who looked like the successful manager of a nightclub. Under questioning, however, Kuron impressed Wolf with his razor-sharp intellect and impressive command of detail.

Kuron reiterated his basic conditions: he wanted a one-time payment amounting to three of his net annual BfV salaries, a total of nearly DM 150,000, and a monthly salary of DM 4,000. Wolf agreed that Kuron's salary would be equivalent to that of an East German intelligence colonel in "field operations," and that after fifteen years of service for the HVA, Kuron would be entitled to a pension at 60 percent of his former pay. The social-mindedness of this arrangement was very German.

Kuron suspected that a number of Western moles inside the KGB could be dangerous to him, so he stipulated that the information he provided to the HVA was not to be passed on to the KGB or other Warsaw Pact intelligence services without his approval. He also insisted that under no conditions were the double agents he was about to disclose to be arrested by the Stasi. Wolf agreed to everything.

Kuron proceeded to name two of his double agents, Horst and Gerlinde Garau, who had switched sides in 1976. Wolf, who had recently suffered the defection of Stiller, showed few signs of emotion on learning of their "treachery." The Garaus' defection was in no small part the result of their exposure to the West, an ideologically corrosive factor that East German intelligence struggled with from its earliest days. Since 1963 Horst Garau had worked for the HVA as an instructor responsible for maintaining contact with a handful of East German agents in West Germany. Instructors were part-time employees of the HVA who were recruited on the basis of their professional qualifications and ideological conviction. Garau agreed to work for the Stasi in return for the promise of a rapid promotion from his job as a school superintendent. But like so many others who were lured into working for the HVA, Garau was also tempted by the chance to get a look at the forbidden world beyond the Berlin Wall. He signed a pledge to serve State Security. Garau's wife, Gerlinde, a school director, also joined the HVA as an instructor.

On his frequent visits to the West, Garau explained the HVA's instructions to his agents, listened to their problems, and relayed them back to headquarters along with espionage material.

Despite making many dangerous missions to the West using forged West German identity papers, the Garaus grew disappointed over their lack of career opportunities. Even more telling was the impact of the West on the couple. They were no longer as docile as their compatriots. On an assignment in the West in 1976, Horst Garau contacted West German counterespionage and was put in touch with Klaus Kuron. The two men got along famously. Garau disclosed all that he knew about his agents in West Germany and let the BfV copy the espionage material he had gathered from them. For once, West German counterintelligence had penetrated Wolf's lair and knew exactly what he was getting from several of his agents. The BfV had no intention of arresting the East German spies as this would have given away Garau.

As the afternoon wore on at the Stasi mansion, Wolf and Kuron hammered out the details of their work arrangement. Once Kuron began working for the Stasi, Wolf would tell him broadly what he wanted to know about West German counterintelligence and its double agents. But he would leave it up to Kuron, the counterintelligence expert, to decide what information to pass on to East Berlin. Kuron was flattered and impressed. He told Wolf about his superior, Hansjoachim Tiedge, a bon vivant and alcoholic who, like Kuron, lived well above his means. The information would prove valuable to Wolf in a few years' time.

Kuron was told that Gunther Nehls would be his controller and that he would have *treffs* with him once or twice a year in another Western country. Courier *treffs* for handing over information would be arranged whenever and wherever Kuron wished. Kuron would also be able to transmit information in high-density taped format via telephone. He was not asked to sign anything and was given the code name Berger.

With business out of the way at their first meeting, Wolf and Kuron turned to the pleasurable part of the evening. Drinks and dinner were served by discreet, specially trained State Security waiters. Wolf laughed heartily at the jokes Kuron cracked in a droll Rhenish dialect that reminded him of his father's. Afterward, in the basement bar, Wolf presented a slide show of his own photos of scenic sites in the GDR. Wolf catered to Germans' deep-seated yearning for security and order that made them plan their lives in such detail. He left his Western moles with the reassuring belief that they would have a harmonious, long-term relationship with the HVA. Wolf took leave of Kuron the next morning after breakfast, saying that he was looking forward to meeting him again in 1984. Kuron left Dresden for home, using the same roundabout route by which he had come.

Back in Cologne, Kuron busily relayed inside information to East Berlin, including the code names of more East German agents who had defected to the BfV. One of them was Joachim Moitzheim, a portly worried-looking man, who had spied on the BfV in Cologne for more than twenty years before he was caught in 1980 and "turned" by Kuron and Tiedge. Moitzheim was given the choice of either working as a double agent for the BfV at DM 2,000 a month or spending the next six years in prison in Cologne. He agreed to spy for West Germany. Overly eager to convince Wolf's intelligence administration, the HVA, that Moitzheim was still East Berlin's man, the BfV made a disastrous mistake: it fed him confidential data on more than eight hundred West Germans, which came from the top secret Nadis computer system operated by the West German security services. Among the names he was given to pass on to East Berlin were those of West Germans who worked on secret defense projects as well as candidates for recruitment by the BfV. This information gave East Berlin an opportunity to recruit these people even before West German counterintelligence had a chance.

Moitzheim, however, was wracked with guilt over having betrayed the socialist cause, and he reported back to East Berlin that he had been turned. Galvanized by this latest challenge to his ingenuity, Wolf approved a complex plan for Moitzheim to serve as a triple agent. Moitzheim was to continue pretending to work for the BfV while the HVA tested his true allegiance by asking him questions about the BfV to which it already had the answers. Such were the satanic games that intelligence agencies in East and West played with each other using weak, often broken individuals. Wolf played with verve, pleased with his cleverness and the ineptitude of the West German intelligence services.

Kuron hatched a fiendish plan with his new ally, Lieutenant Colonel Trögel, who headed the section that conducted espionage against the BfV. They would use Horst Garau, the double agent Kuron had recently betrayed to the HVA, as an instructor for Wolfgang, the double agent Kuron had also betrayed. Wolfgang had returned from South America with a new identity. Neither he nor Garau suspected that they had become the marionettes of Kuron and Wolf.

At his second meeting with Kuron in 1984, Wolf presented his mole with the Fatherland Order of Merit in Bronze and DM 5,000 in award money. At the cookout afterwards, Wolf promised Kuron and his wife that the HVA would give them the DM 90,000 they had asked for to buy a vacation apartment in Spain.

It should have been obvious to Kuron's superior at West German counterintelligence that Kuron was living far beyond the means of a man bringing home a salary of DM 4,000 a month. But his superior, the high-spending Hansjoachim Tiedge, was scarcely in a position to judge. By the early 1980s, Tiedge was deeply in debt, and his addiction to the bottle was so serious that he could barely drag himself through the working day. But even this significant problem went unnoticed for a long time in the amazingly lax atmosphere of the BfV; officials there even bragged about their East European girlfriends.

Gradually Tiedge's debts rose to the point where he could no longer keep them a secret from his employer and old friend Heribert Hellenbroich, president of the BfV; the two had joined the counterintelligence agency together in the mid-1960s. On August 19, 1985, after playing cards in his regular beer parlor in Cologne, Tiedge caught the train to Helmstedt, the West German border station, and boarded the 2:02 P.M. train bound for Berlin. He left the train at Marienborn, the first station in the GDR, where he identified himself to a captain in the border guards. "I want to defect," he told the astonished officer. Shortly after the defection, Tiedge's old friend Heribert Hellenbroich took the blame and resigned.

Tiedge was taken to a Stasi guesthouse outside Berlin, where he was welcomed like a long-lost son. He disclosed the names of all his double agents and the details of some eight hundred operations against the GDR. He held back nothing, knowing full well that if he omitted even the smallest detail or distorted anything even slightly he ran the risk of not being trusted by Wolf. He was not told that Klaus Kuron, his subordinate and drinking companion, had switched sides three years earlier and had since disclosed most of what Tiedge was now spilling to the HVA.

Wolf was only mildly surprised when he learned of this latest high-level defection from the West German intelligence community. He had learned all about Tiedge's weaknesses from Kuron. But Tiedge's main value to Wolf was that he freed Wolf to take action against the "treacherous" double agents at the BfV. After three years of exercising restraint in order to protect Kuron, Wolf could now spring his trap. As far as West German counterintelligence knew, the agents were betrayed by Tiedge.

Meanwhile, Kuron had promised Gerlinde and Horst Garau, his East German double agents, that he would help them escape to West Germany in late 1985, because the HVA planned to send them to the West as instructors for its agents. On August 15, 1985, the Garaus' HVA controller appeared at their weekend cottage in Cottbus and told them to accompany him to East Berlin, where they were to be prepared for a special assignment in the West. But when they arrived in Berlin, husband and wife were separated. Gerlinde Garau was taken to a Stasi safe house where a colonel bluntly told her, "You have lost your husband. Now tell us everything." After being interrogated for three days and nights she was formally arrested, taken to prison, and given a lawyer. He advised her to save herself by telling the Stasi everything; her husband was beyond help.

Horst Garau was sentenced in December 1986 by a military court to life imprisonment as a West German spy and thrown into an isolation cell at the infamous Bautzen II prison. Severely ill, Gerlinde was released four months later. The Stasi ordered her to leave Cottbus and make no contact with friends or acquaintances there. She was to tell anyone who inquired about the whereabouts of her husband that he was abroad and that they had been separated. She returned to her hometown of Torgau to live with her sister, the only person who knew what had happened.

During the visits that she was allowed to have with her imprisoned husband, Gerlinde Garau saw a broken man who spoke with her as if in a trance. In July 1988 she was called to prison and told that her husband had committed suicide. In the morgue she saw her husband's head covered with blood but could detect no sign that he had hanged himself. Only after insisting was she given a death certificate by the prison warden. No death notice was permitted, and no one except Gerlinde Garau and her sister was allowed to attend the macabre burial ceremony held at her husband's unmarked grave. Frau Garau was convinced that Wolf and the Stasi had murdered her husband, and she vowed that one day she would take revenge on Wolf.

Kuron said later that although Wolf had assured him that the Garaus would be allowed to leave the GDR, he gave in to pressure from Mielke and senior HVA officers who were against showing any leniency toward a traitor. Gerlinde Garau was kept under close observation by the Stasi until the collapse of the Communist regime. Only then did she dare seek out the help of someone she trusted, her former controller at BfV headquarters in Cologne, Klaus Kuron. The man who had betrayed Gerlinde Garau and her husband received her warmly, listened sympathetically to her story, and promised to help.

Harsh as Horst Garau's sentence was, State Security dealt even more severely with its staff officers who betrayed the GDR or were suspected of doing so. The oath they had taken for the Stasi ended with the words "If I ever violate this my solemn oath, may I be punished severely under the laws of our Republic and with the contempt of the working people." The death sentence was not abolished in the GDR until 1987.

After the Stasi failed in its efforts to track down and kidnap Werner Stiller, after his defection early in 1979 the agency and the East German leadership were determined to set an example of what would happen to any future traitors. In a meeting attended by Wolf and other senior Stasi officers in 1982, Mielke spoke openly about what would happen to traitors, using the pithy language of his old working-class neighborhood in Berlin: "Unfortunately we are not immune to having an occasional bastard among us. If I knew who it was now, he wouldn't be alive tomorrow. I'd make very short work of it. That's my opinion because I'm a humanist. All that crap about not executing and no death sentence — all rubbish, Comrades."

The first victim of the GDR's wrath was Winfried Zakrzowski, a former naval captain in East German military intelligence. Zakrzowski, like so many major and minor espionage players, had sunk into an alcoholic stupor and was fired by his employer. In 1979, the same year that Stiller absconded to the West with damaging details of Wolf's espionage network, Zakrzowski disclosed to West Germany's Federal Intelligence Agency (BND) the names of several GDR military intelligence agents operating in West Germany. He desperately hoped that in return the BND would help smuggle him out to the West along with his girlfriend.

Buoyed by Stiller's defection and the arrest of his betrayed HVA agents, Klaus Kinkel, head of the BND, had visions of a repeat performance. Although Zakrzowski's alcoholism had virtually paralyzed him, a BND courier was dispatched to Poland in an attempt to smuggle him and his partner out to the West. The Stasi, however, intercepted Zakrzowski's invisible ink communications with the BND and arrested him and his girlfriend in East Berlin only a few months after they made contact with the BND.

After interrogating the couple, the Stasi located the BND courier, who had been sent to Poland, and discovered that he was a former East German intelligence courier who had been turned into a double agent by the BND. Wolf and several aides personally flew to Warsaw to get the Polish authorities to arrest the man. With the courier in tow, Wolf returned to East Berlin. During the flight the double agent made one last desperate attempt to convince Wolf to allow him to work as a triple agent for the HVA. But his request was met with icy silence.

Zakrzowski, in his last words to the GDR military tribunal in early July 1980, in East Berlin, called on the court to give him the "possibility to die" because he could not bear the thought of a life sentence. But the Stasi had long since determined that he would be put to death in Leipzig by the Stasi's executioner, Major Hermann Lorenz. On July 18, 1980, Zakrzowski was shot at close range in the back of the head. He was buried in Leipzig in an unmarked grave. His girlfriend was sentenced to fifteen years in prison and was released in a spy swap in 1987.

At least ten Stasi officers were sentenced to death by the High Court of the GDR. Nearly a year after Zakrowski's execution, on June 26, 1981, Captain Werner Teske, one of Wolf's officers from the same department as Werner Stiller, was executed in Leipzig for espionage and desertion. Teske had smuggled documents out of HVA headquarters and concealed them in the basement of his house. At his trial he admitted that he had planned to defect to West Germany's BND. The East German authorities forbade him to reveal that he had not yet made contact with the BND. Teske's widow served a ten-month sentence in a Stasi prison.

Frau Teske was less censorious than Gerlinde Garau about Wolf's role in the death of her husband: "The way I look at it, you cannot place the sole responsibility on him. He was part of a group, and the whole trial was preprogrammed. It was a warning to other officers who might have had similar ideas." Wolf later insisted that not only had he played no part in Teske's execution and that of the others, but also he had never even been told what had happened to them.

Americans, too, spied for East Germany. Specialist James W. Hall III worked in the U.S. Army's top secret electronic surveillance installation in West Berlin. Field Station Berlin, as the listening post was innocuously named, employed 1,300 skilled technicians around the clock and was located on top of the city's highest hill, Teufelsberg, which was built after 1945 using the bombed ruins of Berlin. Just below the facility, children flew kites in the summer and sledded in the winter. It was common knowledge in West Berlin that the facility's "big ears" — its enormous radar domes — were able to eavesdrop on the Warsaw Pact's military forces in

East Germany and Poland. But in reality the surveillance equipment could penetrate far into the western part of the Soviet Union. The United States used the Teufelsberg electronic warfare installation to listen in on Soviet military communications during the critical months in 1981 when Soviet forces appeared to be poised for an invasion of Poland.

The enormous range and versatility of Field Station Berlin were known only to the ultrasecret National Security Agency at Fort Meade, Maryland, the nerve center of America's electronic eavesdropping. That, at least, was what U.S. intelligence officials had been telling themselves until 1988. Thanks to Specialist Hall, senior analyst of intercepted radio and telephone traffic and coded messages, Markus Wolf and his Soviet friends discovered just how thoroughly the Americans had electronically tapped the Warsaw Pact's defense communications.

By 1982 Hall had been in West Berlin long enough to know that even with the cushion of the Army PX, his pay as an E-4 was not going to get him very far. The declining U.S. dollar had boosted the price of a whiskey in the Berlin bars to the equivalent of $4.00. He told Hussein Yildirim, a Turkish-born mechanic in the U.S. Army auto repair shop, that he needed money. The army's auto shop was open to U.S. soldiers and civilians, and my eldest son, Tom, often worked on his car there. He knew Yildirim as a good-natured, helpful man who was nicknamed Meister (for master craftsman). But Yildirim had another employer, the HVA in East Berlin. After he told his controlling officer about Hall, GDR intelligence made Specialist Hall a financial offer that he could not resist and gave him the code name Ronny.

Col. Klaus Eichner, the middle-aged deputy head of HVA counterintelligence, was the analyst who evaluated Hall's top secret information. His department dealt with the Western intelligence agencies and was directly accountable to Markus Wolf. The mild-mannered Colonel Eichner quickly realized that with Hall the HVA had struck gold. The highly classified data the American could pass to the HVA dealt with Soviet military communications that were being intercepted by the Teufelsberg installation. Once Hall's information was handed on by Wolf to the KGB, the Soviets would have several options. They could attempt to protect the content of their radio communications, stop using the monitored channels altogether, or deceive the Americans by sending altered data over the air.

The HVA paid Hall up to $30,000 a year for his information, twice what he was earning at the time from the U.S. Army. Yildirim acted as his courier and paymaster. Hall would hand over stolen documents to Yildirim in the Army PX in Frankfurt and at other U.S. Army facilities. The two would copy stolen documents by day and by night in a small apartment Hall had rented in Frankfurt. The copies were then packed into a car, which the Turk drove back to Berlin. Hall then returned the original documents.

Once Hall mentioned to Colonel Kenneth Roney, commander of Field Station Berlin, that he had bought a Volvo for $25,000 cash. Colonel Roney began wondering about Hall, since he himself was finding it difficult to purchase the same car on a higher salary. But the colonel's doubts were assuaged when Hall told him that he and his wife had managed to save the money by dint of their thriftiness. Judged by his superiors to be a talented analyst of electronic intelligence, Hall was quickly promoted to supervisor.

After further training in the United States in 1985, Hall was assigned to a military intelligence battalion of the Fifth Army Corps in Frankfurt, where he served in supervisory positions. Eventually he was appointed to head the battalion's electronic warfare and signals intelligence operations section. Among the classified defense information Hall passed on to the HVA was the National Sigint Requirements List (NSRL), a four-thousand-page manual detailing how the armed forces could use electronic surveillance to gain military and political information on America's enemies and friends for U.S. intelligence and the State Department. The documents named military installations, companies, and research institutes in Warsaw Pact and NATO countries that were of particular interest to Washington. But perhaps the most important document stolen by Hall was Canopy Wing. It listed the types of electronic warfare needed to neutralize the strategic centers of the Soviet Union and the Warsaw Pact countries, as well as the measures required to deprive the Soviet High

Command of the ability to effectively use high-frequency communications to control its armed forces. Once the Russians knew what to expect, they were able to take countermeasures. In the eyes of the KGB and the Soviet military command, Markus Wolf and the HVA had helped prevent a potentially lethal blow to the Soviet motherland.

In the five years that he spied for the GDR, Hall was subjected to only one army security clearance, just before he began spying. Yildirim never needed clearance, since he had no access to classified information. They were ideal partners in treason, normal as could be and well liked. But they grew addicted to the money and started to believe that they were immune from detection. It was an illusion to which most spies succumbed after working undetected for several years.

Wolf was only mildly surprised when he learned that his former top American spy, Warrant Officer James W. Hall III, had been arrested in December 1988 in the United States together with Yildirim. It was greed that finally did them in. Having tasted big money from the HVA, Hall could not resist when an FBI agent posing as a Soviet spy proposed that they meet at a hotel in Savannah, Georgia. When he arrived for the meeting, Hall was arrested on the spot. Yildirim was also brought in.

Hall pleaded guilty to ten counts of espionage at a court martial in Washington D.C. During his trial it was revealed that he had given his fellow officers six conflicting stories to explain his lavish lifestyle, without ever arousing suspicion. In addition, a routine lie detector test he was to have taken in 1985 was never administered because of an army shortage of examiners. After admitting to receiving more than $100,000 in espionage pay from 1983 to 1988, Hall was sentenced to forty years' imprisonment and fined $50,000. Yildirim was also convicted of espionage at his trial in Savannah, Georgia. The prosecution disclosed that he had been far more than a simple courier; he had used his job as an army automotive repair instructor in Berlin to "run" several other spies in addition to Hall.

As for American spies in East Germany, Colonel Eichner was later scathing in his opinion about the CIA's clumsy attempts to penetrate the GDR. He said that virtually all the CIA's agents in

the GDR — most had been recruited among East Germans serving abroad — were, in fact, double agents who worked for Wolf's
counterespionage against the CIA.

Even while Wolf's espionage feats continued to dazzle both his
enemies and his allies in the 1980s, he was growing skeptical
about the value of the intelligence his HVA was gathering, given
the enormous cost. At the same time he saw himself as a prisoner
of the system and felt he could do nothing to discourage the
ballooning of his espionage service. The truth was that after more
than thirty years, espionage had lost its fascination for him.

He had achieved as much as he could ever have hoped for.
Friend and foe alike recognized him as one of the foremost
practitioners of his craft. Kuron and Gast had laid the West
German security agencies bare. Wolf's man inside NATO headquarters in Brussels, Rainer Rupp, alias Topas, was providing him
with the rundown on defense capabilities of all NATO member
nations. Vladimir Kryuchkov, the KGB chief, was fascinated by
the German translations of Rupp's material that Wolf's agency was
sending him, and begged to be given the original English version.
It was not until 1994, after twenty-one years of spying for the East,
that the repentant forty-nine-year-old Rupp was sentenced to
twelve years in prison and fined DM 300,000 for betraying secrets
that, in the event of an East-West war, would have had "disastrous
consequences" for NATO, in the view of the court.

Wolf was painfully aware that despite all the top secret
military, political, and industrial documents his agents had managed to obtain, East German industry was decaying, and the
economic gap between the Warsaw Pact countries and the West
was widening inexorably. Yet what could one do without playing
into the hands of the enemy? One could only hope, he told his
family, that the sclerotic leaders in East Berlin and Moscow would
soon pass away so that younger, more intelligent officials could
guide the countries out of their decline.

His brother Koni finally lost his long, agonizing battle with
cancer in 1982, and his courage left a deep impression on
Markus. Koni had been the conscience of the Wolf family, help-

ing intellectuals in political hot water by putting in a good word for them with the leadership. As a former Red Army officer, president of the Academy of Arts, and the GDR's leading film-maker, Koni was one of the few intellectuals respected by Erich Honecker, East Germany's leader. Markus knew how despondent his brother had been about the stranglehold the Party's hardliners had on the country. But Koni had managed to heed his father's admonition to "act on the courage of your convictions," Markus told himself. He and Koni had often spoken about the fossilized leaderships in Moscow and East Berlin, reverting to Russian whenever the conversation got especially heated. Koni had been his own repressed conscience, the sole person to whom he had been able to express his political doubts. Markus was proud of his brother, his achievements, and the respect in which he was held.

Koni's death made Markus think seriously about how much longer he would remain on as head of the HVA. He had reached the pinnacle of his career, and Mielke, despite his advanced age, showed no sign of stepping down and making way for a younger man. Besides, Markus had no ambition to head a monstrous domestic repression machine.

Wolf was determined to break away from intelligence work and try something new. As a "Combatant against Fascism," he was entitled to early retirement and was sorely tempted to take it. During one of his last conversations with Markus, Koni had spoken about the film project that he would be unable to finish. The film was to be about the lives of three boys who had been friends in Moscow; one of them was Koni. Wolf decided that taking on such a project might be a good change for him. He thought back to his early postwar years as a journalist, the profession the Party had forced him to abandon. He recalled the satisfaction he had gained from writing his commentaries for Berlin Radio, finding just the right word. It had made him appreciate his father's writing even more. The idea of once again trying his hand with words took hold.

Mielke scowled when Wolf told him that he was interested in working on a TV film about his late brother, Koni, together with the leading documentary filmmaker Lew Hohmann. Intelligence chiefs did not make films, Mielke remarked bitingly. But in the end he reluctantly consented, and the film was completed. Wolf found the work a welcome change from his normal routine and decided that he would soon apply for early retirement. Werner Grossmann, his deputy, was perfectly capable of assuming his functions, he said.

Wolf had a special reason to smile as he opened the Party newspaper, *Neues Deutschland*, on the morning of January 19, 1983, his sixtieth birthday. Prominently displayed on page 2 was a message of congratulations from Erich Honecker. In it the leader extolled Wolf for "struggling untiringly" to carry out the Party's decrees, "smashing" the enemy's subversive plans, and playing an important role in developing and strengthening the State Security Ministry. The Party thanked "dear Comrade Wolf" for his long-standing work and preparedness in the defense of the German Democratic Republic and awarded Colonel General Markus Wolf the "Hero of Labor" medal. Could there be a more opportune time for Wolf to relinquish his post?

When Wolf submitted his application to "retire from service" in the MfS (Stasi) shortly afterward, Mielke flew into a rage. Where would we be if everyone abandoned his work in order to follow his leanings? he barked. Wolf replied that he would always be available to the MfS whenever it needed his advice. Mielke objected that Honecker and the Soviets would not approve of his plans. Yet the more Mielke thought about it, the more the idea began to appeal to him. Grossmann, after all, was far more pliable than Wolf and would be easier to control. All the same, Mielke was in no hurry to work out the extraordinary arrangements of Wolf's retirement.

It would be three years before Markus would gain his separation from the Stasi. In the meantime, his second marriage began to founder. Christa had long sensed that something was wrong in their marriage, but she told herself that things would be better once Markus retired. She did not yet realize that she had already lost him to another woman. In March 1985 when the Wolfs invited Christa's lifelong girlfriend, Andrea, and her husband to spend a weekend with them at their lakeside dacha in Prenden,

Christa discovered what had come between her and Markus. During that weekend Markus and Andrea unabashedly made love, and Markus made no attempt to deny the affair when Christa confronted him with the evidence. Trembling with anger, Christa recalled that Markus had once told her about the gypsy who had predicted that he would marry three times. She could not get over how unfairly she had been treated. Above all, she was incensed that her closest friend had deceived her. She was certain that Andrea had taken up with Markus because her own marriage was a failure and because she saw that Christa had found happiness with Markus.

Markus tried to console Christa, but he also admitted that he was unable to live without Andrea. He urged Christa to consult a neurologist, recalling that his own mother, Else, had spent time in a mental clinic after the war. Christa did not need to be told that Friedrich Wolf's affairs had been the root of the problem. Ironically Markus was telling her that she would have to take antidepressants if she, too, wanted to avoid being sent to an institution.

In early 1986 Mielke learned of Wolf's marital problems and told him that he would have to choose between Christa and Andrea. State Security could not tolerate the slightest moral taint on its deputy minister, he said disapprovingly. In June he summoned Christa to his office. "Christa, you know what Mischa is like," he told her. He said he would make sure that Mischa (Markus) reached a decision soon, and, in the event of a divorce, he promised that the ministry would see to it that she was provided for. When the divorce followed, soon afterward, Christa lacked the strength to display any emotion; she felt only that her life was meaningless. The final blow came when she was told that Markus insisted on taking custody of Sascha, their son.

Mielke assigned two Stasi officers to Christa to make sure that she did not do anything foolish, like seeking contact with the BND. He was certain that the West Germans would do anything to get their tentacles around her. What ensued could have sprung from the overly fertile mind of a spy writer.

Christa managed to evade her Stasi chaperones and, during a vacation in Bulgaria with Sascha, met a West German businessman who fell in love with her. When he asked her to marry him,

Christa turned him down without explaining why or who she was. Back in East Berlin, where her telephone was bugged by the Stasi, she placed a call to her West German suitor from an outside phone. Not long afterward he saw a photo of her in a newspaper, along with an article about her divorce from Markus Wolf. He contacted the BND in Pullach and told West German intelligence that he had to get Christa out of the GDR. The BND, sensing a propaganda coup, promised to help.

Unaware of his ex-wife's predicament, Wolf worked out his separation from the HVA in late 1986 with the blessings of Mielke and the Politbüro. But both Mielke and the GDR leadership were anxious to retain Wolf's expertise, and he was eager to keep a number of benefits. He was given an MfS (Stasi) office and provided with two assistants, a driver and a secretary, all State Security employees. Even his maid belonged to the Stasi, which paid 700 GDR Marks toward her 1,100 GDR Marks monthly wage. Wolf was also entitled to medical treatment at the MfS hospital, as well as access to the agency's special shops.

But the pièce de résistance was the apartment at 2 Spree-ufer, in the newly rebuilt historic Nikolai district of East Berlin, that Wolf and his new wife, Andrea, moved into. The MfS picked up the hard currency portion of the bill—DM 200,000 out of a whopping total of 545,752 GDR Marks—for furnishing and equipping the luxurious duplex that overlooked an arm of the Spree River. For that, Wolf got a solarium, assorted electronic gadgetry, and the latest West German kitchen equipment and bathroom fixtures. Wolf's monthly rent for the flat was a mere 298 GDR Marks. His pension amounted to 6,500 GDR Marks a month; the average East German pension was less than 300 GDR Marks a month.

During this time Wolf buried himself in Koni's notes. The book that emerged, The Troika (three), was ostensibly about Koni and his two boyhood friends in prewar Moscow. One of the friends was Lothar, the son of Wilhelm Wloch, the Comintern agent who died on his way to one of Stalin's gulags. The third boy was Viktor Fischer, son of Louis Fischer, an American correspondent who was based in Moscow. Despite their separation by the Second World War, the three managed to renew their friendship in defeated Berlin in 1945. Koni wore the uniform of a lieutenant in the Red Army; Viktor's brother George, who took his place in the troika, was a U.S. Army officer; and Lothar Wloch, who had returned to Berlin after fighting for Hitler on the Eastern front, was back in civilian clothes.

It was not the tale of the three friends that made Wolf's book a sensation when it appeared in March 1989, at a time when the East German regime was vigorously resisting and warning against Mikhail Gorbachev's policy of glasnost in the Soviet Union. In The Troika Wolf broke an East German taboo by describing Stalin's mass arrests. Worse still, the account came from the former deputy head of the Stasi, an institution that owed its origins to Stalinism. Although he had shown no sympathy with dissidents in the GDR, Wolf wrote that he opposed using force against them and explained that two of Koni's boyhood friends in Moscow later became dissidents. One of them, Julius Hay, took part in the Hungarian uprising in 1956, and the other, Andrej Sinyavski, the oppositional Soviet writer, was sentenced to a long prison term in Moscow. Wolf wrote in The Troika that it had always been "our opinion"—his brother's and his—that politics should be rendered more transparent. He criticized the leadership for ignoring Koni's advice that East German youth be subjected to less control and be given more independence.

With The Troika a new Wolf emerged, and millions of East Germans liked what they were hearing. Among Wolf's supporters were several of his former moles in the West who by this time were also living on pensions in the GDR. During a visit to Johanna Olbrich in Bernau, Wolf spoke about the need for political and economic reforms. Although skeptical, she said that she hoped he would succeed in his work for change. Wolf arranged a reunion with his former "spies on the invisible front" in an unusual setting—an exclusive new Chinese restaurant located only a few hundred yards from Checkpoint Charlie. The ex-spies, who had often eaten Chinese food in the West, gave the food high marks for authenticity. But they were caustic in their criticism of Honecker and the other fogies who were driving East Germans out of the country in record numbers.

Overnight, Wolf was miraculously transformed into a

standard-bearer for reform, a disciple of former KGB chief Yuri Andropov (by then deceased), who had become a critic of the orthodox leadership because of his intimate knowledge of the Soviet empire's fatal economic backwardness. In his 1989 diary, published in 1991, Wolf admitted that perhaps his own belated attempt at reform was "too cautious, too tame and much too late."

The question was, did Wolf, the tactician par excellence, turn reformer out of pure calculation? After all, he must have known that with Gorbachev in power in Moscow, the days of the orthodox East German leadership were numbered. Wolf may well have hoped that a reform Communist regime would come to power in East Berlin, and that he would play an important, if not the most important, role in the new administration, especially when his close friend, Hans Modrow, the reform-minded Party chief of Dresden district, became the new East German prime minister.

Wolf reveled in his new role as a dissident, condemning the GDR's banning of the pro-glasnost Soviet magazine *Sputnik* in interviews with the West German media and taking part in public readings from his book, in which he would cite his father's letter urging his sons to act on the courage of their convictions. For the first time in his life, Wolf was able to follow his father's advice. He was secure in the knowledge that his high-level contacts to the KGB and the Central Committee in Moscow protected him from retaliation by the Honecker regime. Even the American ambassador in East Berlin, Richard C. Barkley, sought Wolf's views on the future of the GDR over dinner at his residence — which was bugged by the Stasi. And Wolf dutifully asked Mielke's permission before accepting the invitation.

Wolf succeeded in getting custody of his ten-year-old son, Sascha, who went to live with his father and Andrea in their new penthouse. Christa's nerves were in shreds. In 1987 her West German suitor wrote her a letter, passed to her via one of West Germany's BND safe drops in East Berlin, in which he promised to get her out to the West and said the details would be forthcoming. Christa suspected that the letter was a forgery concocted by the Stasi and designed to test her. She showed it to a girlfriend, who turned it over to the Stasi. Christa was told that she would remain under twenty-four-hour surveillance and that no letter or telephone call from her would ever reach the West.

Christa's depression worsened, and in July 1988, after a massive overdose of pills, she was rushed to the hospital, where she remained in a coma for five days. Mielke feared that if Christa were to die, the West Germans would launch a campaign blaming the Stasi. But Christa pulled through and returned to her apartment, still under Stasi surveillance. During a lull in the observation later in the year, Christa managed to telephone her West German friend. He told her that he had written Chancellor Helmut Kohl in a dramatic bid to get her out to the West. But her surveillance resumed, and, after a renewed fit of depression, Christa was hospitalized for three weeks.

After Christa was released, a girlfriend placed an ad for her in the lonely hearts column of an East German newspaper. Klaus, a loyal subject of the regime, replied and entered Christa's life. Wolf and the Stasi were much relieved that she had finally found someone in the GDR who cared about her.

As always, Wolf turned out to be fortunate in his choice of women. His new wife, Andrea, was dedicated to him, just as Emmi and Christa had been before her, and she would prove a devoted partner in the stormy years that lay ahead.

9

Wolf began the year 1989 firmly convinced that he was a driving force in the opposition to East Germany's dogmatic Communist leadership. He saw himself as a former Stasi general who had become a symbol of hope among East Germans. By the end of the year, though, he would once again be a Stasi general in the eyes of his people.

Throughout the year Wolf looked on with dismay as the two pillars of Communist rule in East Germany — the secret police and Moscow's military support — crumbled. This was not what he had had in mind when he spoke of reforms.

Paradoxically, as Communist rule in East Germany hurtled toward its end in late 1989, the Stasi went about the routine of informing, harassing, and coercing as if nothing had changed. One Stasi file on me was filled with warnings to the fraternal secret police services about the suspicious trips I made to Prague and Budapest up until late 1989.

In spite of its repeated operations, the Stasi was deeply vexed at not having been able to produce a shred of evidence that I was an imperialist intelligence agent. MfS counterintelligence closed and sealed its main operative dossier on me, all 237 pages, on October 9, 1985, and deposited it in the windowless nine-story archives building. Why had it taken so long? After the collapse of the Stasi, burly ex-Colonel Gerhard Behnke of the HVA gave me the absurdly simple reason: mindless bureaucracy.

Closing an operative dossier on either a victim or an "informal collaborator" of the State Security Ministry meant that a Stasi officer was required to get approval from his superior for placing the contents into the archives, page by excruciating page. For each file the procedure could take at least three weeks. The Stasi bureaucracy avoided such thankless tasks like the plague.

Behnke shook his massive head sadly when I showed him a copy of my file. "It's typical of the mentality of MfS counter-espionage, which saw nothing but spies everywhere," he said. "That is the difference between them and the HVA. I would have treated you in a completely different way. I would have cultivated you. After all, you were a correspondent for an influential news-paper and head of the Foreign Press Association in Berlin. You had many high-level contacts, and I would have tried to find out as much as I could from you." He seemed to genuinely regret that he had not had a crack at me.

A separate Stasi file on me was kept alive until late 1989. It contained the reports of border controllers at Schönefeld airport outside East Berlin who questioned and searched me on my way to other East European countries. The most grotesque entry of all I found in a report dated August 29, 1989, and submitted by the passport control unit at the airport. (By this time East Germans were fleeing to the West by the tens of thousands, via the virtually open border between Hungary and Austria, and by climbing over the gate surrounding the West German Embassy in Prague and seeking asylum. Less than two months later Communist rule in the GDR would effectively collapse.) In the late August report the controller wrote that he had determined that I was a correspon-dent bound for Prague. The "fraternal organ," again the Czechoslovakian secret police, the StB, was alerted, and it was noted that I was to be thoroughly controlled when I returned to East Germany.

But when I was in Prague, the StB was occupied with more pressing matters — a mass demonstration in the heart of the city by thousands of supporters of the opposition. When baton-wielding riot police moved to break up the crowd, I was chased along with some demonstrators into one of the arcades lining Wenceslas Square, down three staircases, and into a movie theater located in the bowels of the arcade. Sitting huddled in the near darkness among a handful of drunks and lovers as the riot policemen stormed down the aisle, I suddenly knew where Czech film-makers had gotten their inspiration.

If anything, East German leaders were even more paralyzed by the rising mass discontent than were Czechoslovak authorities. Each Monday in Leipzig the opposition was staging ever bolder and larger rallies to demand civil liberties. By mid-September 1989 I was determined to witness them.

In an effort to prevent eyewitness reports about the opposition movement in East Germany's second largest city, the government barred Western journalists from going to Leipzig. As a ruse I booked a tourist trip to Dresden, an hour's drive from Leipzig. Armed with my hotel voucher and visa, I drove on a Monday afternoon to the GDR border outside West Berlin, and less than two hours later I turned off the Autobahn at the Leipzig exit. A police control unit was waiting for me at a roadblock. The senior officer informed me sternly that I could not proceed to Leipzig. I pulled out my hotel voucher for Dresden and said that I only wanted to have lunch at the famous Auerbach's Keller in Leipzig on my way to Dresden. He studied the hotel voucher and the tourist visa in my passport, grunted, and began inspecting the tires of my car. One of my rear tires had too little tread, he decided, and it would have to be replaced immediately. All but saluting, I assured him that I would comply as soon as I reached Dresden. With that he returned my hotel voucher and waved me through the roadblock.

I parked my car at the side of the Leipzig Opera House and walked across the strangely silent street toward Nikolai Church, where a "peace" service was being held before the rally began outside. Thousands of people from all over Saxony were gathered in the small square outside Nikolai Church, listening to the service. A voice boomed over the loudspeakers of the city's public address system: "Citizens, remain calm and follow the orders of the organizers. . . ." It was one of the prominent citizens in a group that included Kurt Masur, the conductor of Leipzig's Gewandhaus orchestra, and a local Communist Party official. They were appealing to the crowd and the State Security forces for restraint.

I had begun to take notes when a young man cautioned me to put away my notebook.

"The Stasi is watching. Do you see those cameras up there?" he said, pointing at the cameras aimed at us from a nearby building.

But I felt secure surrounded by so many young East Germans. This was the "unity in protest" that I remembered experiencing in Prague after the Soviet-led invasion in 1968 and in Gdańsk (Danzig) in 1980. I had never thought that I would one day witness it in the GDR.

The crowd slowly began to move toward the opera house and the ring boulevard that encircles central Leipzig. Banners were unfurled, and chants of "Legalize New Forum," the opposition movement, rang out. The sky above was streaked red with gaseous pollution. The only uniforms in sight were occasional policemen watching from the side of the street. I turned to interview the man walking next to me, Herbert John, a scientist from nearby Halle. He had joined the New Forum to protest the massive water and air pollution in the chemical-producing region where he lived. Little did either of us imagine that in less than six months he would be elected mayor of the blighted city of Merseburg.

The number of marchers swelled as more and more Leipzigers who had been watching from the sidelines joined in. By the time the protesters passed the huge main railroad station they numbered several hundred thousand people. I looked into the side streets for signs of the security forces, but there were none. At the corner of Dittrich Ring we passed the large curved building known locally as the Round Corner, Leipzig district headquarters of the Stasi. The crowd began shouting "Security out!" to a row of jack-booted guards outside the building. If there was going to be violence, it would happen here. But all of a sudden several young demonstrators walked over to the guards, lit candles, and placed them at the guards' feet. The guards gazed nervously at the candles and into the faces of the young men and women who smiled reassuringly. The crucial moment passed without incident.

I ran toward the nearby Hotel Stadt Leipzig to write my story for the first edition of the *Financial Times* in London. First, I stopped to speak with the hotel's middle-aged telephone operator, who would be the key to my success or failure. I convinced her that she was an important link between Leipzig and the outside world. Without pause, she repeatedly dialed the area code for Britain until, some twenty minutes later, the line suddenly came alive and my newspaper answered. I rushed into the phone booth in the lobby and dictated my story. By the time I emerged, steaming, from the airless booth, the peaceful protest march by a record number of East Germans was over, and the crowd was dispersing. I had been the only Western newspaperman to make it to Leipzig that day.

A few weeks later, on September 27, 1989 — only eleven days before the fortieth and last anniversary of the GDR — the final page was entered in my Stasi file of the GDR. I was the subject of a letter from Major General Damm to the head of counterintelligence, Lt. Gen. Günther Kratsch, informing him that he was getting a report from the border controllers at Schönefeld airport on the above-named American citizen for "your information and operative analysis." By this time, however, the Stasi's analysts had nearly come to the end of their rope.

As of September 1989 Wolf was still going strong. His opposition to the orthodox leadership in East Berlin was enthusiastically backed by many Party functionaries who had silently hoped for decades that the system would renew itself. Even many East German intellectuals, long browbeaten and compromised by the Stasi, regarded Wolf as the key to future reforms. But what did ordinary East Germans think of him?

The answer came on November 4, 1989. On that day I stood in a crowd of more than half a million East Germans at a rally for Freedom of Opinion, Press, and Assembly on East Berlin's Alexanderplatz. Not a policeman could be seen. Among the speakers, Wolf waited, wearing an open raincoat, sweater, and tie. When his turn came, like an early Soviet revolutionary he mounted the rear of the truck that was serving as a makeshift speaker's platform. His left hand stuck nonchalantly in his trouser pocket, he began to speak. In the stilted, wooden language he often adopted in public, he criticized the former Communist leadership under Honecker for living in a make-believe world and for failing to act even when East Germans began to leave the GDR in droves. "That was bitter for us Communists," he said.

The crowd began to whistle disapprovingly. Ignoring them, Wolf went on to criticize the regime for holding a torchlight rally and military parade the previous month to celebrate the fortieth anniversary of the GDR. Wolf's flow of words was interrupted by ever louder catcalls. He spoke of the people having won their freedom of expression in the streets and squares. This time the crowd applauded. He recalled the hundreds of thousands of Communists who had worked "honestly and actively" and now expected a clear new direction. The whistling resumed and grew more intense as he spoke of renewing socialism. I began to feel sorry for him.

He mentioned the book he had written in which he advocated openly discussing the truth, acting on the courage of one's convictions, and working for the humane treatment of dissidents. There was a ripple of applause. Was Wolf's tactic working?

"If we want to continue on the path of renewal with reason and prudence, then I must object to the way many employees of this ministry, whom I have known for many years, are now to be turned into the whipping boys of the nation," Wolf said in the face of a rising chorus of whistles and deafening catcalls.

Refusing to give up, he paid tribute to his hero, Mikhail Gorbachev, but the crowd, which idolized Gorbachev, signaled that it had had its fill of Wolf. "*Aufhören!*" (stop) the citizens who stood around me chanted. Yet Wolf, the veins bulging in his neck, went on about perestroika and glasnost while the crowd loudly vented its displeasure. His face white with shock, he finally stepped down from the truck platform. Evidently the people refused to accept his claim that he and his fellow Stasi officers had acted in good faith. East Germans would not forget or forgive so easily.

Later he would acknowledge this decisive defeat in his brief career as a reformer, but in his published diary of the events of

1989, Wolf wrote that after the rally he viewed the video of his speech at home, and he told himself that it had been "right." Here was the old Wolf, the indefatigable Communist trooper.

Less than a week later I was surrounded by tens of thousands of East Germans swarming through the glittering center of West Berlin like small children in a toy store. Many of them, including East German officials, were lined up in front of the banks to receive their "welcome money" of DM 50 from the West German government.

The evening before, November 9, 1989, the new Party leader, Egon Krenz, in a last desperate attempt to gain support, announced an innocuous-sounding bureaucratic arrangement that would allow citizens to visit the West. Only a few hours afterward, faced with thousands of boisterous citizens who were clamoring to cross into West Berlin, East German border guards hastily opened the frontier barriers. Thousands of East Berliners, on foot and in Trabant and Wartburg cars, surged across the border that had divided Berlin for twenty-eight years.

The opening of the Berlin Wall caught Wolf as much by surprise as anyone. He criticized the decision as an expression of "panic" by the new Party leadership and condemned the "spontaneous reunification" that took place when East Germans streamed across to see, touch, and even to buy the forbidden fruits of the West. His sights firmly fixed on Gorbachev, Wolf was confident that a reformed Party would be able to keep East Germans where they were best off, in the warm, sticky nest of the socialist GDR.

But even Wolf's reforms looked like a vague prospect as long as Erich Mielke and his Stasi were still going strong. After Mielke gave his final performance on November 13, 1989, in the rump GDR Parliament, Wolf had nothing but scorn for his former boss. The Stasi chief brusquely introduced himself as "Mielke, minister of State Security" to the other deputies, then he defended the Stasi's brutal crackdown on demonstrators the previous month. His remarks that the employees of the MfS, the "sons and daughters of the working class," had "extraordinarily close contact with all working people" evoked loud laughter from the deputies. But the eighty-two-year-old Mielke could not be stopped. He praised the Stasi for having provided the leadership with excellent information about "everything that was aimed against peace," everything that had brought things "to where they are now, comrades, not only in the GDR but the socialist camp." Called to order for addressing the deputies as "Comrades" — members of the noncommunist bloc parties were also present — Mielke objected that this was merely a "formal question." His remark met with heated protest.

"But I love everyone, every human being!" Mielke insisted. His fellow deputies laughed derisively, so did the many Stasi informers among them. He claimed that State Security had dutifully informed the leadership about all the difficulties and shortcomings in the GDR, but no one had listened. It was his last public remark that anyone would remember.

Less than a month later he was arrested and detained until his scheduled trial in February 1992. To the astonishment of his former subjects, at first Mielke was charged not with crimes against his fellow citizens, as might have been expected, but in connection with a case the prosecution believed would be easier to win. It was his alleged murder of two Berlin policemen in 1931, details of which had been locked up in Mielke's safe since the end of the Second World War. Ironically, his former "friends" in Moscow provided the prosecution with Mielke's own damaging account which he had written in 1931 after his escape to Moscow. In the document, he bragged that he had indeed committed "terrorist acts" for the German Communist Party and had "taken care" of two policemen. The trial ended in October 1993 in a six-year prison sentence for Mielke, by that point nearing his eighty-sixth birthday. After serving four years in detention, he was freed from Moabit Prison in Berlin on August 1, 1995, as obdurate and unrepentant as when he entered.

For Wolf the opening of the Berlin Wall and the border between East and West Germany meant that in the eyes of most East Germans he was identified with the dark past. Citizens were incensed by a flood of revelations about Stasi human rights violations, the wheelings and dealings of KoKo (Commercial Coordination), and the moral corruption of the old Communist leadership. At the weekly demonstrations in Leipzig, the battle cry switched from "We are the people" to "We are one people." East Germans were in no mood for further socialist experiments and were looking to Bonn for their economic salvation.

Wolf's embattled former colleagues from State Security were seeking his advice and support as never before. He gave them his counsel in person and in writing, urging them to remain loyal and not to commit "treason" by defecting to the Western security services. He also advised the interim Communist government, under the leadership of his reform-minded friend Hans Modrow, on how to reform the new Office for National Security — the old Stasi in a new guise. Wolf's ideas on retaining a democratized intelligence service even found support among some former East German dissidents.

But the hopes for a new intelligence agency crashed to oblivion in the final weeks of 1989 when angry citizens decided to occupy the regional branches of the Stasi. Surprisingly they met with virtually no resistance. The once terrifying might of the Stasi melted away once its leadership lost the will to defend the corrupt and discredited system. On January 19, 1990, the Stasi's last bastion, in East Berlin, came under assault.

Lt. Col. Horst Wittke, who was in charge of security at East German intelligence headquarters, will never forget that day. At five that afternoon he sat and waited tensely inside the totally darkened HVA building. Outside the Normannenstrasse gate of the State Security Ministry, a crowd of several thousand irate East Germans chanted, "Let us in." Wittke and the handful of officers who were with him had handed in their pistols to the HVA weapons room earlier in the afternoon. They had been given ample time to prepare for this day. The Citizen's Committee had announced three weeks earlier that it planned to take over MfS headquarters. An HVA officer thought he could prevent the crowd from breaking in by identifying the purpose of the building. A sign posted outside read "Aufklärung" (intelligence).

The heavy steel gate, guarded by fifteen ordinary policemen instead of the normal detachment of the MfS guard regiment, swung open to the cheers of the demonstrators who spilled onto the grounds like a crowd of crazed soccer fans. The demonstrators showed not the least interest in HVA headquarters, where Lieutenant Colonel Wittke sat waiting for them. Instead they broke into the long services building of State Security, smashing windows and ransacking offices. Bottles of Western liquor that had been found were held up triumphantly as proof of the Stasi's decadence.

But at the same time a handful of men posing as demonstrators were making their way across a glass-enclosed bridge and entering the MfS counterintelligence department. Guided by instructions from recent Stasi defectors, they broke open filing cabinets and rifled through the contents until they found and removed the documents that were of interest to Western intelligence agencies. CIA agents managed to corner a large number of the pilfered documents, putting the West Germans in the humiliating position of having to ask Langley, Virginia, for information on individuals in the Stasi files.

For the time being, though, the Stasi's inner sanctum, the concealed Central Archives building, remained undiscovered. The windowless nine-story building erected in 1984, contained nearly eighteen and a half miles of files on nearly four million East Germans and two million West Germans (and a sprinkling of foreigners like myself). Victims and informers lay back-to-back on the shelves. The Central Archives building could be detected only by an aircraft flying overhead, surrounded as it was by a twelve-story office building housing the archivists. Access to the archives was from a wing of the outer office building that consisted solely of passageways. An outsider would be unable to find his way into the archives without help from the inside. The first to discover the archives was the Citizen's Committee, which in the following months took over control of the files. The committee and its successor, the German Office on the Stasi files, headed by Joachim Gauck, a former Protestant minister, found itself entirely dependent on former Stasi archivists to find the names for which they were searching.

At nine o'clock on the night of January 19, when the demonstration was over, Lieutenant Colonel Wittke telephoned the police detachment to inform them that he and a few other HVA security officers were still in the building. Later in the evening MfS (Stasi) officers and their families ventured out from nearby apartment buildings to view their ransacked offices firsthand. They shook their heads, muttering about the "senseless" reprisal. Mainly, though, they were afraid that the people would now vent their anger against MfS employees.

The Round Table (responsible for governing East Germany until the first free elections on March 18) set up a committee on February 8, 1990, to dissolve the Stasi, and Lieutenant Colonel Wittke was appointed a member. With Germanic thoroughness, even in defeat, the committee arranged for every last *treff* by a HVA controller with his agent to be reported on and approved by the committee, along with the officers' final payment. The HVA's agents still active in the West were to be discharged and protected from arrest. Wittke and his fellow officers were to make certain that the HVA's files were totally destroyed so that the names of agents would not fall into the hands of the West German intelligence services.

By the time the committee was set up, though, the secret police had had months to get rid of its most incriminating records. The Citizens Committees had showed unbelievable naiveté in trusting in the "security partnership" they had formed with former senior Stasi officers, the People's Police, as well as the state prosecutor. Stasi officers helping to dissolve the MfS were allowed to leave their former offices, uncontrolled, carrying bulging, briefcases. In this way they were able to remove and reduce to pulp many files on prominent East Germans who had worked as Stasi informers.

By the end of March the Central Intelligence Administration, the HVA, was dismantled, its files destroyed, and most of its officers dispersed. Former Colonel Klaus Eichner was among the officers who helped disband East German intelligence under the supervision of the Round Table. "I destroyed my life's work, so to speak," Eichner said glumly.

But the Stasi's filing system was so extensive and intricate that it was difficult to expunge all the evidence. Some ex-Stasi officers had pilfered the files on their ex-informants and busily peddled them to the highest bidders in the German media. One after another, East German notables were uncovered as former unofficial collaborators of the Stasi. The head of the new Social Democratic Party of the GDR, Ibrahim Böhme, was exposed as a long-serving informer. East Germans were also shocked to learn that the modest little man they revered as the first and last democratically elected GDR prime minister, Lothar de Maizière, had a long history of contacts with the Stasi under his code name Czerny. Most ex-Stasi officers were refused employment in factories and offices in the GDR, so some staffers, using stolen MfS funds, formed private companies offering security services.

Although several Stasi counterintelligence officers defected to the West German side, remarkably few former HVA intelligence officers succumbed to West German offers of money and pledges of nonprosecution if they disclosed the names of their former agents in the West. The overwhelming majority remained loyal to their dismantled intelligence agency until the end, heeding Wolf's repeated warnings not to emulate the "few traitors." It was extraordinary. GDR espionage, like all intelligence services, was based on a perverse morality, on the deception and the manipulation of human beings, yet Wolf called on his officers not to become "traitors," and they obeyed him.

Wolf and Andrea left Berlin in February 1990 for Moscow, where they were given an emotional reception by his half-sister, Lena, the daughter of Friedrich Wolf and Lotte Rayss. Ever since Lenutchka had lived with the Wolfs as a little girl in their tiny Moscow flat, she remained a favorite of her elder half-brother, Mischa. The Wolfs remained in Moscow for nearly a month, giving rise to a spate of rumors: he was negotiating with the KGB on unfinished business, arranging his eventual asylum in Moscow to avoid prosecution in a united Germany, or — his version — escaping the glare of publicity in Germany and completing a book. The contract he signed to produce three books was worth more than $400,000, one publishing source said. But after the first book was finished and it became apparent that Wolf faced prosecution by the German authorities, the publisher backed out.

In September 1990 Wolf, with his back to the wall, wrote Willy Brandt and West German president Richard von Weizsäcker to ask them to intervene on his behalf and that of other

HVA officers and spies who were facing arrest on charges of espionage and treason. He apologized to Brandt, the ex-chancellor he had helped to topple, asking forgiveness for the "personal pain" he had caused him.

On unification day, October 3, 1990, agents of the German Federal Criminal Office bounded up the steps to Wolf's apartment on the top floor of 2 Spreeufer. But Wolf had already fled united Germany, having informed the Federal Supreme Court that he had decided not to take part in the media "event" of his arrest. He had not made the decision lightly, for he had no wish to leave "my home, where my family lives and where the graves of my parents and my brother lie in Berlin."

After his arrival in Moscow with Andrea, Wolf said he did not want to seek a second exile in the Soviet Union, that he had only one goal — to return to Germany. But once Germany was united, officialdom took its revenge. The 1,700 GDR Mark honorary pension Wolf had been receiving as a "Combatant against Fascism" was eliminated from his retirement pension of 6,500 GDR Marks per month. Later his benefits were slashed to DM 802 per month, the maximum for a Stasi pensioner.

Wolf's flight to Moscow to escape prosecution generated disappointment and outright bitterness among many of his hitherto admiring officers. Ex-Colonel Eichner, once a glowing admirer of his boss, said he began to have misgivings about Wolf when he fled to the Soviet Union. "In a way it was desertion, which made me and my colleagues bitter," he observed. "We had the feeling that we were abandoned by him. Wolf should have spoken for the MfS as a whole and taken responsibility for it."

Eichner's former HVA colleagues grumbled that Wolf had disappeared and that they had to take the brunt of the attacks on the Stasi. The criticism of Wolf only mounted when he left Moscow in late August 1991 for Vienna after the attempted overthrow of Gorbachev and the resulting demise of Wolf's friend Vladimir Kryuchkov, the KGB chief. Realizing that he faced eventual extradition to Germany, Wolf made his way to Austria, where he applied for political asylum. His application was rejected. While waiting in Vienna he entertained the media with interviews, such as one in the giant Ferris wheel of the Prater amusement park, which was featured in the postwar spy film *The Third Man*. His ex-subordinates back home in Berlin were not amused by the way he appeared to be relishing the media attention.

Wolf's Hamburg lawyer, Johann Schwenn, arranged for his client to surrender to the German authorities with style. Schwenn was eager to gain an assurance that Wolf would not have to spend time in pretrial detention. But the German officials would give no assurances. Wolf and Andrea were met on the morning of September 24, 1991, at the Bavarian side of the small Austrian-German border crossing point of Bayerisch Gmain by Federal Attorney Joachim Lampe, who was later to conduct the prosecution against the master spy.

"*Guten Morgen*," Lampe said, offering his hand.

"My name is Wolf," Europe's by now best-known espionage chief responded nonchalantly. He got into Lampe's armored Mercedes limousine and was driven to the Federal Court of Justice in Karlsruhe. There he appeared before a judge, gave personal information, but added that he would "name no names." It was evening before the judge confirmed the arrest warrant against Wolf, but he suspended it under the condition that Wolf pay DM 50,000, report to the police every week, and surrender his identity card and passport so that he could not flee. Twelve hours after his surrender, Wolf was conditionally a free man. The contrast with the methods used by the Stasi could not have been more striking.

While eating a late dinner in a Karlsruhe restaurant, however, Wolf was informed that he would have to be placed in custody after all. The jailer locked his cell door shortly after midnight; it was the first night Markus Wolf would spend behind bars. Eleven days later he was released after new conditions were imposed by the Federal Court, which was concerned that he might flee. Bail was raised to DM 250,000, and Wolf was not allowed to leave the Berlin borough of Mitte, where his apartment was located, without permission. Under no circumstances was he to have any contact with former officers of the MfS. Asked about his experiences in custody, Wolf replied that he adapted remarkably quickly to his new surroundings and had many interesting contacts with other prisoners—"people of a kind that I did not previously know," he added tongue in cheek.

Wolf's moles in the West, the major and the lesser ones, would gladly have exchanged positions with their former chief. When the Communist system collapsed in early 1990, each of them was assured by his or her HVA controlling officer that their dossiers had been destroyed and that no trace of his or her espionage activities remained. But how trustworthy were such assurances, the moles wondered? What about the danger that some disgruntled former controllers might try to earn a handsome reward by betraying the spies who were still in the West?

Such thoughts raced through the mind of Gabrielle Gast, senior official of the Soviet Union department of the West Germany's BND in Pullach, as she watched, half-dazed, the TV coverage of thousands of East Germans storming East Berlin's Stasi headquarters and ransacking the offices on January 19, 1990. How long would it be before her role as Gisela, Wolf's top mole in the BND, was betrayed to the West Germans?

Gast's controller, Col. Karlheinz Stephan, arranged for a final meeting with her in Austria in late March of 1990. Unlike with most of his other Western agents, there was no question of making a final payment to Frau Gast. She had never accepted a pfennig from the HVA, working out of conviction and her infinite love for the most unlikely Romeo agent that Wolf had ever helped to create, the bumbling Karliczek, alias Karl-Heinz Schmidt, whose real name was Schneider.

Karliczek was with Colonel Stephan when Gast arrived on March 27 at the meeting place, a restaurant near Salzburg, Austria, the town where crowds of tourists are herded through Mozart's birthplace. No one among the few guests found anything remarkable about the well-dressed German lady and her two companions. The fact that the Stasi had been disbanded and that Stephan was now an ex-colonel did nothing to diminish his pride in having served the HVA. He solemnly thanked Gast for her years of service in the cause of peace and assured her that everything even remotely connected with her work for the HVA—reports, personnel files, and photos — had been destroyed under his personal supervision. She wanted to believe him.

Four days before German unification, on September 29, 1990, a Saturday, Gast drove off bright and early from Munich for a rendezvous in Austria with her beloved Karliczek. But on the German-Austrian border at Mittenwald, she was met by officials of the Bavarian Criminal Investigation Department who arrested her on suspicion of treason and espionage for the GDR.

Gast and a number of other top moles in the West had been betrayed to the BfV in Cologne by the ruthlessly ambitious ex-Colonel Karl-Christoph Grossmann of the HVA, whose department had been responsible for penetrating West German intelligence services. Only during her interrogation did Gast learn that her lover's real name was Karl-Heinz Schneider, and worse, that he was not the friendly technician and sometime driver he had pretended to be all those years. Her career wrecked and her personal life in shreds, Gast spent fourteen months in solitary confinement. In sheer desperation, she wrote a letter to Wolf, telling him that she was filled with bitterness. Whenever she had tried to terminate her work for the HVA, Wolf's officers had refused. Was Schneider's relationship with her nothing but a tactic used by the HVA to retain her as a "source"? she asked. "Please give me an answer. With great affection, your Gaby," she wrote.

She never got an answer. Wolf's meetings with her in Yugoslavia and the GDR, the solicitous questions about her welfare, the conversations about his father and brother had all been a sham, an act, she felt. She had been a tool, a helpless female accessory, nothing more.

The High Court of Bavaria put her on trial, and Schneider testified that he had merely been a lure to get her to work for the HVA. This was the final blow, even worse than a life sentence. On December 19, 1991, Gast was found guilty of espionage and treason and sentenced to six years and nine months in prison. Schneider and Stephan got off lightly by comparison. Both were given probationary sentences, Schneider eighteen months and Stephan twelve months.

Wholly unlike Gabrielle Gast, the brash Klaus Kuron,

Wolf's other top intelligence mole and double agent at West German counter intelligence (BfV) in Cologne, was jolted into action by the threatening developments in late 1989. He destroyed his camera, high-speed tape recorder, and other espionage apparatus and arranged a *treff* with his former controller, Major Stefan Engelmann. Kuron was less interested in hearing his controller explain that his file and all traces of his work for the HVA had been destroyed, and more eager to get to the business at hand. Engelmann agreed that the HVA would give Kuron a final payment of DM 45,000, and Kuron signed and returned the receipt. Even in its death throes, the HVA was a stickler for procedure.

As his situation had grown more perilous, Kuron, the BfV's man responsible for double agents, had sought to cover himself by becoming even more valuable to the West. He was given responsibility for testing the trustworthiness of HVA officers who had expressed an interest in defecting to the West. After years of being outfoxed by Wolf and his officers, West German counterintelligence was dead set on gaining revenge as the GDR began to implode.

In late autumn of 1989 Kuron met one such HVA officer on barren Potsdamer Platz in the shadow of the crumbling Berlin Wall. The man had previously informed the BfV that he was prepared to divulge valuable East German intelligence information. Kuron tested the would-be defector. Could he name HVA agents in the West, reveal what parts of the HVA were still functioning and what contacts still remained with the KGB? If so, the BfV was prepared to offer him a considerable bundle of deutsche marks.

Kuron also informed East Berlin about the HVA defector; in fact, he was informing on others who turned colors until well into 1990. Ironically, Kuron's reports landed on the desk of Col. Bernd Fischer of the HVA, who had been put in charge of disbanding GDR intelligence by the Round Table.

On October 5, 1990, two days after German unification, Kuron made another hurried trip to Berlin, where Engelmann broke some bad news. He had learned from a reliable source that retired colonel Karl-Christoph Grossmann was preparing to betray Kuron and other top moles to the BfV. Engelmann handed over the HVA's last payment to Kuron, DM 10,000, and offered to put him in contact with the KGB in Berlin-Karlshorst. Without hesitating, Kuron agreed.

He was escorted by the KGB to one of its safe houses in Karlshorst, and a senior KGB officer offered him asylum in the Soviet Union. Kuron accepted. Joined by his wife, he was driven to Zossen, headquarters of the Soviet Air Force in the former GDR, from where the Kurons were to be flown to Moscow. But in the meantime, Kuron had some second thoughts. He was afraid that once he was inside the Soviet Union, he would be prevented from ever leaving. His mind whirred and came up with a deal, which he offered his KGB hosts. It was a last desperate plan, ingenious in its simplicity.

He proposed that he return to Cologne and work for the KGB as its mole inside the BfV, just as he had done so successfully for Wolf. The KGB officers smiled. They were confident that the idea would gain them points in Moscow. Even though the Soviet Union was collapsing, the KGB had not by any means lost its appetite for agents. Kuron was given a cover name, and he and his wife were bid a fond *Auf Wiedersehen* as they drove off in their car toward the Autobahn and west Germany.

During the two-hour drive through east Germany, Kuron drew up a mental balance sheet on his chances of escaping. He knew that Grossmann would betray him to the BfV, and that all hope of finding refuge anywhere in Europe, now without East-West borders, had been eliminated. He stopped the car at a hotel near Braunschweig and telephoned a friend in the security section of the BfV. Kuron explained what he called his "problem." He was arrested shortly afterward, bundled into a car, and taken to Cologne. The three-hour drive gave him more time to mull over his next move, which clearly had to be a brilliant one. On arrival at counterintelligence headquarters, he demanded to see the president of the BfV, Gerhard Boeden. Kuron planned to make Boeden a proposition that he hoped would prove irresistible, even to Boeden's plodding, bureaucratic mind: Kuron would offer his services as a triple agent, helping the BfV to discover what it was that the KGB wanted to find out.

But to Kuron's chagrin, Boeden refused to see him. That

same evening Kuron confessed to his interrogators that since 1982 he had "served only one side, the HVA." He reeled off the names of eight top HVA spies in the West, all of whom were arrested shortly afterward. Several of the spies had already been handed over to the KGB by their former HVA controllers. Among the arrested spies was the untiring Joachim Moitzheim, Kuron's double agent who had been tripled by the HVA. He was sentenced to two years and six months in prison.

The High Court in Düsseldorf sentenced Kuron on February 7, 1992, to twelve years in prison for treason and bribery. The meager remains of the nearly DM 700,000 he had earned by working for Wolf were impounded. Kuron had lost his treacherous game, yet in a prison interview he avowed that it had been worth it. "Compared with the pitiful lives some people endure, staring at a filing cabinet the whole day, I lived five lives," he said spiritedly.

Thousands of Stasi informers also waited in dread to be revealed by their victims, who had begun reading the recently opened Stasi files. One of the frightened informers was Olaf, who as a schoolboy had been forced to inform on his parents. Over the years Olaf had progressed from being a Stasi informer at home to ratting on his colleagues in the factory where he later worked. He made careful notes of the remarks they made at lunch in the canteen and passed them on to Hans, his controlling officer.

Olaf acted in a time-honored German tradition, denouncing errant strangers or even neighbors and workmates to the police. Such behavior had been used to the hilt by the Nazi Gestapo. The secret police had exploited the readiness of Germans to denounce their fellow Germans for everything from failing to draw their air-raid curtains at night to having illegal sexual relations with Jews. The Stasi, like the Gestapo, could not have succeeded in suppressing dissent without widespread help from the population.

Hans had repeatedly warned Olaf as a teenager that his contacts with State Security had to remain clandestine or his reports would no longer be of use to the agency. Hans was especially interested in getting Olaf's eyewitness reports on weekend soccer games. The drunken teenagers who filled the stands would brazenly chant antistate slogans. Tensions were especially high when the MfS team, Dynamo, played, with fans of the opposing team taunting the Dynamo players. Since Mielke was a fanatical Dynamo fan, he had ordered that the stadiums be packed with policemen and Stasi officers. Informers such as Olaf were ordered to be on the alert for "hostile, antisocialist" outbursts.

Actually, Olaf eventually tired of informing on other people. He wished that he could get up the courage to tell Hans that he no longer wanted to be an unofficial collaborator, an IM. He had "cooperated" with the MfS (Stasi) for nearly five years, and that was enough, he told himself. He promised himself that at his next *treff* with Hans in the safe apartment he would bring up the issue more forcefully.

But Olaf never did ask to be released from service. His last *treff* with Hans took place in late December 1989 at a safe apartment of the MfS in Cottbus. Hans brought Olaf's monthly payment of 300 GDR Marks which Olaf signed for, as always, and then Hans told him that this would be their last meeting. Opening a bottle of Armenian brandy, Hans splashed out two large shots and lifted his glass in a toast.

"Olaf, in the name of the MfS I want to thank you for your devoted service in the defense of socialism and the GDR. I wish you all the best for the future," he said formally.

"*Danke*," Olaf replied. He could not think of anything else to say.

After they had downed the smooth brandy, Hans reminded Olaf never to violate the pledge of secrecy he had taken. He promised that the MfS would do everything to ensure that Olaf's past cooperation with the state authorities remained confidential. "Perhaps we will meet again one day," Hans said with a somewhat forced smile as they shook hands on parting.

Although Olaf had wanted to quit for a long time, the abruptness of the break with the MfS left him with a strange emptiness. Informing on his fellow citizens had given him a role, a sense of importance that was now gone. A few weeks later, one of his workmates at the factory told him about a meeting of "national-minded" West Germans that was scheduled in the youth center. Free beer from the West was going to be served, he said. Olaf said he would try to come.

The "Kameraden" (comrades) from West Germany had draped the former black, red, and white "Reichs war flag" at the rear of the largest room in the youth center. A stocky young man with short dark hair, who wore a leather bomber jacket, introduced himself as Frank Hübner. He had been imprisoned in the GDR for illegally corresponding with an ultraconservative West German TV commentator and was bought free in 1985 by the Bonn government. In West Germany he had joined Michael Kühnen's neo-Nazi storm troopers, and after the Wall fell he had been sent back to the GDR to organize the Deutsche Alternative (DA). The way he described it, the DA was a patriotic movement of Germans against left-wingers and foreigners, especially gypsies, blacks, Turks, and Jews.

"What about Vietnamese and Poles?" a young man in the audience wanted to know.

"Yes, Vietnamese and Poles too," Hübner said.

Olaf applauded enthusiastically along with the others. He despised the Vietnamese workers who hawked Western cigarettes at the railroad station, and the Poles who were buying up goods cheaply in East Germany and reselling them at a huge profit in West Berlin. As for the Jews, everyone knew they were somehow disgusting.

Hübner went on to say that since the Communists had been finished off, citizens of the GDR could once again be "proud of the fatherland, proud of Germany."

As the young listeners cheered and stamped their feet, Olaf found himself carried along with them. The formal part of the meeting was closed with the singing of "Deutschland, Deutschland Über Alles," as one of the organizers held up large cue cards with the words to the old banned first stanza of the national anthem. Olaf felt a lump in his throat as he sang of Germany "above everything in the world." Application forms to become a member of the Deutsche Alternative were passed around, and Olaf folded his carefully and put it in his pocket.

Afterward the beer flowed, and there was talk of defacing a

nearby memorial to the Soviet soldiers who fell in 1945. A few days later the newspapers carried a photo of the Soviet memorial daubed with red paint.

In July 1990 Olaf learned that his entire department at the machinery plant was to be closed down. He handed in his application form to join the Deutsche Alternative and soon found himself volunteering to help "shake up" a Jewish cemetery that had escaped destruction by the Nazis. In the early morning hours, Olaf and two other young men, armed with heavy iron bars, clambered over the stone wall of the cemetery. When they were finished less than twenty minutes later, gravestones with faded German and Hebrew inscriptions to Hans and Sarah Friedländer, Fritz and Else Bernstein, and others lay smashed and strewn on the ground. The authorities pledged to hunt down and bring the desecrators of the Jewish cemetery to justice, but Olaf and the others were not caught.

Slavishly obedient, disoriented, and radicalized young men like Olaf were an easy target for recruitment by the Western neo-Nazis working in the former East Germany. Here the right-wing extremists terrorized gypsies, Vietnamese, Poles, and even the few Jews who remained. For this, the former Communist leadership and Erich Mielke bore a heavy responsibility. The warped socialist vision they force-fed East Germans, the mistrust and fear they engendered through the pervasive network of Stasi informants, the intolerance of any dissenting opinion they bred with their totalitarian regime — all produced a sharp backlash of right-wing extremism when the old dictatorship collapsed.

10

Hundreds of spies who had worked for Wolf's intelligence service were still lying low one year after German unification. They stubbornly refused to respond to repeated appeals by the German authorities to surrender voluntarily. Justice officials, boasting they had captured one hundred of the five hundred HVA (Central Intelligence Administration) spies who they said were still at large, warned that they would not rest until the remaining four hundred had been tracked down. This number would appear to have been wishful thinking. More than three years later the German Federal Attorney's Office would announce that preliminary legal proceedings had been launched against another 1,231 suspected former East German agents.

I was in my office in Berlin, reading the *Frankfurter Rundschau* newspaper in late October 1991 when my attention was riveted by a lengthy article under the headline: A SPY IN THE SPD: TOP AGENT OR SMALL FISH?

The alleged spy was Armin, my friend who had escaped from East Germany. While serving as an advisor to the Social Democratic Party in Bonn, he had been arrested and accused of spying for "more than thirty years" for the State Security Ministry in East Berlin. Armin was said to have admitted to the authorities that he had signed a pledge to work for the MfS (Stasi) while in prison.

Shaken, I read and reread the article until it blurred. Armin appeared in my mind just as I remembered him in late 1960, crossing the Friedrichstrasse in East Berlin in his somewhat too elegant gray overcoat. I had often asked myself in those days what Armin, a refugee from East Germany, was doing in East Berlin. But I had virtually forgotten about my doubts.

I tried to find out where Armin could be reached, and was told that he was already in pretrial detention in a prison near Cologne. In the coming weeks and months I pieced together what had happened to him by speaking with his friends, acquaintances, and former Stasi controllers. After his release in early 1992, pending his trial as a suspected spy, I telephoned him at his home, and we arranged to meet in a hotel overlooking the Rhine River in Bonn.

Armin looked pale but smiled thinly and waved his crutch in welcome. The gesture reminded me of the time he had first knocked on my door in the Student Village. Although his face was puffy, he looked remarkably youthful for a man of sixty. He introduced his wife, Norys, an attractive, petite Colombian who I could see was extremely devoted to him. Her stylish outfit contrasted sharply with his tieless shirt and corduroy trousers. We remained in the hotel the entire day, and Armin once again told me about his past. Only this time, he assured me, he was telling the truth.

Speaking rapidly, in a voice that rarely rose above a monotone, he avoided answering most of my questions, instead launching into lengthy, circuitous monologues that made my mind reel in confusion. But bit by bit I was able to reconstruct what seemed to have happened.

In 1959, several months into his twelve-month prison term for alleged economic crimes in Leipzig, Armin was called away from his work in the prison tailor shop one day. He had a visitor, a neatly dressed middle-aged man who introduced himself formally as "Gärtner, Leipzig district administration of the Ministry of State Security."

Armin said Gärtner was intelligent and listened respectfully to Armin's opinions while plying him with cigarettes. Gärtner was worlds apart from Armin's prison attendants, who were coarse-looking, vile-mouthed men. A few days after his first visit, Gärtner returned with an ominous message. A red postal receipt had been found in Armin's portable chess set; it was the receipt for the letter he had sent to the Yugoslav Embassy requesting political asylum. Gärtner angrily accused Armin of wanting to flee to Yugoslavia. Armin nodded, knowing that if he denied it he might even be accused of spying for Tito's Yugoslavia.

"Look, you are an intelligent young man," Gärtner had begun. Instead of fleeing to Yugoslavia, he said, Armin could serve the cause of peace and socialism much better by obtaining political information for the GDR in West Germany. Gärtner's voice hardened as he described the alternative. If the state prosecutor were to get his hands on that red postal receipt, he would accuse Armin of illegal contacts with Belgrade. Armin would end up with a far longer sentence than the one he was already serving. "That would be a pity," Gärtner said, standing up to leave. He urged Armin to think it over in the quiet of his cell.

Armin said that he had then agreed to cooperate with the MfS, but on his own terms. Instead of taking orders from the MfS, he would decide what information he would give them. He assured me that State Security, and in particular Markus Wolf, had been more open than the Communist Party to the idea of reforming socialism.

Did he really believe this? I wondered.

Norys fidgeted and appeared ill at ease as her husband spoke.

After signing the pledge, Armin was released from prison two months ahead of time and assigned a furnished room. Back in his favorite Leipzig haunt, Café Schmalfuss, he met a young woman, Bärbel, who took a liking to him. Mindful that the Stasi had informers everywhere, he told Gärtner about her. He was instructed to reveal to her that he was an "informal collaborator" of State Security and to get her to work for the Stasi.

Before Armin had a chance to develop his pitch, though, Bärbel smiled knowingly. "Armin, stop, don't say any more. I've been working for them longer than you have." After the Berlin Wall was built, the Stasi would use Armin to feign an escape by Bärbel to the West, where she was to work as an agent. Ali, my former neighbor in the Student Village, was to play a role in the bogus escape.

In January 1960 Armin packed a small brown vinyl suitcase containing his spare peg leg and was driven to East Berlin by Gärtner. At an MfS safe apartment, Gärtner introduced Armin to Werner, his future Stasi controller from counterintelligence. Werner gave Armin a series of assignments in West Berlin in order to test him before his scheduled "escape." Under the pretext of seeking legal advice as a disabled East German, he was instructed to contact the militantly anti-Communist Investigating Committee of Free Lawyers (the UFJ) and report on its employees and many East German visitors.

One of the Westerners Armin reported on was Günter Buch, the deputy head of the UFJ, who would later become Armin's boss. When I spoke with Buch he told me that he had suspected that something was "wrong" with Armin from the start, and that when Armin later changed jobs, Buch had warned Armin's future employer in Bonn against hiring him.

Like many UFJ staffers, Buch had escaped from East Germany for political reasons yet retained excellent unofficial contacts in the East. Over a period of decades, the Stasi used every trick in the book to try and lure him back to the GDR, once even coercing his father into writing Günter that he was on his deathbed and wanted to see his son one last time. Although the letter was in his father's handwriting, Buch instinctively sensed a Stasi ruse and refused to return.

Armin had no way of knowing it at the time, but another of the UFJ's employees was already intimately known to the Stasi. For many years the office next to Buch's in UFJ headquarters at 29 Limastrasse was occupied by Dr. Götz Schlicht, a sallow-faced man, with thick glasses and the smooth unlined face of a bureaucrat, who had a reputation for knowing more about internal developments in East Germany than anyone in West German intelligence. Noted for wearing the same two threadworn jackets to work all year long, Dr. Schlicht had a remote, pompous manner, which was reinforced by his habit of dropping weighty Latin and Greek aphorisms in his conversation. From 1960 to 1968 Schlicht headed the UFJ's Legal Advisory Office at Marienfelde refugee center, where tens of thousands of newly arrived refugees from the GDR were screened and processed before getting their Western identity papers and being resettled in West Berlin and West Germany.

Whenever East German refugees needed legal or other advice, they were referred to Schlicht's office at the Marienfelde center. After the Berlin Wall was built in 1961, men who had just risked their lives to escape from the GDR sought Schlicht's confidential advice about less dangerous ways of helping their wives and children who remained behind to escape. Schlicht told them where to go for help, and they trusted him. Schlicht also enjoyed the complete confidence of the UFJ and its American backers and was ferociously attacked by East Germany for using the most "insidious means" to conduct espionage. But East Berlin knew otherwise. Schlicht, operating under the code name "Dr. Lutter," was one of its most diligent moles.

During the seven years that Schlicht headed the UFJ office in the Marienfelde refugee center, his neatly typed reports to his controller in East Berlin betrayed the escape plans of between three hundred and five hundred East Germans. The exact number may never be known. Schlicht was secretly awarded several of East Germany's highest medals for his services as an "Informer with Enemy Contact," or IMB. He was given the Combat Medal for Service to People and Fatherland (in bronze, silver, and gold) and the GDR Medal of Merit, and Mielke personally pinned the Merit Award of the State Security Ministry on him. For each medal Schlicht received a large sum of money, in addition to being handed 5,000 GDR Marks several times on the anniversary of the founding of the MfS (Stasi).

But his services to West Germany were no less outstanding. He was awarded West Germany's highest decoration, the Distinguished Service Cross, presented by a senior West Berlin official. No lesser personage than Richard von Weizsäcker, Germany's president, in 1991 personally awarded Schlicht his second Distinguished Service Cross, this time First Class. His former colleague, Günter Buch, admitted sheepishly that he had recommended Schlicht for the award. Götz Schlicht achieved the near impossible by becoming the only German ever to be decorated for his services to the state by both East and West Germany.

Schlicht's information earned him DM 288,000 over the years (about $90,000) and 288,000 GDR Marks ($90,000 at the official rate). He continued to report to East Germany's Central Intelligence Administration (HVA) until one day before the opening of the Berlin Wall. In 1993 — Schlicht was eighty-five years of age and too infirm to face prosecution — he told me how he had been blackmailed into spying for the Stasi. In 1957, midway through serving a ten-year sentence in the GDR after being caught distributing anti-Communist leaflets for the UFJ, he was visited in prison by a Stasi recruiter who gave Schlicht the choice of completing the remaining five years of his sentence or serving "peace and the counterespionage service of the GDR."

Schlicht shrugged his narrow shoulders. "I was a poor swine and had no choice," he said, recalling his decision. Armin would have agreed.

Once Armin had successfully carried out his preliminary assignments in West Berlin, he was deemed ready to "defect." His MfS controllers were confident that once he had been fully compromised by spying in the West, he would continue to serve East Berlin faithfully.

Told by his controller, Werner, to choose a code name, Armin decided on Talar (gown), an allusion to his academic background. The disgraced young ex-Communist, expelled student, and prison inmate did not quite fit Wolf's picture of the ideologically steeled, highly motivated Communist agent suitable for infiltrating into West Germany. But Werner was pleased with his new recruit. He gave Armin the feeling that he was appreciated, fulfilling Armin's deep-seated craving for recognition. They went over every detail of Armin's forthcoming bogus "escape" to West Berlin and the kind of questions to expect when he was processed at Marienfelde refugee center. All three Western Allied counterintelligence services as well as West German intelligence would be there to screen him and other refugees.

I reminded Armin that we had met shortly afterward in the

Student Village, where he had first told me about his "escape." He nodded and resumed his story.

He encountered no problems at Marienfelde processing center, where, for a moment, he even considered defecting to the West. But he resisted the impulse. Freshly recruited East German spies who immediately turned themselves in to the Western authorities were rarely prosecuted. Werner, however, had warned Armin that if he violated his MfS pledge, State Security would find him and bring him back to the German Democratic Republic, where he would be given his just punishment. Armin explained that this was no empty threat, since the Stasi had kidnapped several of its political opponents and defectors in the West.

Once in West Berlin, Armin obtained part-time work at Informationsbüro West, one of the many anti-Communist organizations in the city, which, like UFJ, was financed by the West German government. Using his studies at the Free University as a cover, he carried out Werner's instructions to report about the staff and visitors to the UFJ, his professors at the Free University's School of Political Science, and others who were of interest. Using his physical impairment to gain the confidence of others, he reported their every human weakness to the Stasi. Every third Monday or Saturday he would meet his controller in East Berlin.

I must have seen him crossing Friedrichstrasse on just such an occasion, I decided.

Interrupting his account of the past, Armin fixed his gaze on me and said that there was one thing he had to tell me. "I never informed on you," he said.

I wanted to believe him. But when he resumed his story, it was riddled with exaggerations and gaping omissions. Despite all the evidence that he had been paid for spying, Armin insisted that he never accepted money from his controller, reminding Werner that he was not an agent of the MfS but an "observer" of West German political life.

In desperation, I decided that perhaps I could convince Armin to stop evading the truth by revealing something from my own past in order to gain his confidence. "I was working for the Americans when we were in Berlin together," I told him. "I want to try to understand what you did and why, but I can only do it if you are open with me."

"You were working for the Americans?"

"Yes."

Armin's voice took on a distinctly hard edge. "Joachim Menz from the Student Village told me that you mentioned seeing me in the Friedrichstrasse in late 1960," he said.

What he said took me completely by surprise. He had touched a raw nerve, and I instinctively defended myself. "Armin, I don't remember who it was, but someone asked about you. I said that I thought I had seen you in the Friedrichstrasse. That was all."

He said nothing, but it was clear that at the time he had felt acutely threatened by my remark. For a long time, he had remained haunted by the knowledge that I had seen him in East Berlin.

The building of the Berlin Wall, a little more than a year after his "escape" to West Berlin in 1960, took Armin by surprise as much as it did anyone. It meant that he could no longer enter East Berlin without attracting attention. He began handing his information to Werner in a shed on the sealed-off Western platform of East Berlin's Friedrichstrasse station, which was accessible only to Westerners — and the Stasi.

During his early years in the West, Armin operated under the control of MfS counterintelligence, and not Wolf's HVA, because he had been targeted to eventually become a mole inside the Ostbüro (Eastern Bureau) of West Germany's Social Democratic Party (SPD). East Germany regarded the Ostbüro in Bonn as one of the most dangerous of the "enemy espionage centers." But Armin showed little inclination to be drawn into this seamy and dangerous side of the cold war. Instead, he enlisted in a postgraduate program run by the SPD's Friedrich Ebert Foundation and went to Colombia as a researcher. The Stasi gave Armin DM 1,000 toward the trip and instructions to write to an address in West Berlin three months after his arrival in Bogotá.

He spent two carefree years in Colombia, where he met and fell in love with Norys, who came from a well-situated family and taught literature at the University of Bogotá. He had long dreamt of finding a woman like Norys, so once he had won her, his fear of losing her was constant. Although he told me that his contacts with the Stasi were suspended while he was in Colombia, I later learned that in between courses at the University of Bogotá and introducing bemused students at the Catholic University to Marxist theology, he airmailed seven reports in invisible ink to his East Berlin controller. One of them, dated October 25, 1964, informed Werner that Armin was going to get married in December and ended with the words: "I'm with you in my thoughts. . . . think of another kind of invisible ink I can use. Talar."

After returning to West Germany in 1966, Armin and Norys moved into an austerely furnished room in a suburb of Bonn. He told me about his shock at being visited by a Herr Kaiser from West Germany's counterintelligence agency, the BfV. Kaiser confronted Armin with a report that in late 1960, after his escape, he had been spotted in East Berlin. Armin denied that he had ever gone back to the East.

Norys by now knew about her husband's commitment to the MfS. He had told her that he was providing the GDR only with political material, and that the more the two Germanys knew about each other, the better. She made him promise never to take money from them.

Armin's controller, Werner, paid him between DM 500 and DM 700 for each of his reports that was passed on to East Berlin. Armin was fully aware, though, that to give Norys the life of comfort and style she deserved, he would have to make a great deal more money. But how?

The fallout from the questioning by Herr Kaiser from West German counterintelligence came in 1967. Armin was hired by the quasi-official All-German Institute in Bonn to run its Unity in Freedom House, which informed visitors about the reality of the Communist menace. His first day on the job, Armin told local newspaper reporters that the Freedom House, with its life-sized puppets dressed up as East German border guards armed with Kalashnikov machine guns, reflected an outdated view of the GDR. Angered after reading the newspaper interview, a prominent anti-Communist politician queried the BfV about Armin. He was told that Armin was an ex-Communist from the GDR, and that there was a report that Armin had been sighted in East Berlin in 1960 — after his escape.

Herbert Wehner, a prominent German politician, the Social Democratic Party's (SPD) foremost strategist, and the newly appointed Minister for All-German Affairs in the Bonn coalition government, was called on to discipline Armin for his remarks. Wehner took pity on Armin, because he was a disabled orphan and, equally important, an ex-Communist, like himself, who had seen through the Stalinist swindle.

Wehner harbored a secret from his own murky past that made him of particular interest to the Stasi. He had been a prominent member of the German Communist Party's leadership in exile in the Soviet Union during the 1930s and early 1940s — when the Wolf family also lived in Moscow. During Stalin's purges, Wehner and other members of the Party leadership denounced several German Communists in Moscow as "traitors," and as a result the accused were executed by the Soviet secret police or died in one of the gulags. During those years Wehner had been terrified by the prospect that early one morning he would hear a knock by the secret police on the door of his room at the Hotel Lux in Moscow, where prominent foreign Communists lived. He convinced the Comintern that he should be sent to the West to keep tabs on the Communist underground in Nazi Germany. Not long after arriving in Sweden, though, Wehner was arrested by the Swedish police, interrogated, and imprisoned. While in Sweden he underwent a transformation into a Social Democrat, returning to Germany after the war to play a major role in the rebuilding of the SPD.

But Wehner's interrogation report by the Swedish police contained some highly incriminating details about his past. This report, as well as other sordid details of Wehner's activities in Moscow during the purges, had been personally turned over to Wolf by Soviet intelligence. For a long time Wolf planned to use this information to put Wehner "under pressure." Ironically, he had to drop his plan when Wehner became one of the chief architects of *Ostpolitik*, Bonn's policy of relaxing tensions with Moscow and its East European allies.

After deliberating Armin's fate, Wehner ordered that he be

moved out of the public eye and into the research department of the All-German Institute, where from 1967 to 1968 he analyzed Soviet military and political strategy in the Middle East.

The MfS (Stasi) assigned Armin a new courier in 1969, a young East German woman code-named Helga, who met him in restaurants and cafés near Bonn. He gave her rolls of film containing photographs of his typewritten reports. She deposited them in the overused but still undetected "dead drop on wheels," the hiding place in the toilet of the interzonal train to East Berlin. In the event that he had to cancel a *treff* with Helga, he was instructed to send a postcard containing the words "Grandmother died" to an address in East Berlin.

Armin promised his vivacious young wife that she would soon be amply rewarded for her patience and faith in him. He planned to build her a luxurious home. In West Germany the potential builder of a house had to commit a considerable chunk of cash to obtain a building society loan. Where was he going to get this money, not to mention the monthly mortgage payments for the house, on his paltry salary? East Berlin had flatly refused to give him the DM 7,000 he had asked for toward the purchase of a house.

Armin proudly told me about how he had come up with an idea to earn extra money. He and Norys had developed a thriving business selling antique clocks and art objects. He neglected to mention that the merchandise came from an innocuous-sounding company in the GDR, Art & Antiques, which bought up artwork and antiques cheaply from East Germans who had been arrested for tax evasion. Art & Antiques belonged to the sprawling Commercial Coordination (KoKo) network of companies under the direction of Alexander Schalck-Golodkowski.

Armin bought a small bungalow in Rheinbreitbach, a charming village south of Bonn, and in 1970 he and Norys moved into the house. But it soon proved too modest for their soaring aspirations. So he purchased a plot of land in a small settlement of homes on a wooded rise outside Rheinbreitbach and made plans to build his dream house with a view of the Eifel Mountains in the distance. But making this dream come true would require a great deal of money.

At work Armin's problems mounted. His superiors scoffed at his professor's title from Colombia and questioned his right to be addressed as Herr Doktor. Armin spoke with Wehner, and in 1972, on the recommendation of one of Wehner's aides, Armin joined the parliamentary group of the SPD as an advisor on East Germany. At the time Chancellor Willy Brandt was still in power.

Armin was relieved to discover that his new job with the SPD did not entail even the most cursory security check. Finally, he was in a position to provide the insatiable MfS with important background information on the governing party's policies toward East Germany. He had no way of knowing that East Berlin was already getting much the same information from a dozen other agents operating within the SPD or close to it.

It was almost impossible to pass the open door of Armin's office in the SPD without being beckoned in for a chat and a drink, or several. One of his fellow employees recalled Armin's unkempt beard, chalky complexion, and alcohol-laden breath. Armin regularly attended the working groups that helped to formulate Willy Brandt's *Ostpolitik* (Eastern policy). As he later admitted, he took copious notes on nearly everyone, typing up the information for East Berlin and then carefully laying out the pages on the floor of his apartment. Fixing his Porst reflex camera on a tripod and turning on a floodlight, he mounted a ladder, peered through the viewfinder, and released the shutter. He had been trained to produce "*Mikrate,*" tiny negatives of documents, which he deposited inside a pair of hollow cufflinks. Armin passed the cufflinks to Lothar, his new courier, at *treffs* every six to eight weeks in Bonn and Cologne.

In contrast to the wily and inspired Klaus Kuron, Wolf's top mole in West German counterintelligence, Armin was a plodder. Like a vacuum cleaner, he sucked up every bit of dirt from his vantage point in Bonn and turned it over to the appreciative Stasi.

After the arrest of the Guillaumes in Bonn on April 24, 1974, Armin's controller in East Berlin informed him that in the future they were to meet less frequently, and in neighboring Holland. Every four to six months Armin drove alone to *treffs* with Lothar in Amsterdam.

The first time Dr. Walter Zöller, a colleague of Armin's with the SPD, visited him in his newly completed home, he was struck by its sheer size and the costly materials. With more than 250 square yards of floor space, the house was far roomier than the cramped dwellings occupied by many West German cabinet ministers. The exquisite antiques — albeit with a bit too much gilt on the chairs — the oriental carpets, and the fine paintings reflected Armin's exalted taste. A large fireplace rounded out an atmosphere of upper-class comfort and style. Armin had told Zöller that he was planning to build an indoor swimming pool, a luxury that only well-to-do Germans could afford. A Mercedes 230SL sports car was parked in the garage. Norys would drive Armin to work in the two-seater each morning and pick him up in the late afternoon. No one, not Dr. Zöller, least of all his SPD employers, wondered where Armin was getting the money for all this.

Had he ever considered turning himself in during those years? I asked.

Armin guffawed. Did I not realize how dangerous that would have been? The West German authorities demanded that East German spies who defected "betray" at least three other Stasi employees in order to escape prosecution. One of them, Armin's courier, lived in West Germany. Armin added that he was still terrified by the prospect of being kidnapped by the Stasi. But it was clear that he was most afraid of losing what he had achieved since coming to the West: his house, his job with the SPD, and, above all, Norys.

In 1977 MfS counterintelligence transferred control of Armin to Wolf's espionage service, the HVA, and Dr. Kurt Gailat, head of the section that dealt with the SPD, assumed overall responsibility for him. Gailat enjoyed a phenomenal reputation among his fellow officers as the former controller of the Guillaumes. He agreed that Armin was to be allowed to retain Lothar — his courier but also one of his few close friends.

In 1979 Armin met his new operative controller, Col. Gerhard Behnke, during a *treff* in Dubrovnik, Yugoslavia. Behnke was a bruiser of a man to look at, but he was soft-spoken and had a gentle manner.

Although Armin was unaware of it, once he started working for the HVA, Maj. Gilbert Schneider of Department 7, analysis, played a pivotal role in his espionage career. Schneider, a tall, bespectacled man, had the bookish appearance of someone who spent long hours poring over documents. His section in analysis evaluated intelligence reports solely from the moles inside the SPD, the party in power in Bonn. Schneider analyzed Talar's reports and gave them an average grade of 2, or "good." State Security's evaluation scale for information went from 1 (very good) to 4 (satisfactory). As an analyst, Schneider was caught in a dilemma that beset the entire socialist system. His department, and every other one in the MfS, had to fulfill its target within the annual plan, which set out goals for ever better espionage results. His superiors had no objections when an agent was given a grade of 2 by one of the analysts, but they frowned when a spy was handed down a 4, since this was a virtual admission that the agent was providing worthless pap. Thus the MfS came to resemble the giant state factories that routinely evaluated their products as world-beaters, although everyone knew they were inferior.

The SPD's defeat in 1982 by the conservative-liberal coalition under Helmut Kohl should have further downgraded Armin's value to the HVA. Yet Armin's reports continued to earn an average grade of 2 from Major Schneider. His superior, Major Peter Richter, a deputy head of analysis, explained this striking contradiction to me. He placed the blame squarely on Wolf for giving his analysts the impression that the East German leadership could not get enough clandestine information on the Social Democrats. This was Wolf's way of getting controllers and analysts to keep up the flow of material from his moles in the SPD. The consequences would prove severe: Armin's artificially high ratings meant that he was kept on long after he should have been retired.

When Professor Horst Ehmke, Willy Brandt's former aide, took charge of the SPD parliamentary group in 1982, he had many more suspicions about Armin than he had had a decade earlier about Wolf's master mole, Günter Guillaume. Ehmke removed Armin as an advisor on inner-German politics and shunted him off to set up a new archive on security and defense affairs.

Here Armin filed clippings and hatched new plans to make money.

Inundated by the monthly mortgage payments for his house and the bills for costly furnishings, Armin decided to put all his chips on one number. Using bank loans, in 1985 he bought a sprawling, twenty-six-room nineteenth-century mansion overlooking the Rhine between Bonn and Koblenz for DM 850,000. While waiting to resell the mansion at a hefty gain, Armin opened a gallery in the house for Norys, so she could sell clocks and watches, antique furniture and carpets, mainly from the East German warehouses of KoKo.

Getting rid of the mansion profitably, however, proved much more difficult than he had imagined. Finally, a company called Delta in West Berlin answered one of Armin's newspaper ads and said it was interested in buying it. Armin told me that he discovered later that Delta was a front for KoKo. KoKo was apparently shopping for castles and mansions to convert into high-class brothels for businessmen and politicians. Armin flew to West Berlin, where he negotiated a contract with Delta to sell the mansion for DM 1.7 million. But Delta later broke the contract, claiming they did not have the money, he told me.

As Armin continued his story, it all sounded as if he had once again been made an innocent victim of Stasi duplicity. But Colonel Behnke of the HVA said that he had repeatedly warned Armin against doing business with KoKo. He was afraid that if Armin was arrested for shady dealings with KoKo, the authorities would discover that he was a spy.

Armin was forced to close down Norys's gallery and sell his mansion on the Rhine at a loss of DM 350,000. He was again gripped by the fear of losing Norys and was prepared to sell or buy almost anything if it meant keeping her love and respect.

Unknown to Armin, East German intelligence had been tapping his office telephone — 165716 — in Bonn. East Berlin had listened in on the phone conversations he had had with one of Delta's employees in West Berlin. What the Stasi heard was remarkable to say the least. On September 16 and 19, 1988, the Delta representative called Armin about possible deliveries of 120 tons of gold bars, worth DM 2.8 billion, to a "customer in the

GDR" and in another Communist country. Armin told him that he had developed excellent business contacts "over a period of many years" with the Soviet Embassy in Bonn. They arranged to meet at three o'clock on September 28, 1988, at the International Congress Center in West Berlin.

What did these bizarre dealings mean? I asked Armin during a telephone conversation.

He snorted contemptuously. "I made believe I was interested in selling MIG fighter planes and Russian gold," he replied.

I got a possible answer from a member of the parliamentary committee investigating KoKo. He told me that "conclusive" evidence existed that West Germany's intelligence services had known all along about KoKo's purchases of embargoed Western electronic devices from leading West German companies. They also knew that KoKo was selling Soviet-made military hardware to Third World countries, with official West German connivance. Chancellor Helmut Kohl's government, however, had refused to act on this information because in the 1980s Bonn had no wish to endanger its highly confidential political and financial negotiations with KoKo's boss, Alexander Schalck-Golodkowski. This would explain why, when Schalck fled East Berlin in 1989 after the demise of his political masters, he was given a safe haven in Bavaria by grateful West German authorities.

In the mid-1980s Armin was assigned a new controller, Hans-Jörg Ullrich, a colleague of Colonel Behnke, and a new courier, Bernd Lähn, who was ten years younger and lived in the nearby Ruhr region. Lähn, when not working for the HVA, was a minor West German trade union official. He had been recruited in 1966 by Peter-Dieter Hausstein, the HVA officer who was to play a decisive part in the final chapter of Armin's espionage career. Just as Behnke had hoped, Armin and his new courier hit it off extremely well.

Armin told me that he grew so disappointed over the lack of enthusiasm in the HVA for his ideas on reforming East German socialism that in 1985, at a *treff* with Colonel Behnke and Ullrich in Cyprus, he demanded that his espionage for the HVA be terminated. He said that East Berlin had agreed, but I had my doubts.

In 1987 Armin notified Colonel Behnke that he had to see him on an extremely important matter. They met in one of the HVA's safe apartments in East Berlin, and Armin excitedly told Behnke of his disgust over recent remarks made by Kurt Hager, a Politbüro member, that the GDR would not emulate Mikhail Gorbachev's perestroika. Behnke told Armin to write it all down in a report for him, assuring him that his views would receive careful consideration.

Behnke then gave Armin a medal for twenty-five years of faithful service to the State Security Ministry, which Armin was to have received in 1985. Armin fingered the cheap gilded medal with the shield of the MfS and returned it to Colonel Behnke for safekeeping. There was one more matter, Behnke said, handing Armin the cash bonus that went with the medal.

Behnke was convinced that Armin's main reason for visiting him in East Berlin was not political frustration but his acute financial straits. Before Armin left, he asked Behnke for help in establishing direct contact with Art & Antiques, the KoKo company. Behnke warned Armin to keep his hands off Art & Antiques, because the company was crawling with shady operators in the pay of hostile intelligence services.

In 1989 Armin looked on with a mixture of astonishment and foreboding as Communism in the GDR collapsed like a house of cards. He sensed that his life was hurtling toward a cataclysm. In the spring of 1990, after East Germany's first and last free elections, Armin got a telephone call from Bernd Lähn, his courier. For the last time, he heard Lähn utter a sentence with the code word "grandmother." It meant that he wanted a *treff* with Armin. Lähn, Armin, and Ullrich, his controller, met in an Italian restaurant in Bad Honnef, near Bonn, where Ullrich assured Armin that there was no need to worry, and that his files had been completely destroyed. Armin desperately hoped that Ullrich was telling the truth. Ullrich also warned Armin that under no circumstances was he to turn himself in to the West German authorities, who were regularly issuing appeals to former GDR spies to give themselves up. Armin nodded. He knew that to do so would mean losing Norys, the house, his job, and everything he had worked for for so many years.

Germany was unified on October 3, 1990, in a brief burst of joy and sweet harmony. Armin, lonelier than ever, telephoned Behnke and Ullrich in Berlin and said he was coming to Berlin. He wanted to see them and refresh old memories. They met in a restaurant near Alexanderplatz, in what had until only recently been East Berlin; they drank beer and reminisced about the past. But Armin's gnawing doubts about his safety would not go away.

On October 21, 1991, at 8:00 A.M. sharp — German officials are precise in such matters — the doorbell of Armin's villa in Rheinbreitbach rang, and Norys opened the door. Six men in civilian clothes stood outside along with a policeman. Norys did not need to be told why they were there. Armin shuffled to the door in his pajamas, and Chief Detective Heinz Fiedler flashed a search warrant.

"You are accused of espionage activities," Fiedler announced as the other officials fanned out through the house in search of incriminating evidence.

Armin told Norys not to answer any questions. As he ate his breakfast, the men filled three boxes with his files and notebooks, which contained Bernd Lähn's name and telephone number. Armin was bundled into a large BMW and taken for interrogation to the State Criminal Investigation Office in Düsseldorf.

"Are you going to talk or not?" Fiedler said, fixing him with a steely gaze. Armin talked. Norys phoned and said she had found a lawyer. The next morning Armin was driven to Karlsruhe, where a warrant was issued for his arrest by the Federal Court of Justice. He was taken to a prison in Koblenz, not far from his luxurious home overlooking the Eifel Mountains.

I asked Armin how the former West Germany's BfV had tracked him down after he had been assured by East Berlin that his files had been destroyed.

He gave a short, bitter laugh. "Hausstein betrayed me," Armin said. "That swine."

Peter-Dieter Hausstein was the HVA officer who had recruited Bernd Lähn. In 1984 he had been given the diplomatic cover of first secretary and sent to the GDR Permanent Mission in

Bonn. Armin said he and Hausstein had had frequent contacts in Bonn but none involving espionage. Hausstein told me that he had learned only in late 1989 that Armin worked for the HVA. Colonel Behnke had told him that Armin was a "long-time source," an "old man," as Behnke had put it.

Hausstein in the meanwhile had already gained considerable notoriety among former HVA officers and their spies who were certain that he had betrayed them in return for a promise from the authorities that he would not be prosecuted.

The news of Armin's arrest, carried by the German news agency and most major newspapers, landed like a bombshell in the SPD parliamentary group. At first, his fellow staffers were skeptical. He was the last person they would have suspected of espionage. Armin a spy? Armin, the eternal clown, that blundering, chaotic ne'er-do-well who never completed his work? Incredible. After the initial reaction, coworkers began remarking that they had known all along that Armin was a rotten egg. He was immediately fired by the SPD, whose officials darkly hinted that they had long suspected him of untoward behavior.

Dr. Walter Zöller, Armin's colleague and friend, was one of the few who denounced Armin's treatment by the SPD as a "tragedy." Zöller said that he had felt a terrible, sinking feeling on learning about Armin's arrest on espionage charges.

"Armin is being tried after he was blackmailed into spying when he was only twenty-one years old," Zöller said earnestly. He played down the value of the "secrets" that Armin had passed to the GDR, noting that his friend had been in no position to gain much valuable information.

Hans Büchler, who was Armin's immediate superior from 1979 to 1983, agreed. "Armin's forthcoming trial is rubbish!" he said. "What was he supposed to have divulged? With certainty I can say that he could not have revealed anything of importance. Of course, he did misuse our confidence, which is why the SPD fired him and stripped him of his special pension. The only reason he wasn't fired earlier was that he was handicapped, and Wehner had taken pity on him."

Nearly three and a half months after his arrest Armin was released from pretrial detention because of his physical disability.

One day not long afterward, a former SPD colleague ran into him on the street in Bonn. "You are a criminal," he blurted out to Armin's face. He reported that Armin, stung by the remark, had replied melodramatically: "They beat me in Bautzen [one of the GDR's worst prisons] for so long that I was ready to do anything." Armin had never seen the inside of Bautzen prison.

Epilogue

After speaking with Stasi perpetrators and their victims, as well as those who were both, I decided to seek out the spymaster himself and the woman who for more than thirty years had known him most intimately. But first I was to encounter his most likable mole and my own Stasi informers.

I stood in 1991 under leaden skies in Leipzig, where a rally was under way against mass unemployment in former east Germany. The speaker was a militant west German labor union official who warned that if the rate of factory shutdowns continued, the east would become a postindustrial wasteland. The few hundred locals on the square applauded listlessly. The vacant expressions in their faces told me that they were in no mood to fight back. Now, as before, when the Stasi trampled on their rights, they were largely resigned to their fate.

I was startled to hear someone call out my name and turned to see Beate standing there with her parents. She seemed pleased to see me again after so many years and said she was visiting her parents in Leipzig. She had married a Dutchman and was living in the Netherlands, where she was working as a translator. I wanted to ask her whether she had been allowed to leave the GDR as a reward for her years of informing for the Stasi. But I decided against it.

"It's awful what is taking place here. Everyone wants to work, but they aren't being given a chance," she remarked.

"This is not what we demonstrated for in 1989," her father, a morose-looking professor, added.

I looked at Beate, but she lowered her gaze.

I arranged to meet Gisela Münzenberger on a gray January day in 1994 in a coffeehouse opposite Leipzig's Old Town Hall. My former landlady said that after German unification she had joined the ranks of the many losers, despite having taken part in the demonstrations for unity in early 1990. What was the use of having freedom of the press if she no longer had enough money to subscribe to a daily newspaper? she grumbled. Her son had been released from prison but was out of work. Toward the end of our conversation, I mentioned that she had cropped up in my Stasi file as the informer "Münze."

She stared at me, dazed, slowly murmuring, "I had no idea," several times. After regaining her composure, she gave me a lengthy explanation of why she had had no choice. Her neighbor had worked for the Interior Department, which oversaw the police.

Münzenberger insisted that she had reported only "positive" things about me, since she and her late husband had treasured our talks together. We walked over to the Old Town Hall, where she wanted to show me a photo exhibit of Leipzig as it had looked after the war in 1945.

"You are an American, correct?" she said after we had viewed the exhibit. "Well, nowhere was there any mention that American and British bombers wrought most of the war damage. The Russians are blamed for everything, but they only arrived in Leipzig after the Americans withdrew in July 1945," she remarked, with a hint of malice in her thin smile.

"But Frau Münzenberger, that was the Second World War . . . ," I objected.

"I know, which Hitler began," she replied.

"With a good deal of help from the population," I added.

I visited Johanna Charlotte Olbrich, alias Sonja Lüneburg, in mid-1993 in her tastefully furnished apartment in Bernau. It had been her reward from State Security for sixteen years of outstanding service as an HVA mole inside the Free Democrats and the Bonn government. Her hair streaked with gray, her gaze firm, she reminded me of one of my favorite Upstate New York teachers.

"I was betrayed," she told me matter-of-factly. One of her earlier HVA controllers, Ingolf Freyer, had revealed her identity to West German counterintelligence. Olbrich was arrested in June 1991 on espionage charges and, after two months in custody, was released on bail to await trial in Düsseldorf. But she displayed no hint of bitterness. Unlike Gabrielle Gast, Johanna Olbrich was self-assured and strong. She had never needed a man to define her role in life.

A housewife now, she looked back fondly on her relationship with Wolf. After stepping down as head of the HVA, he had been as thoughtful toward her as before, visiting her in Bernau with Andrea. She had served them coffee and cake, and they had chatted about her travels, their common friends, and his writing.

Wolf could not have changed anything in the GDR or he would have been immediately arrested, Olbrich told me. Besides, he would have betrayed himself had he done so. "The society we aimed for was a good one," she told me with the clear and steady voice of a true believer.

At her trial in February 1994 her ex-boss, Martin Bangemann, the former West German economics minister, praised Olbrich, alias Lüneburg, as an "unusually capable secretary — very open, very friendly, very helpful." She had taken care of his apartment and other personal matters and even accompanied his family on a sailing trip in the Aegean. Grateful for his words of commendation, she told the court that she had felt somewhat guilty about misusing Bangemann's trust in her, and that she had tried to make it up to him by giving liberally of her time and energy.

Johanna Olbrich was sentenced on February 24, 1994, to two and a half years in prison for espionage.

I sought out the spymaster himself on a bleak November day in 1992. Shorn of his Communist benefactors and facing the prospect of imprisonment for a considerable part of his remaining years, Wolf was vulnerable for the first time in his life.

Wearing sandals, Wolf opened the door of his duplex on the top floor of 2 Spreeufer. I automatically extended my arm to shake hands, but he smiled nervously.

"One shouldn't shake hands across a doorway," he remarked, looking genuinely worried. Was Markus Wolf, the cold war's preeminent espionage chief, superstitious?

Murmuring apologies, I entered his lair. After years of being pursued by the Stasi's officers and informers, I was now the hunter and Wolf was my prey — in theory, at least.

Wolf, lean and ruddy-complexioned, looked as if he had just emerged from his private sauna. He was free on bail but was unable to venture beyond the former East Berlin district of Mitte, where he lived.

In only a few months, his trial on charges of espionage, high treason and bribery would begin. We hardly spoke about the trial, however, and that was understandable, since as far as I was concerned, the trial was both hypocritical and absurd. After all, the BND, Wolf's West German counterpart, had also conducted espionage, yet no one was suggesting that the head of the BND be put on trial along with his senior officers. Ultimately, of course, it was the superpowers, America and the Soviet Union, that had called on their German client states to conduct espionage against each other in the first place.

As for high treason and bribery, Wolf, at the time, had been a citizen of the GDR and not the Federal Republic of Germany, the state he was accused of having betrayed. And he was accused of having bribed his moles? If so, then every intelligence chief from Washington to Bonn was guilty of the same crime. Here was a case of the law being bent to fit the aims of the victors of the cold war. West Germany's conservative leadership, sailing to victory in the wake of the Americans, was determined to take revenge on Wolf and other Stasi officers.

Ironically, no one was showing the least interest in whether Wolf, as former deputy minister of State Security, bore responsibility for the Stasi's massive human rights violations.

We sat below the modern paintings in his living room, and I

told him that I wanted to write about his father. It was a ruse, but harmless compared with the deceptions that he and his agents had routinely used to snare their victims. I was determined, like an HVA agent, to gain the confidence of my quarry before stalking him. Wolf gazed at me calmly with his small, dark brown eyes, betraying no hint of whether he believed me.

He spoke in that mellow voice with a touch of Swabian dialect that immediately won over his listeners. But not me. I was not going to be lured into complacency by his genteel ways.

Suddenly, without the least prompting, he began speaking about his father's Jewishness. It was uncanny; he had anticipated the first question I was going to ask him.

"My father never denied his Jewish descent, but he felt himself to be a German," Wolf said thoughtfully. "It would have been an advantage for him to have Jewish nationality on his internal Soviet passport during the Second World War, but instead he chose to be German."

"What about you?" I asked.

"I felt myself to be Jewish," he said without hesitation, lighting a cigarette. Having rediscovered his Jewish roots, Wolf took to the subject.

"The kibbutzim interested me, and I read *Exodus* in the early 1960s with great sympathy and interest," he remarked, adding that he had rejected the policies of the Israeli government while viewing those of the Arab states with detachment.

"The truth lay elsewhere," he said, leaving no doubt that he was referring to the objective, Marxist truth. He spoke about the many prominent East Germans who had been of Jewish background, mentioning Lt. Gen. Paul Kienberg, who he had "heard was Jewish or partly Jewish." He did not say that Lieutenant General Kienberg's Department 20 of the Stasi had used an army of informers to hound and suppress all forms of internal opposition in the GDR.

"Today one says that there was anti-Semitism in the MfS, but this is untrue. I would never have become what I was otherwise," Wolf argued.

The reason for Wolf's Jewish rebirth only became clear to me a few months later during his trial in Düsseldorf. In his opening plea, Wolf diverged for a moment to remind the court that the Nazis had once placed his family on their wanted list: "I was fourteen years old. My brother was eleven. Had the 'sound instincts of the people' borne fruit, our names would have ended up on some tombstone, perhaps in Yad Vashem Memorial in Jerusalem."

Normally, such appeals from Jewish victims of Nazi atrocities found a positive response among Germans and foreigners alike. But on that occasion there was an embarrassed silence. No one, inside or outside of Germany, was prepared to regard Wolf as a renewed victim of anti-Semitism.

Seated on the couch in his living room, he briefly spoke with Andrea, his young wife, who was about to go out shopping. After she had left, Wolf leaned back on the couch, nimbly anticipating a question I was going to ask about his spies.

"Blackmail never played a role in getting people to work for us. Sometimes money played a role, but conviction was the main reason," he said.

I thought of Armin. He continued.

"Western intelligence emphasized quantity, not quality," he maintained, implying that his agency did precisely the opposite.

I could not help recalling the never-ending gossip and dirt his moles had passed on to him from inside the West German political parties. He and Mielke and the rest of the Politbüro could not get enough of it. And what about the surveillance reports in my Stasi file and the mountain of trivia informers had gathered about me? No doubt Wolf would have answered that this had been collected by Mielke's infernal counterintelligence, for which Wolf said he bore no responsibility.

"I often had fierce discussions with Mielke when we were alone," he said. "But it was an advantage for me that Mielke did his work, and my organization stayed relatively apart from his. We had nothing directly to do with it. By means of my work, I had this niche where I alone had responsibility. The intelligence work was necessary, and I was convinced I was doing the right thing. As for the other matters, I told myself that I was not responsible for them. I always followed the appeal of my father to live up to my convictions."

I resisted the temptation to interrupt him.

"We were genuinely convinced that we were promoting the cause of peace," he said. "I believe that our information helped convince the GDR leadership that Bonn's *Ostpolitik* (Eastern policy) was in the interest of détente. Yes, I was a successful commanding general," he said, pausing for a moment. "But what was the use of winning the battles if the war was lost?"

I had a mental picture of Wolf in his white general's uniform at which he had often poked fun, but which he proudly wore on the anniversaries of the MfS and the KGB. And his medals: the Fatherland Order of Merit in Gold, the anniversary medals of the KGB, the Order of Merit of the MfS, the Red Star of the Czechoslovak Interior Ministry, the Red Banner Order of the Soviet Union, the Karl Marx Order, the Commemorative Medal of the Working Class Militia, the engraved General's Dagger, and all the rest.

"I increasingly doubted the sense of this work. Of course, my resignation was not only the result of my opposition," he explained. The leadership's refusal to react on the information it was getting from the HVA, he said, made him realize that it was time "to do something."

The telephone rang. It was his daughter, Tanja. He spoke warmly with her, calling her *Tochter* (daughter), and advising her on some matter before taking another cigarette from a box and returning to the couch.

"As a person who was persecuted by the Nazis, I was entitled to early retirement. But even this pension was taken away," he said more in sorrow than in anger.

Here he was, another former top official of the regime, forced to subsist in high-cost Germany on a DM 800 monthly pension and the slim proceeds from his two books. Money had meant little to him in the old days when the MfS took care of his needs. But now he faced huge lawyer's fees and hotel bills for the forthcoming trial, as well as the hefty rent for his plush apartment. Small wonder that he was asking tens of thousands of deutsche marks for a single interview with the German media.

I was about to ask him about his cooperation with German and international terrorists, but again, uncannily, he had already read my thoughts. He said he had only seen Mielke's reports on terrorism and contacts to the PLO, which East Germany had wanted to keep at arm's length. But he had not seen any of the Stasi's reports on the Evangelical (Protestant) Church. In other words, he was claiming to have been unaware of the Stasi's campaign against the Church and Church-backed civil rights groups. I wondered whether he could sense my incredulity.

"We knew what the civil rights movements were doing only by reading the accounts in Western newspapers. I was in favor of the Swords into Plowshares movement," he said glibly, referring to the young East German protesters who had been sorely harassed by the Stasi in the 1970s. It appeared that his questioning and doubting of the regime had begun long before that time.

"I read the publications of [Robert] Havemann with interest and found the ideas of [Alexander] Dubček and [Andrei] Sakharov very sympathetic. But they only seemed to be a small group of people, and what would it have helped. . . . The effect of internal protest was exactly the opposite. The dogmatists used it in order to become even more repressive," he insisted.

Wolf turned to the underlying reasons he had kept silent about his own opposition for so many years. "I was trained to follow a certain Party discipline. In addition, during the cold war, if a Party member criticized the system, then this played into the hands of the West. And then you must remember that one felt an obligation to our cause. We were tied as if with chains, and our mouths were sealed shut," he said.

I was struck by the image he had of himself: helpless, bound and gagged. I had hoped that Wolf would assume at least some responsibility for the Stasi's crimes against East Germans. Instead, he was taking refuge in self-pity, describing himself as a victim of an ideology that had gone berserk. What made him so unwilling to acknowledge his own guilt?

Emmi Wolf, Markus's first wife, lived in Leipziger Strasse in one of the high-rise apartment houses that had been built in East Berlin to block out all sight of nearby West Berlin. The tenants, however, were thought to be sufficiently steeled, ideologically, to withstand their view of West Berlin. Now a huge Coca-Cola sign loomed high over the wide boulevard, a constant reminder of the new order. As I rode the elevator to her apartment on the twenty-first floor, I mulled over my line of approach. As with Wolf, I would first try to gain her confidence.

Emmi was a plump, matronly woman, so plain-looking that she might have been mistaken for her nonexistent maid. Her apartment, filled with drawings by her grandchildren and Russian knickknacks, reflected her humble background. Only in passing did she mention that her father, a Communist deputy in the Reichstag, had been murdered in Dachau by the Nazis. Although she had a doctorate in Russian literature, she had none of the arrogance and stuffiness of German academics. While we talked, she occasionally switched to Russian to speak with her younger sister who was visiting her from Moscow. Hearing her speak Russian, I realized the closeness of Emmi's and Markus's Russian ties.

Emmi spoke about her childhood in Moscow, her mother's arrest in Moscow in 1937, on suspicion of opposing Stalin, and of meeting Wolf and falling in love with him at the Comintern school. She had been afraid to meet his parents, noted intellectuals that they were, but was relieved to find out that they, like Markus, were totally unpretentious.

I was attracted by her complete lack of guile. There was something touching about Emmi Wolf's steadfastness, her refusal to abandon the beliefs for which her father was killed by the Nazis and her mother interrogated by the NKVD. Emmi sometimes still felt more Russian than German, she told me. Was it not bitter that the Soviet people who had liberated Poland, Czechoslovakia, and Hungary in 1945 were now the humiliated losers, she asked me.

I found myself taking a liking to her. This was no act; she was genuine. But how could I sympathize with someone who had a reputation for having been a ferocious Stalinist?

Emmi was stubbornly loyal toward Markus Wolf. She frequently referred to him as "my husband" when she told me about their more than thirty years together, and she condemned his upcoming trial as "political revenge." Erich Mielke had taken credit for Wolf's successes and left the HVA alone after he realized that Wolf had no designs on his job. But no, her husband had never talked shop at home.

"It was better that way because of the children," she explained.

Gradually, like an informer winning the trust of his victim, I felt that I was gaining her confidence.

"How much did Wolf know about the excesses of the Stasi?" I asked.

"I do not know what he knew, but he surely knew more than I did," she replied ambiguously.

"And what about his renewed Jewishness?" I asked.

She seemed to be hearing about this for the first time, and said she had not been aware that Wolf had ever felt himself to be Jewish.

"We were all Russified," she remarked succinctly.

Emmi assured me that Wolfgang Leonhard's accusations about her having informed on him at the Comintern school were untrue. She denied having taken notes on the "suspicious" remarks he made in Comintern school, and then reading them off at the meeting that Leonhard had described as his "interrogation."

"We had discussions in seminar groups, debates about behavior and studies. The others didn't like the way Leonhard showed off, either. But there were no interrogations, only discussions," she repeated. Her dark eyes peered at me out of an open, honest face.

I forced myself to remember that nothing was what it seemed.

I watched Wolf at his trial, which began on May 4, 1993, in the High Court in Düsseldorf, a hulking Prussian pile built in 1911 during the reign of Kaiser Wilhelm II. Room A01, where the proceedings took place, was windowless and had been specially constructed in 1975 for the top security trial of the Guillaumes. Bare of any ornamentation — there was not even a German flag or eagle — the room was spotless, antiseptic, entirely cleansed of the sordidness of Germany's past division and the forty years of squalid intra-German espionage.

One after another of Wolf's top moles was summoned to testify. Günter Guillaume, aged almost beyond recognition, was feisty despite a serious heart ailment. After testifying, he demonstratively grabbed Wolf's hand and shook it vigorously while his former boss flashed a winning smile.

Klaus Kuron, then some months into serving his sentence, depicted himself as a counterintelligence official of such consummate skill that he could serve only the ultimate intelligence service, Wolf's HVA. He displayed phenomenal recall of every double agent he had ever controlled for West Germany.

Johanna Olbrich, alias Sonja Lüneburg, was dignity personified as she spoke modestly of how she tried to do her best, both for her employers in East Berlin and in Bonn.

The moles all nodded to Wolf or shook hands with him as they passed the table where he sat with lawyers on either side. The one exception was Gabrielle Gast. She avoided even a glance in his direction. The pain was still too great.

The trials of Wolf's moles were even more dubious than his. They had been cogs in the machinery of the cold war that had divided their nation. Now that the German state was unified again, what purpose could their prosecution serve except retribution?

Judge Klaus Wagner, who presided at Wolf's trial, was a florid, haughty man with an uncanny resemblance to Charles Laughton. He had made a brilliant career out of trying nearly a hundred arrested East German spies. Finally he had the spymaster in his net. Yet Wolf was refusing to act like a man on trial for espionage and treason. Patrician in appearance, dressed in an impeccably tailored light blue suit, he busily took notes, conferred with his two lawyers, or simply looked bored. Apart from his opening statement, he refused to speak during his nearly seven-month-long trial. Throughout the proceedings, the stalwart support and unswerving loyalty of his wife, Andrea, and the presence of his children, friends, and supporters helped buoy his spirits.

During a break in Wolf's trial in the late summer of 1993, we spoke again in his apartment in Berlin. This might well be my last chance to confront him before the verdict and his imprisonment, I told myself. But first, I decided to take a detour by asking some questions about his childhood.

He reminisced about his stubbornness as a child, his inability to excuse himself or display shame even today. He had been a very headstrong boy, a product of his antiauthoritarian upbringing.

This, ironically, had produced one of the world's most fiendishly inventive spymasters. Had he ever regretted not being able to complete his studies and become an aircraft designer? I asked him.

"I obeyed the Party's instruction to attend Comintern school, and later I went to work for the radio station in Moscow, although I had no inclination for radio work or writing. I did it because of the Party order, and I grew to like the work."

This was the same way he became fascinated with intelligence, I thought, only because the Party ordered him to. The contrast between his antiauthoritarian upbringing and the Party's commands could not have been greater.

The time had come to close in on the spymaster. Did he know who Talar was? I asked, giving Armin's HVA alias.

His expression betrayed no surprise. He began to reel off data on Armin as if he had just retrieved it from a computer file. "He was Social Democratic Party, originally was dealt with by MfS counterespionage, but since he was close to the SPD he was turned over to us. He had a wooden leg if I remember correctly. *Ach ja*, and he sold antiques," Wolf added. "He was fairly important, otherwise I would not have remembered the name Talar," he assured me.

But Wolf's memory was selective. He made no mention of Armin being coerced in prison into working for State Security.

"Does the name Caesar mean anything to you?" I probed.

"Who was Caesar?" he replied, appearing genuinely unaware.

I pointed to myself and told him that the Stasi had kept an operative file on me for more than twenty years. Wolf smiled and shrugged his shoulders as if to say: That was the way it was. He offered no apologies, nor had I expected any. We went to a nearby restaurant for lunch.

He was open, engaging, and sparkling as he recalled incidents from his childhood, as well as a visit to an Armenian pilgrimage site in 1970 during which he registered the incipient nationalism that would later destroy the Soviet Union.

As we were sipping coffee, a young waitress approached Wolf, bent over, and spoke in an audible whisper: "I want to express my contempt for you," she said, then turned on her heel.

What struck me was that Wolf never for a moment lost his composure.

"It's the second time this year that someone has said that to me," he remarked calmly. "In Düsseldorf, a man came over to tell me how much he disliked me. But most people here support me, which is what you would expect in the East."

It all sounded so disarmingly frank, just as he had been taught by his father. Yet it was fraudulent. He knew as well as I did that his prominent role in the Stasi had discredited him in the eyes of the waitress and a lot of other former East Germans.

He went on to speak about his ancestors, who, among other Jews, had been invited by a liberal leader to settle in the Rhineland, because of their money. Even in defeat, Wolf, the master tactician, remained in complete control.

Wolf's expression betrayed not the slightest hint of surprise on December 6, 1993, when Judge Wagner sentenced him to six years in prison. He had been found guilty of severely endangering West Germany's security by his espionage activities and of committing high treason. But Wolf was free to go home until his appeal was ruled on, the judge added charitably. Outside the courthouse, a crowd of supporters cheered their fallen hero. Among them was Hans Modrow, the last Communist leader of the GDR, and Gregor Gysi, then head of the Party of Democratic Socialism, the party that replaced the old Socialist Unity Party of East Germany, of which Wolf was a member.

The final verdict on Wolf still had to be spoken. For over a year he waited anxiously for a ruling on the appeal of his sentence. He complained about his freedom of movement being restricted to Berlin, and of having to seek permission from the authorities before visiting his weekend dacha in Prenden. I thought about the many victims of the Stasi who had languished for years in dehumanizing prisons. Some had not survived long enough to be released.

More than two years had passed since the Berlin High Court dismissed the espionage case against Wolf's successor, Werner Grossmann. The Berlin court argued that to prosecute former GDR spies and spymasters while West German spies and spymasters enjoyed immunity, violated the Constitution's principle of equality before the law. The court had called on the Federal Constitutional Court for a ruling, and that decision was still awaited.

It was difficult to imagine that Wolf would land in prison. But his supporters had prepared for that eventuality, issuing a thinly veiled threat to the German authorities. They hinted that Wolf was privy to acutely embarrassing secrets about prominent West Germans, and that if he told what he knew the entire German establishment might never recover.

At least for the time being, Wolf was spared the ignominy of imprisonment. But his debts left him no peace. In a highly paid TV interview, he hinted that in the future he might well disclose his past mistakes and those of the Communist system. Wolf's Communist world had collapsed along with his ideals. Now, in the new capitalist world, he girded himself to make a living from the ruins of the past. He decided that his fellow Germans were less eager to hear his political revelations than to sample his fabled recipes, which he published in a cookbook with the tongue-in-cheek title "Secrets of Russian Cooking."

On the morning of May 23, 1995, Wolf, his face deeply etched by months of worrying that he would soon serve a prison term, heard the long-awaited ruling by the Federal Constitutional Court. The judges in Karlsruhe decided that former East German intelligence officers who had spied exclusively from GDR territory could not be prosecuted for their espionage.

Visibly relieved over what amounted to an amnesty, Wolf said that he expected his sentence to be annulled and that the years of uncertainty and slander against him and his former associates would be ended. He could not resist adding that the decision was also encouraging for all those "such as myself who had doubts about the rule of law" (in united Germany).

I spoke with Armin and Norys in the spring of 1994 at their luxurious home in Rheinbreitbach overlooking the Eifel Mountains. Armin was still awaiting trial but had been summoned to appear in a few days as a witness at another espionage trial in Düsseldorf. He sat on a gilded sofa in the spacious living room lined with somber paintings. The left leg of his trouser was neatly pinned up, and his crutches were resting next to him. I reminded him that there were still a great many inconsistencies in the story he had told me.

He replied with his familiar, rambling discourse in a voice that was alternately emotionless, then trembling with indignation. Norys, who hung on every word, began chanting, "His parents were poisoned," like a Greek chorus, until Armin sharply told her to be silent. In spite of his attempt to conceal more than he revealed, what emerged was a tale of the desperate, chaotic search for recognition by a cripple who had been robbed of his youth by the Nazis and of his illusions by the Communists. But greed and cowardice had also played a role, as had the constant fear of losing Norys.

On my way out, Armin proudly showed me one of his expensive golden clocks that stood on a shelf in the richly appointed dining room.

Driving from his house toward Bonn, I wondered how I might have reacted if I had been in prison and a Herr Gärtner had visited me and presented the Stasi's grim terms for my release. The answer was not long in coming.

Slowly, a frayed and yellowed picture of the thin man appeared before me as I stared at the winding road leading toward Bonn. I heard the thin man asking me if I knew anyone who might want to earn some money by doing a small, harmless errand. I heard myself tell him about Ali. I stared at the road but saw only Ali. He was asking me, with that perpetually mild smile, to join him for coffee in his room, next to mine, at the Student Village. With all the might that I could summon, I tried to cancel out the memory of him. But it only sank back slowly into the depths of my mind.

A few days later, I was in the courthouse in Düsseldorf when Armin, seated in a wheelchair, was dramatically rolled into room A01 by his lawyer. Armin had been summoned as a witness in the trial of four senior HVA officers on charges of espionage and treason. Among them were ex-colonels Gailat and

Behnke, Armin's former controllers. Unlike Wolf's trial the previous year, though, no newspaper photographers or TV cameras were present.

The florid-faced Judge Wagner asked Armin about what had happened back in 1959 when Gärtner had visited him in prison. Armin spoke rapidly, his voice rising as he described his refusal to sign the pledge to work for the Stasi on Gärtner's terms. Stabbing the air with his finger, he said that he had told Gärtner he would work only for the working-class movement and his own ideals.

"Did he accept that?" Judge Wagner asked incredulously.

"Yes," said Armin.

The judge reminded him that when he was taken into custody in 1991, Armin had told his interrogator that during his meeting with Gärtner he had agreed to provide information to the MfS in the form of regular situation reports.

Armin stared glumly into the distance.

Judge Wagner persisted. Had Armin actually believed that there was a reformist group around Markus Wolf in the HVA? he asked.

"I did not exactly believe that they were a reformist group but . . . ," Armin replied, his voice trailing off.

Outside the courtroom, I witnessed a remarkable display of the human bonds forged between controller and spy, which had been a vital ingredient in the HVA's success. Ex-Colonel Behnke put a fatherly arm around Armin, who was seated in his wheelchair, and asked him how he was faring. They confided in each other, like two old friends, talking about their present situations and the past. The existence of such a tie was all the more astonishing because of the endemic mistrust that pervades the world of espionage.

Returning to my hotel room in Düsseldorf, I thought about Armin and his bleak future. Granted, he had been dealt a raw deal in life. But he had made things far worse for himself by giving in to his most destructive instincts.

When Armin's trial for "especially serious" espionage and that of his courier, Bernd Lähn, for plain espionage, opened in room

A01, I was one of only three people in the visitor's gallery. I had seen no reason for their trial from the start, but because they were citizens of West Germany at the time of their spying, they were being held accountable under West German law.

Armin, his face chalky, entered on crutches. Norys, doleful but smartly attired, left Armin's wheelchair in a corner of the room. From the wheelchair dangled a tag from a travel bureau giving Armin's title as "professor" and his destination: Moscow. Had he taken the trip or planned to before his arrest? I wondered.

Armin's previous lawyer had resigned out of frustration, and the new attorney appeared no happier with his client.

Judge Günter Krantz, a mild-mannered man who peered shortsightedly through glasses, took down Armin's personal data. I was surprised to learn that Armin had been married twice before coming to the West and had two grown daughters.

Asked why he had signed the pledge to work for State Security, Armin said in a firm voice that he had wanted to prove that he was not an "enemy" of socialism. Judge Krantz's bland expression never changed. Queried about the people he had informed on in West Berlin and Bonn since 1959, Armin said he had provided information on thirty-two people to his controller.

"I described most of them positively," he said. "I was not unscrupulous."

Judge Krantz reminded Armin that all of his reports from 1960 to 1989, filling sixteen Stasi files, had been found. He inquired about the role Armin had played after the Wall was built in the feigning of an escape by Bärbel, the young woman from Café Schmalfuss in Leipzig, to West Berlin, where she had worked as a Stasi agent.

Armin said that his controller had asked him to name someone in West Berlin who could get Bärbel a passport for the contrived escape. "I gave him the name of an Arab student named Ali," Armin said.

I was startled to hear the name of my former neighbor in the Student Village. What did this mean?

As if in reply, the judge quoted from a report by Armin's controller, which stated that Armin had reacted "positively" to the arrest of Ali in East Berlin, saying that it would "tie him closer to the MfS."

"They duped me," Armin burst out loudly. "It was a dirty trick to arrest him even though they wanted to get Bärbel over to the West."

Slowly it became clear to me that I had not been responsible for Ali's arrest after all. I felt an oppressive weight lifting off me.

In a pause in the proceedings I went over to Armin and asked him whether I had been among the people he had informed on back then in Berlin.

"I had to," he replied dully. "There was no other way. I only told them you were going to Leipzig for the fair."

Strangely, his disclosure scarcely affected me. I had long since expected the worst.

Frustrated by Armin's refusal to concede that he had been regularly paid by the Stasi, Judge Krantz reminded him that he had already admitted to his interrogator that he had been paid. Armin remained impassive. He did not seem to realize or care that he was harming his own case with his deceptions.

He arrived late when the trial resumed the following week. His face was bloated, and he stared through puffy eyes as Judge Krantz cited reports from Armin's Stasi file in which Armin had disclosed a planned escape tunnel under the Wall, as well as the names of persons who had helped East Germans to flee.

On the next to last day of the trial Armin's increasingly distressed-looking lawyer rose and said he had been authorized by his client to say that Armin had been paid between DM 100,000 and DM 125,000 by the MfS, minus expenses, between 1960 and 1989.

Judge Krantz had saved up the most devastating evidence for the end. He read from a report submitted by Armin in May 1963 on a group of professional escape organizers that he had infiltrated in West Berlin. In the report Armin informed his controller that one of the key figures in the organization, Max Sovik, planned to enter East Berlin on June 1, 1963, to arrange details of an escape by an East German to West Berlin. Sovik had been arrested in East Berlin.

The federal prosecutor turned to Armin. "Did you betray Max?" he asked.

"Why are you so spiteful?" Armin murmured. "I am not denying it, Herr State Prosecutor. But I did not think that he would be arrested."

In his final summing up, the federal prosecutor said that Armin had worked with great intensity for the MfS for thirty years and had been responsible for Ali's arrest and delivering Max into the hands of the Stasi, but that Armin had not been a top spy. His punishment, nonetheless, should act as a deterrent to other Eastern espionage agencies. He called for a four-year sentence — out of a possible ten years — and a fine of DM 150,000.

Armin gasped loudly, and tears welled in his eyes. His lawyer asked for a break before Armin read his lengthy final statement. I anticipated the worst. As I watched Armin, a pitiful human wreck who had once been my friend, I decided that I could no longer remain a detached observer. I approached him in the hallway and urged him to discard his prepared statement. I pleaded with him to admit his guilt, say that he deeply regretted what he had done, and throw himself on the mercy of the court.

"You're right, Leslie, I will," he promised.

But back in the courtroom he did just the opposite, arguing that he had agreed to spy for East Germany out of gratitude for the "food, education, and home" it had given him. He said his first emotional break with the Stasi came with Ali's arrest, after which he began to "doubt" the orders he was getting.

"I made great mistakes, that I know. But I didn't betray anyone," he insisted, bursting into tears.

Armin sat dejected as the judge read out his sentence: four years and a fine of DM 100,000. It was well above what he might have been given if he had acknowledged his guilt. Armin appealed the sentence. His courier, Lähn, was given a twelve months' probation after admitting his role, and he was fined DM 3,000.

But even more devastating to Armin than the prospect of going to prison, paying the fine, and losing his SPD pension was the prosecution's conclusion. All the espionage material that he had passed to the Stasi for thirty years, and which had given him such a sense of importance, had not caused "discernible harm" to West Germany. It had been worthless.

Armin was a broken man in spirit and body, his future bleak after the Constitutional Court ruling. The judges had urged leniency for East Germans, such as Frau Olbrich, who had spied in the West. But they approved of punishment for West German citizens who, like Armin, had engaged in espionage against their own country for the GDR. This was perhaps the cruelest irony for Armin, who had become a West German only after the Stasi arranged his "escape" in 1960. Now he clung desperately to Norys, fearful of what would happen to her while he was in prison. In spite of all he had done, I felt pity for him.

His spymaster, Wolf, will remain in a class of his own as one of the supreme intelligence players of our time. Yet even Wolf had admitted that his espionage triumphs were Pyrrhic victories. He and countless others in similar positions of influence had known that the real enemy lay within, but they had lacked the courage to combat it.

As for myself, I had been lucky. As a Westerner, I had come out on the winning side in the gigantic East-West struggle. Yet there was no reason to feel triumphant. I had never been subjected to the crushing pressures of a dictatorship that had morally paralyzed Wolf, Armin, and the many others. Whether I would have shown greater courage and moral strength I would never know.

Sources

Contrary to what I had expected, Markus Wolf was surprisingly cooperative during my interviews with him, which began on November 16, 1992, in his apartment in Berlin-Mitte. I was able to continue observing Wolf at close quarters throughout his trial in Düsseldorf, where he was nearly always accompanied by his wife and often one or more members of the Wolf clan. His seeming openness toward me, an American, may have been a reaction to the overwhelmingly negative treatment he received in the German media. My interviews with Emmi and Christa Wolf, his former wives, as well as many of his ex-officers in East German espionage, provided me with further insights into Wolf's nature.

Lew Hohmann, the Berlin documentary filmmaker who worked closely with Markus Wolf in the late 1980s on a film project about his brother, Koni, was extremely helpful in evaluating Wolf and his multifaceted, impulsive father, Friedrich. I also profited from the views of Wolfgang Leonhard, who had known young Markus and Emmi at Comintern school. Karl-Wilhelm Fricke, the dean of experts on the intelligence establishments in East and West Germany, who himself served a long sentence as a political prisoner in the GDR, also was helpful.

The spymaster himself helped me locate Emmi Wolf when I told him I wanted to see her. I interviewed Emmi in her living room, and she also took my wife and me to the house in Lehnitz where Friedrich Wolf and his wife had lived, and which Markus frequently visited. His own weekend dacha is located in nearby Prenden.

Jörg Drieselmann of the Stasi memorial located in State Security's former Berlin-Lichtenberg headquarters, let me roam at will through Erich Mielke's office. He told me about the four-year sentence he was handed in 1974 for distributing leaflets protesting Aleksandr Solzhenitsyn's arrest.

Ex-colonel Horst Wittke, who was in charge of security at HVA headquarters and a veteran of thirty years' service under Wolf, provided me with details of the atmosphere at the agency after Werner Stiller fled to the West, a description of the relationship between Wolf and Mielke, and an account of the storming of MfS headquarters on January 15, 1990.

Klaus Eichner of the HVA was invaluable on many details of daily routine in the espionage service and in explaining the agency's emphasis on "human intelligence" over electronic spying and other means. As James Hall's controller, Eichner provided me with firsthand information on the case. To my consternation, I later discovered that in my Stasi file he was listed as the MfS officer who, earlier in his career, had been involved in the Stasi alert issued on me after my expulsion from Czechoslovakia in 1977.

I looked up Gerhard Heidenreich, the sole survivor among the founding fathers of East German espionage, in his apartment in Berlin-Pankow. He proudly told me that he had left everything as it was when the GDR collapsed in 1989: a wooden plaque on the wall from Rudolf Abel, the Soviet spy, along with a large tapestry of Ernst Thälmann, the prewar German Communist leader, and a lithograph of Lenin. Also displayed in his apartment was a photo of Heidenreich with the Soviet KGB residence chief in East Berlin.

I had several long and difficult sessions with Armin before his trial. As much as I pitied him, I knew that our earlier relationship would be difficult if not impossible to restore. I spoke with several of Armin's colleagues at the SPD, as well as his bosses, Hans Büchler and Horst Ehmke. I interviewed Günter Buch, formerly deputy head of the United States–backed Investigating Committee of Free Lawyers (UFJ) in West Berlin. He was Armin's boss when he worked for the Informationsbüro West in West Berlin. Buch was also a colleague of Götz Schlicht, East Berlin's mole inside the Marienfelde refugee center. I spent a bone-chilling afternoon with the aged but highly alert Schlicht at his home in Berlin-Zehlendorf. In addition to giving an account of his espionage career, he told me about his macabre battle under the Nazis to refute suspicions that his Romanian father was Jewish. He did this in order to become an officer in the Wehrmacht, in which he served in one of many police units that dealt brutally with the civilian population on the Eastern front.

I had several conversations with Gerhard Behnke, Armin's former HVA controller, and met Kurt Gailat, who had overall responsibility for Armin and had earlier been Günter Guillaume's controller. After interviewing them I was able to follow their testimony at their trial in Düsseldorf. Behnke was given a one-year suspended sentence, and Gailat got a suspended term.

I spoke with Peter Richter, former head of the HVA section that analyzed intelligence reports from the West German political parties, who offered his theory as to why Armin's reports were consistently given such a high grade by analysis although they contained little of value. I also talked to Peter Hausstein, the former HVA officer who Armin was convinced had betrayed him to the German authorities.

During their appearances as witnesses at Wolf's trial, I closely followed the testimony of his supermoles: Guillaume, Gast, Kuron, Olbrich, and others. By this time Kuron had already been convicted and had begun to serve his sentence. His lawyer, Werner Leitner, patiently explained to me the fascinating details of how Kuron had operated. Frau Olbrich, alias Sonja Lüneburg, turned out to be a pleasure to interview. I cannot say the same about Günter Guillaume. Less than a year before his death in April 1995, he testily accused me of "working for a Western intelligence service" when I asked him about the identity of the HVA emissary he met in southern France shortly before his arrest.

Heidemarie Brauer, who contacted me after reading the account I wrote in the *Financial Times* about my Stasi file, told me why the Stasi failed to penetrate her defenses with its informers, and to weaken her and her husband by its tactics over a period of many years.

As for the East Germans who informed on me, I learned who they were when my Stasi file was released to me in 1992 by the Federal German agency in Berlin headed by Joachim Gauck. Although I met the two women informers again, despite repeated efforts I was unable to locate Bodo, who had tried so hard to gain my confidence in Leipzig. He had apparently left the city without a trace. While I had been made aware on one occasion in Leipzig that I was under overt Stasi surveillance, I had no idea of the massive scale of the observation until I read my file. I have made every effort to ensure that this account of the spymaster's life is free of the lies, misinformation, and indigestible trivia contained in the bulky file that the Stasi kept on "Caesar."

Notes

pages 21–22   Letter from Markus Wolf to Friedrich Wolf that begins "Pappele, do you remember . . .": quoted with permission of SAdK, Friedrich-Wolf-Archiv, Berlin.

page 23   *"Nemets, perets, kolbassa, kislaya kapusta . . ."*: from Markus Wolf, Die Troika, Aufbau-Verlag, Berlin and Weimar, 1989.

pages 24–25   Letter from Friedrich Wolf to Markus Wolf that begins "In order to combat abuses . . .": quoted with permission of SAdK, Friedrich-Wolf-Archiv, Berlin.

page 29   "In mid–1937, without warning. . . . 'nothing of this' ": from Markus Wolf, Die Troika, Aufbau-Verlag, Berlin and Weimar, 1989.

page 32   Letter from Friedrich Wolf to Markus Wolf that begins "Now Mischa, good night": quoted with permission of SAdK, Friedrich-Wolf-Archiv, Berlin.

page 36   "Mischa casually extended . . . code name, Linden": from Wolfgang Leonhard, Die Revolution entlässt ihre Kinder, Verlag Kiepenheuer & Witsch.

page 36   "Comrade Klassner. . . . in the action themselves": from Wolfgang Leonhard, Die Revolution entlässt ihre Kinder, Verlag Kiepenheuer & Witsch.

page 38   "Klassner lashed out. . . . expelled from the Party": from Wolfgang Leonhard, Die Revolution entlässt ihre Kinder, Verlag Kiepenheuer & Witsch.

page 39   "Wolfgang Leonhard would never forget. . . . his remarks in the future": from Wolfgang Leonhard, Die Revolution entlässt ihre Kinder, Verlag Kiepenheuer & Witsch.

pages 44–45 "A few days after his arrival.... Moscow film academy": from Markus Wolf, Die Troika, Aufbau-Verlag, Berlin and Weimar, 1989.

page 45 Letter from Markus Wolf to his parents that begins "Strange as it sounds...": from Markus Wolf, Die Troika, Aufbau-Verlag, Berlin and Weimar, 1989.

page 46 "Markus complained ... roasted coffee": from Markus Wolf, Die Troika, Aufbau-Verlag, Berlin and Weimar, 1989.

page 114 "West Germany would present a list.... via Vogel to the West Germans": from Craig R. Whitney, *Spy Trader*, Times Books/Random House, New York, 1993.

pages 123–125 "Early one wintry morning.... into the GDR": from Richard Meier, Geheimdienst ohne Maske, Gustav Lübbe Verlag, Bergisch Gladbach, 1992.

page 151 "...one of the 'fathers' ... computer age": from Werner Stiller, Im Zentrum der Spionage, Hase & Koehler Verlag, Mainz, 1987.

page 152 "Gerhard Arnold was another ... payment": from Werner Stiller, Im Zentrum der Spionage, Hase & Koehler Verlag, Mainz, 1987.

page 152 "Stiller was most impressed ... East Berlin": from Werner Stiller, Im Zentrum der Spionage, Hase & Koehler Verlag, Mainz, 1987.

page 153 "... 'fulfill your wish' ": from Guido Knopp, Top-Spione, C. Bertelsmann Verlag, Munich, 1994.

page 154 "... 'undeliverable' ... would soon be trapped": from Guido Knopp, Top-Spione, C. Bertelsmann Verlag, Munich, 1994.

page 154 "... were on the stubs": from Guido Knopp, Top-Spione, C. Bertelsmann Verlag, Munich, 1994.

page 161 "Erzsébet Stiller was interrogated.... when they caught him": from Guido Knopp, Top-Spione, C. Bertelsmann Verlag, Munich, 1994.

pages 204–205 "On August 15, 1985.... she would take revenge on Wolf": from Alexander Reichenbach, Chef der Spione, Deutsche Verlags-Anstalt, 1992.

page 231 "... for the 'personal pain' he had caused him": from *Der Spiegel*, 20 March 1995.

Index